THE
MANAGER'S
Desk Reference

THE MANAGER'S
Desk Reference

Cynthia Berryman-Fink

amacom
American Management Association

Library of Congress Cataloging-in-Publication Data

Berryman-Fink, Cynthia, 1952–
    The manager's desk reference / Cynthia Berryman-Fink.
      p.   cm.
  Includes index.
  ISBN 0-8144-5904-8
  1. Management—Handbooks, manuals, etc. 2. Personnel management—
—Handbooks, manuals, etc. I. Title.
HD30.33.B47   1989
658.3—dc19   88-48035

Printing number

10 9 8 7 6 5 4 3 2 1

Table of Contents

Preface

ORGANIZATIONS OF ALL TYPES need good supervisors, managers, administrators, and executives in order to survive and thrive in a competitive world. Even though management is the most vital function in any organization, many people holding management positions have little or no formal training in managing others. Even those with degrees in management or human behavior have difficulty in obtaining all the information and skills needed to manage effectively in today's complex organizations. Experienced managers must devote much time to understanding burgeoning new requirements, programs, and trends in managing a contemporary work force.

The business information industry has responded to the need for management advice. Indeed, managers are bombarded with a wealth of information and advice on a variety of management issues, much of which is presented in current best sellers, popular magazines, professional and trade journals, newsletters, newspapers, seminars, instructional tapes, and television and radio talk shows. Busy managers often find it difficult to digest the massive amount of information on new issues and methods of managing people. *The Manager's Desk Reference* was written to provide managers with a concise yet comprehensive source of management information. It organizes up-to-date information on a wide range of people-related management topics into a comprehensive reference book. By summarizing current thought on important management issues, *The Manager's Desk Reference* aims to help you cope with the explosion of information needed to manage effectively in an increasingly complex and diverse workplace.

This book grew out of my experience as a management consultant on communication and personnel issues. For over a decade, various clients have been asking me to recommend practical yet substantive sources of information that they could consult on contemporary people-related management issues. Existing sources of information tended to fall into two categories: abstract, theoretical treatments of a particular management topic with perspectives irrelevant to the typical practicing manager, or brief, superficial articles lacking in substance and having little chance of educating the practicing manager. I soon realized how time-consuming it was to locate, review, and evaluate useful books and articles on specific management issues—sources with which I felt comfortable recommending as the best ones available to my manager-clients. Surely, few managers have the time to survey management literature for necessary information. As a manager myself, I feel compelled to stay abreast of management information, yet I have little time to peruse the broad management literature or locate specific information to guide decisions. Thus, the idea of a comprehensive encyclopedia of concise yet substantive information and advice, as well as annotated references on a wide range of people-management topics, emerged.

The Manager's Desk Reference is limited to information on managing people. You will not find information on accounting, budgeting, planning, forecasting, computer programming, conducting research, or other non–people-related tasks that managers may encounter. Instead, this reference presents information on most aspects of human behavior to help you deal with peers, supervisors, subordinates, customers, the public, the press, and others with whom you may have to interact. You will, for example, find information and advice on hiring, orienting, training, coaching, motivating, evaluating, and terminating employees. The reference also covers the full range of communication tasks performed by managers, such as being assertive, writing, dealing with conflicts, giving feedback, interviewing, listening, negotiating, making presentations, and using nonverbal communication.

The Manager's Desk Reference will help you develop and implement innovations such as assessment centers, career-development programs, dispute-resolution procedures, employee-assistance programs, mentoring systems, preretirement counseling, and quality circles. You will also find substantial information on traditional management concerns such as delegating, disciplining, running meetings, appraising performance, managing time and stress, team building, and reducing turnover. Some topics, such as intercultural communication, intrapreneuring, organizational culture, quality, sexual harassment, and women and minorities, are intended to help you cope with a diverse and changing workplace.

This book can be used either as a starting point or as a complete source of information for supervisors, managers, executives, or administrators who want to update their knowledge of management issues and methods, who want advice on dealing with people-management problems, or who want a refresher course on basic supervisory and management functions. Each topic can serve as a self-contained source of information on a particular management issue. In most cases, you will find all the information you need on a topic, but you can also use the cross-references and additional sources listed at the end of each section for further information related to that particular topic. Managers at all levels in the full spectrum of organizations in the private and public sectors should find the *Reference* useful. In addition, the book may serve as a valuable tool for students of management or for management trainees, even though it has not been designed as a textbook or training manual.

Instead of reading *The Manager's Desk Reference* from cover to cover, you will probably prefer to consult particular topics as the need for specific information arises, but if time permits, you may find it useful to read the *Reference* in its entirety and then to consult it in the future as a guide. I hope this book will meet the informational needs of busy managers by providing them with a wide range of information at their fingertips.

I am indebted to several people and organizations for assistance, insights, and support while completing this project. First, without the valuable interaction with dozens of client organizations, I would not have conceived of this project. The Greater Cincinnati Employers Institute was helpful in providing information. I appreciate my colleagues in the Department of Communication at the University of Cincinnati for giving me the opportunity to formulate and test my own management ideas and practices as a university administrator. Three former graduate students, Katherine Araujo, Andrew Gilgoff, and Thomas Joyce, should be acknowledged for their help with background research. I am also grateful to all those at AMACOM Books who advocated on behalf of the project and provided editorial assistance.

My most sincere thanks go to my family. I am indebted to my husband, Chuck Fink, for reviewing and improving the manuscript, for helping me develop as a manager, and for being so patient and supportive during this seemingly endless project. Finally, I give my thanks to my son, Andrew Fink, who, as a "little guy," will never know how much he taught me about human behavior.

CBF

November 1988

THE MANAGER'S
Desk
Reference

Assertiveness

ASSERTIVENESS means standing up for yourself without anxiety and without denying the rights of others. You must communicate assertively when you present and defend positions, negotiate on behalf of a department or work team, and give or receive performance feedback. Many other workplace situations require assertiveness skills—dealing with colleagues, subordinates, supervisors, customers, suppliers, competitors, or the media. The ability to communicate assertively distinguishes the powerful, effective manager whom others respect from the manager whom others take advantage of.

Distinguishing Nonassertive From Assertive and Aggressive Behavior

Some people think they are being assertive when, in fact, they are being indirect, subtle, and vague. Other people are brutally direct and inconsiderate while claiming to be assertive. Thus, not only shy people need to develop assertiveness skills. Aggressive or domineering individuals can also benefit by replacing an aggressive communication style with an assertive one. Assertiveness is behavior that falls midway between nonassertive and aggressive behavior. To better understand assertive behavior, compare it with nonassertiveness and aggressiveness in the following way:

Nonassertive Behavior
- Uses indirect communication.
- Communicates the opposite of what you really feel.
- Lacks honesty.
- Denies your own rights and feelings.
- Makes you feel negative.

Assertive Behavior
- Uses direct communication coupled with tact.
- Communicates exactly what you feel.
- Is honest.
- Balances your own and others' rights and feelings.
- Lets you and others feel positive.

Aggressive Behavior
- Uses direct but untactful communication.
- Goes overboard in communicating what you feel.
- Is brutally or offensively honest.
- Denies others' rights and feelings.
- Makes others feel negative.

Elements of Assertive Communication

To be optimally assertive, the visual, vocal, and verbal elements of a manager's message must be synchronized. You must look assertive, sound assertive, and use assertive language. The following are guidelines for behavior in each of those areas:

Visual Elements of Assertiveness
- *Eye contact*—should be direct and steady. Do not look away when making a point; do not stare.
- *Facial expressions*—should be relaxed but serious. Do not frown angrily; do not smile or giggle.
- *Gestures*—should be natural and relaxed. Do not pound fists or point fingers; do not fidget or wring hands.
- *Posture*—should be businesslike. Do not intimidate or slouch.

Vocal Elements of Assertiveness
- *Voice volume*—should be moderate. Do not shout or mumble.
- *Speaking rate*—should be moderate. Do not show uncertainty by speaking too slowly; do not show nervousness or aggressiveness by speaking too rapidly.
- *Tone of voice*—should be firm, direct, sincere, and calm. Do not use voice tones of anger, sarcasm, excitement, or disinterest.
- *Fluency*—should be such that you speak in complete sentences without fillers such as "um," "ah," "OK," "like," and "you know."

Verbal Elements of Assertiveness
- Statements should be direct, clear, and concise.
- Sentences should be complete.

- Avoid intensifying words, such as "extremely," "very," and "incredibly."
- Avoid qualifying words, such as "sort of," "kind of," "somewhat," and "it's just my opinion."
- Avoid evaluative labels and name-calling, such as "stupid," "lazy," "inconsiderate," and "selfish."

Handling Common Assertive Situations

Specific situations requiring assertive communication are numerous and diverse. However, most assertive situations you face will fall into one of these categories:

- Making requests
- Saying no
- Giving criticism
- Accepting criticism

While the guidelines for maintaining consistency between visual, vocal, and verbal parts of an assertiveness message apply to all four categories of assertive situations, the following are specific suggestions for managers in dealing with each type of situation.

Making Requests

The best way to make a request is to ask, rather than hint, demand, or manipulate. Hints are usually ineffective. Because they are vague or subtle, they are often not perceived. Or, if perceived, they can be easily ignored. Requests disguised as hints are not likely to be taken seriously. On the other hand, ordering someone to do something often leads to resistance. When you phrase a request as a demand, others will resent having to comply. And resentment frequently translates into anger, hostility, and sabotage. Manipulation tricks others into doing something. It takes away the other person's choice and, in the long run, will earn you the reputation of being devious and underhanded.

The assertive style of making a request is to ask specifically and directly for what you want. By asking directly, you take responsibility for your requests and allow others the choice to grant or to refuse them. The clear, direct style is most likely to be effective. Assertively making a request means stating a need, asking for action, and giving a reason for the request. For example, an employee who requests a co-worker to switch a workday says: "Joan, I'm scheduled to work next Saturday morning. Would you be willing to switch with me since you're scheduled for the following Saturday? My niece is getting married and I'd like to be able to attend the wedding." If the request is honored, it is important to express gratitude and to follow through on the negotiated arrangement. If the request is denied, be a gracious loser. Show no resentment and refrain from guilt-producing remarks.

Saying No

An essential element of assertiveness involves the ability to turn down others' requests. Some people have much difficulty saying no. As a result, they find themselves doing favors and resenting it, or feeling trapped in obligations. Some people nonassertively say no by hinting, whining, deceiving, complaining, or blaming others. Aggressive people become outraged or abusive when faced with another's request. Assertive individuals directly say no without hesitation and without giving lengthy excuses or apologies. They do not fall into the trap of feeling guilty, being manipulated, or being coaxed into granting the request. An assertive response to a request to switch work schedules could be worded like this: "No, Ellen, I can't work next Saturday for you. I'm having out-of-town guests. Maybe I can help you out some other time."

Giving Criticism

Frequently, managers have to give negative feedback on the behavior or performance of others. The capacity to be firm but fair when giving criticism is the hallmark of an optimally assertive individual. It is important to be direct, clear, and honest while showing tact and compassion for the person receiving the criticism. Because giving criticism is awkward for many managers, it is seldom handled properly. Weak managers postpone or avoid giving the feedback, use hints or sarcasm, or absolve themselves of responsibility by attributing the message to others. Aggressive managers belittle the target of criticism in front of others, angrily attack the target without getting to specifics, or allow the recipient of the criticism little opportunity to save face.

The constructive communication of criticism entails describing a specific problem, indicating why it is a problem, requesting a concrete change, and conversing nondefensively to work out an agreement for accomplishing that change. For example, an assertive manager delivers the following message: "Rick, this report you wrote doesn't have enough detail on the marketing plan. There's not enough information to prepare a marketing budget that will be approved. Can you redo that section to include all your marketing strategies with a time schedule?" Then, a question to create a dialogue should follow. The manager can ask, "Do you understand what I need? Can you get it to me by Friday?" Giving criticism in such a straightforward, assertive style has many advantages. It is specific, making change easier. It avoids evaluation and name-calling. It deals with work-related behavior rather than people's egos. It encourages two-way communication to ensure understanding and to promote change. Both parties can come away from the criticism feeling positive, and the problem that engendered the criticism is likely to be solved.

Accepting Criticism

Realizing that everybody makes mistakes, accepting your own mistakes, and trying to improve as a result of criticism are essential ingredients of assertiveness. An assertive individual can listen to criticism without becoming defensive, objectively examine that feedback, and then use the information constructively. The nonassertive recipient of criticism whines, cries, pleads, makes excuses, or engages in self-pity. Aggressively handling criticism entails being defensive, making counterattacks, resenting the critic, and stubbornly refusing to change. The assertive approach to receiving criticism involves patiently listening to and paraphrasing the feedback, asking for specifics or examples to ensure understanding, acknowledging the parts of the message with which you agree, stating your position or needs without becoming defensive, and engaging in a dialogue with your critic. For example, a manager gives this response to criticism about the quality of output from his department: "You're saying that our parts aren't meeting specification. Can you tell me which shipments haven't met your specifications and what percentage of error occurred in each batch?" On receiving an answer, the manager continues, "OK, I can see where Batch 103 had problems. I should have had more people on the line since that was a rush order. We're less likely to make mistakes if we have at least two days to prepare an order. We'll replace this shipment. Can you give us at least 48 hours of notice on future orders?" Assertively dealing with criticism solves problems and maintains good working relationships.

[See also Feedback; Nonverbal Communication]

For Additional Information

Cawood, Diana. *Assertiveness for Managers.* Seattle, Wash.: International Self-Counsel Press, 1983. Focuses specifically on managers. The author examines the need for assertiveness, explains the basics of assertive behavior, presents several assertiveness skills, and relates assertiveness to certain managerial functions such as handling poor performers, setting work goals, and coaching employees.

Down, Arden. "Why Assertive Supervisors Are Better Managers." *Supervisory Management*, Vol. 29 (November 1984), pp. 2–7. Contrasts the assertive supervisor with passive and aggressive supervisors and presents communication skills for assertive management.

Smith, Manuel J. *When I Say No I Feel Guilty*. New York: Bantam Books, 1985. The skills of systematic assertive therapy including basic rights in behavior, persistence, self-disclosure, criticism, conflict, and saying no. Smith discusses assertiveness in specific contexts such as financial, authority, workplace, and intimate situations.

Zucker, Elaina. *Mastering Assertiveness Skills: Power and Positive Influence at Work*. New York: AMACOM, 1983. Suggestions, exercises, and self-assessment quizzes to develop assertiveness skills for work situations. Chapters apply assertive behavior to common business situations such as delegating, counseling, appraising performance, giving feedback, participating in meetings, and writing.

Assessment Centers

AN ASSESSMENT CENTER is a program or method using multiple-assessment techniques to evaluate employees for a variety of human resources decisions or purposes. Typically the process is used to make selection, promotion, placement, training, or development decisions in an organization. The method identifies key characteristics needed in a job and in the person who will hold that job. Through the observation of a candidate's behavior in a number of relevant exercises, a team of assessors attempts to measure whether he has the specific qualities necessary for success in that job. Based on the systematic observation and valid measurement of those qualities as prerequisites for job success, hiring, promotion, and development, decisions are made.

The assessment center methodology has been used most frequently to evaluate individuals' supervisory potential. In addition, organizations use assessment centers for promotions to middle and upper management, for management trainee selection, for assessing sales potential and technical capability, and for developing work teams. Although the process is complex, time-consuming, and costly, assessment centers do provide detailed and objective data on which to make human resources decisions. Poor personnel decisions can be costly to companies and stressful to individuals. Informed, logical, and fair decisions in hiring, promoting, and developing key employees characterize sound and humane business practices.

Developing and Implementing an Assessment Center

The following steps and considerations should be followed in setting up an assessment center in any type of organization:

1. *Form a planning team.* Developing and implementing an assessment center is far too difficult for any single individual in an

7

organization. A broadly based planning team, with top organizational support and representatives from key staff and line functions, is necessary. The team should include a competent organizational psychologist or a consultant specializing in assessment center methodology. It is imperative that the team have the technical expertise for translating job duties into behaviorally anchored dimensions, selecting exercises that validly and reliably measure those dimensions, and developing assessors who can objectively observe behavior. Only when those criteria are met will the assessment center be an effective decision-making tool endorsed by employees and protected by legal statutes.

2. *Set objectives.*   This step involves decisions about the purpose and role of the assessment center. Will the center be used for personnel selection, promotion decisions, or employee development? Will it be applied to supervisory, management, or executive personnel? Will certain departments or functions be the primary users? Will there be enough position vacancies to justify the use of an assessment center? Will training and development programs support the assessment center? A survey of these overall issues will determine whether an assessment center is necessary for an organization, and will help structure subsequent decisions in the establishment of the center.

3. *Conduct job analysis.*   Job analysis involves two steps: (1) identifying clusters of job activities that comprise the most important aspects of the job, and (2) determining the behavioral dimensions necessary to carry out those job activities effectively. The first step in a job analysis involves listing exactly what the holder of that job would actually do on a daily basis. For example, a particular supervisor's job might entail scheduling subordinates' work, providing training on new job instructions, disseminating policy and procedures, diagnosing production problems, completing paperwork, ordering materials, maintaining quality controls, and dealing with employee conflicts. There are several techniques available for determining job duties: interviews with persons currently holding those jobs, discussions with superiors and subordinates, reviews of job descriptions, and having job incumbents keep logs of their duties.

   After determining job duties, it is necessary to define the human characteristics required for that specific job. For example, on that same supervisory job, the following behavioral dimensions are deemed necessary: planning and organizing, delegating, interpersonal sensitivity, written communication, oral communication, judgment, problem solving, and leadership. These would be the prerequisite skills and characteristics needed to effectively carry out such job duties. Clearly, it is more difficult to determine behavioral dimensions of a job than it is to identify specific job responsibilities.

There are several methods for determining behavioral dimensions of a job: having managers who are familiar with the target job discuss and brainstorm, having job incumbents articulate key skills and types of behavior necessary for the job, having supervisors recall and describe specific examples of effective or ineffective performance in existing or previous holders of the target job, and finally, on-the-job observations by both incumbents and supervisors over a period of time. Whatever the method of inferring assessment dimensions, it is imperative that the assessment center team develop a complete and valid list of actual kinds of behavior, with specific criteria for making judgments about those types of behavior. Only those duties and forms of behavior necessary for a particular job should be included. Such a job analysis must be completed for each job category included in the assessment center.

4. *Select exercises.* A wide variety of exercises have been used in assessment centers. Some commonly used techniques include in-basket exercises, group discussions with or without assigned leaders, role plays, presentations, interviews, management games, simulations, case studies, projective tests, and paper-and-pencil tests. An in-basket exercise asks the job candidate to sort through a typical array of mail, memos, reports, and other documents to see how the candidate prioritizes correspondence, makes decisions, formulates responses, and delegates tasks to others. Group discussions require participants to cooperatively solve a problem in a specified period of time. This exercise can reveal participants' problem-solving ability, teamwork, division of labor, oral communication, influence, and leadership skills. Role plays attempt to duplicate realistic one-on-one situations such as employee confrontations, customer complaints, coaching employee performance, evaluating employee performance, dealing with grievances, or interviewing prospective employees. The range of role-play situations is broad. Specific role plays should be designed to most closely approximate the interpersonal demands of the job. Thus, assessors can observe the candidate's actual behavior in a hypothetical but realistic job situation. Candidates can be asked to make a formal presentation or be interviewed by the team of assessors. Management games usually involve some group activity with specified roles, an element of competition, and some negotiation for preferred outcomes. This may reveal a candidate's competitive spirit, ability to deal with stress, and persuasive interaction with others. Simulations attempt

to duplicate the complex working environment of an organization by providing participants with detailed role instructions and tasks to accomplish. They work together for a day or more simulating their actual job behavior for assessors to observe. In case-study exercises, participants are given data on a situation and asked to recommend appropriate courses of action. This reveals how a job candidate interprets information and formulates and defends solutions. Personality assessment tools and paper-and-pencil tests do not measure actual behavior, but tap attitudes, values, motives, knowledge, or aptitudes. Licensed organizational psychologists must administer and interpret such tests.

Clearly, a wide range of exercises exist for use in assessment centers. A variety of techniques, rather than just a few exercise types, should be used. The planning team should consider the following criteria when selecting or designing exercises for an assessment center:

- Is the exercise appropriate for the target job?
- Can the exercise demonstrate important behavioral dimensions of the target job?
- Will assessors be able to clearly make judgments about job candidates' behavior in the exercise?
- Does the information gained from the exercise outweigh the complexity, time frame, and manpower cost of the exercise?

5. *Develop qualified assessors.* A key ingredient in the success of an assessment center is the selection and training of assessors. Without a pool of competent evaluators who can objectively observe and rate employees' and employment candidates' behavior for input into personnel decisions, those decisions will be no better than if they are made intuitively or subjectively. Assessors can be drawn from existing management ranks in the organization if those individuals can spare extensive time away from their jobs. They are most familiar with the organization and the requirements of many jobs within the organization. A manager who directly or indirectly supervises an employee should never participate in the assessment center evaluations of that employee, however. An organization can also find assessment talent in the business school of its local college or university, within the membership ranks of professional management and personnel organizations, among recent retirees of the organization, or from consultant organizations specializing in assessment centers.

Once the pool of assessors is obtained, they must be trained to observe and document behavior and to make judgments about specific behavioral dimensions. Willing assessors too ready to offer global or overall impressions of job candidates must instead be trained to follow well-defined criteria for observing and evaluating behavior. Assessors should go through all exercises themselves, familiarize themselves with all materials, practice their observational and evaluative skills, and prepare sample feedback reports. The training of assessors can take several weeks.

6. *Administer the center.* There are several considerations involved in the actual running of an assessment center. These include the physical facility; the scheduling of facilities, equipment, and people; a policy for selecting assessment center participants; orienting participants; a policy for reassessing candidates who perform poorly in an assessment center; publicizing the assessment center to the organization; and ensuring the security of assessment materials. The physical design should be sufficiently large, private, and comfortable to accommodate the number of people and activities involved at any one time in the center. There should be audiovisual equipment for presentations and videotaping, as well as space for relaxation during breaks. Schedules must be established for assessors, participants, and the use of equipment. A group of about six participants can be processed through an assessment center in a day or as long as an entire week, depending on the objective, exercises, and dimensions assessed. After rating all candidates on all dimensions, assessors need time to discuss, reach consensus, and make decisions.

A policy for nominating assessment center participants must be developed and circulated through the organization. Supervisor nominations and self-nominations are common. Once candidates are selected, they must be notified and given some explanations about the purpose and activities of the assessment center. Participants' expectations must be handled and they may be given some advance work to do in preparation for their work in the assessment center.

Some candidates who perform poorly in an assessment center will ask for an opportunity to repeat the process. The organization must specify a policy and perhaps a minimum time interval regarding reassessment. For the program to be successful, it must be publicized thoroughly. Letters, brochures, meetings, or videotapes can be used to explain the concept, to structure expectations, and to allay fears. Finally, there must be a plan for ensuring the security of materials used and the confidentiality of information produced in the assessment center.

7. *Develop feedback procedures.* The type of information about participants developed at an assessment center depends on the objec-

tive of the center. Whatever that objective, participants should be told how the information will be used prior to their participation in the assessment center. Within a two-week period after assessments are made, candidates should receive feedback about their performance on broad behavioral dimensions. Usually, specific ratings are not disclosed to the participants. A member of the assessment center staff should meet with each candidate to present feedback on the candidate's abilities and to discuss recommendations and decisions as they relate to training and career development.

Additional Concerns: Cost, Validity, Legality

Any organization considering the development of an assessment center must examine costs, the validity of information and decisions obtained from the center, and legal questions or liabilities. In analyzing costs, it is important to include both the expense of starting an assessment center as well as the ongoing operational costs of an existing center. Start-up costs typically include consultants' fees, exercise development or purchase, and assessor training. Operational costs include salaries for assessment center staff; assessors' fees; transportation, room, and board for candidates; and the cost of having many employees away from their jobs for a week or more. While assessment centers vary a great deal in purpose, complexity, facilities, and time frame, published costs for assessment centers tend to average $500 per candidate.

The issue of validity of assessment centers is a crucial and complex one that also impinges on legal questions. Equal employment opportunity laws demand that companies with assessment centers collect validity information in order to defend personnel decisions resulting from the method. Assessment centers must demonstrate content validity, which refers to the degree to which exercises used in the center correspond to actual job requirements. An organization cannot evaluate employee skills or abilities that are not relevant to the job the employee has or will have. Likewise, assessment centers must demonstrate predictive validity. That means that the assessment center method must be able to accurately distinguish those individuals who will be successful in a target job from those individuals who will not. Assessors' ratings of a given candidate must be reliable, that is, a given assessor's rating of a particular candidate on a certain dimension must be consistent. Fluctuations would indicate random rather than fair and objective evaluations.

Like most personnel practices, the assessment center must stand up to legal tests. The organization must be able to show that it followed the Standards and Ethical Considerations for Assessment Center Operations in the development, validation, and use of decision-making procedures associated with the center. These guidelines, prepared by a task force of industrial practitioners and academic researchers, can be found in *The Personnel Administrator*, February 1980, pages 35–38. The organization must be able to provide evidence to demonstrate the validity and fairness of job-analysis techniques, exercises and measures used, samples of subjects, statistical analyses, and research techniques.

Selection and promotion decisions based on assessment centers tend to be regarded by companies, job candidates, and the judicial system as fairer and more objective than decisions made by any other means in an organization. Evidence to date indicates that well-designed and effectively run assessment centers are defensible to compliance agencies and to courts. In fact, the Equal Employment Opportunity Commission has used an assessment center in its own agency.

Creative Options

There are other options in addition to developing an in-house assessment center for an organization that wants to use the assessment center process. Some of these options include using outside contractors, prepackaged systems, and interactive computer formats, or combining resources with other organizations to form a consortium of assessment center services.

Outside contractors are available to come into an organization to design and operate an assessment center for the organization. This may be an attractive option for companies without the internal expertise in behavioral assessment or for companies that cannot free the schedules of numerous people who would be involved in developing and running a center. This alternative saves money, but an outside contractor may not be able to tailor its program to meet an organization's specific needs.

Prepackaged systems include videotapes, audiocassettes, standard exercises, and evaluation instructions for an organization to use in an assessment center. This saves time and costs, and exercises usually have undergone extensive validation already. However, a prepackaged system may not include materials to tap certain skills or dimensions relevant to particular jobs in an organization, and the organization still must locate and train a team of assessors. Many companies use, at the very least, commercially available exercises that cost from $3 to $15 for each candidate assessed per exercise. This is inexpensive given the time-consuming task of developing exercises and collecting validity data.

Interactive computer versions of assessment centers are available. Here, the participant performs the exercises at a computer terminal. The computer scores the exercises and provides summary information for feedback purposes. While some critics charge that this technique may violate the standards for assessment centers, the format may have unique applications for certain types of organization jobs.

Small organizations with similar needs can join together to share in the development and operation of an assessment center. The pooling of resources can result in a better-quality center, a larger pool of qualified assessors, and cost savings. Careful coordination is necessary to ensure that the center meets everyone's needs and is available on an equal basis to all member organizations. Methods to maintain the confidentiality of records must be devised. Companies interested in the consortium approach can work through local chapters of professional management or human resources organizations, or through the business school of a local college or university.

Advantages and Disadvantages of Assessment Centers

The growth in the number of assessment centers over the last few years attests to their many benefits. Probably the most obvious advantage is improved decision making regarding personnel selection, promotion, and development. Assessment centers overcome the biases inherent in interviews and supervisor ratings. Published evidence shows that high performance in an assessment center predicts job performance, progress in salary and promotions, and rated potential for high management. In short, assessment centers provide a fair and objective way to make effective decisions about employees.

Participants report favorable reactions to assessment centers. Credible, quality centers approximate real-life work behaviors and allow participants to demonstrate their skills and abilities. When feedback is timely, defensible, and thorough, participants learn a great deal from the center, whatever the immediate decision regarding their career. This feedback lends itself to training decisions and programs. Overall, participants, management, unions, and the courts have accepted assessment centers as a valid and reasonable way to make meaningful and correct evaluations of employee performance.

Another benefit comes from assessor training. Managers who have been part of an assessment team enhance their observation, perceptiveness, and objectivity skills, which can improve both performance appraisals and coaching of subordinates back on the job.

Assessment centers are not without their limitations or drawbacks. Certainly, the process is time-consuming and costly. If the center is used infrequently, the cost may be prohibitive. Good techniques for nominating candidates to the center must exist to ensure a reasonable success rate. If too many participants perform poorly in the center, morale will be adversely affected and grievances or litigation can result.

The center must be part of a larger selection-promotion system. It should not stand alone, should not supplant informal observation of on-the-job behavior, and should not undermine the first-line manager's role in identifying talented people. Some critics argue that the process is too stressful for participants, and that extremely important career decisions should not be made on the basis of a few days' observations of employees.

Tips for Running an Assessment Center

The following are some suggestions for taking care of smaller, yet important, details of an assessment center:

- Position the assessment center as a career opportunity to be welcomed by candidates, not as a make-or-break obstacle.
- The image of the assessment center should reflect competence and professionalism. The center's credibility affects participants' attitudes, performance, and acceptance of outcomes.
- Being involved in an assessment center as a job candidate or as an assessor is hard work. A reasonable schedule, plenty of refreshments, pleasant physical surroundings, and adequate secretarial support are crucial considerations for reducing stress and operating smoothly.

[See also Performance Appraisals; Recruiting and Selecting New Employees]

For Additional Information

Goldstein, Irwin L. *Training in Organizations: Needs Assessment, Development, and Evaluation*, Monterey, Calif.: Brooks/Cole Publishing Company, 1986. Focus is on assessing training needs, but the information on job analysis, criterion development, and validity issues is relevant to general assessment of employee performance. Goldstein provides research data and practical examples related to assessment.

Joiner, Dennis A. "Assessment Centers in the Public Sector: A Practical Approach." *Public Personnel Management*, Vol. 13 (1984), No. 4, pp. 435–450. An overview of assessment centers as they are commonly used in local government settings for employee selection and promotion decisions. An example of a practical model is provided as well as suggestions for developing and administering legally defensible assessment center exams.

Keil, E. C. *Assessment Centers: A Guide for Human Resource Management.* Reading, Mass.: Addison-Wesley Publishing Company, 1986. Information on the history of assessment centers, job analysis, validity, assessor training, and center administration. To illustrate key concepts, Keil provides two fictitious case examples of assessment centers. In addition, the book includes selected portions of The Uniform Guidelines on Employee Selection published by the federal government in 1978.

Klimoski, Richard, and Mary Brickner. "Why Do Assessment Centers Work: The Puzzle of Assessment Center Validity." *Personnel Psychology,* Vol. 40 (1987), No. 2, pp. 243–260. Possible explanations for the predictive validity obtained in assessment centers.

Souder, William E., and Anna Mae Leksich. "Assessment Centers Are Evolving Toward a Bright Future." *Personnel Administrator,* Vol. 28 (1983), No. 11, pp. 80–87. A concise overview of assessment center history, characteristics, implementation steps, trends, and benefits.

Thornton, George C. III, and William C. Byham. *Assessment Centers and Managerial Performance.* New York: Academic Press, 1982. A comprehensive guide to all aspects of assessment centers, including research data documenting the reliability and validity of commonly used exercises and commonly measured managerial dimensions. The book includes questions for future research on assessment centers and thirty-one pages of references.

Business Writing

ALL MANAGERS, REGARDLESS OF THEIR FUNCTION, LEVEL, OR TYPE OF ORGANIZATION, must be effective writers. Workplace organizations produce large amounts of written information in the form of memos, letters, short reports, formal reports, and specialized documents such as employee handbooks, company newsletters, and annual reports for stockholders. While most managers may not be involved in creating these specialized documents, they surely will write memos, letters, and reports on a regular basis. Indeed, a large portion of a manager's time involves writing. Workplace organizations need information to function. A manager's job is to seek and provide information so that decisions can be made, problems can be solved, work can be coordinated, and results can be evaluated. In this information age, with its explosion of knowledge, written communication is even more important. The number of organizations whose purpose is to provide information is increasing in our society.

Writing ability is also an important component of your credibility and success in an organization. Individuals who are competent in specialized fields such as engineering, personnel, or accounting, for example, are passed over for promotions if they cannot communicate effectively. They will not be given managerial responsibility unless their oral and written communication skills allow them to be understood. Successful managers accomplish their goals by being able to communicate in clear and powerful ways. You may also have to edit your subordinates' written work. Knowing and applying the principles of business writing therefore makes your job easier, affects individual and company credibility, and advances careers.

Stages in the Writing Process

All business writing, whether it be for memos, letters, or reports, follows the same process of steps. The three stages in the writing process are prewriting, writing, and editing.

Prewriting

Prewriting is the preparation stage that precedes actual writing. Typically, you should plan to spend more time in this stage than in the other two stages, especially when writing long reports. Attention devoted to the prewriting stage will make writing easier and will increase the quality of your written material. Prewriting includes determining your objective, analyzing the audience, gathering information, and outlining.

1. *Determining your objective.* Deciding on the purpose of a written document is the key to getting organized. All other planning decisions relate to the purpose or objective of the written communication. Knowing the purpose even helps you decide whether to write a memo, letter, short report, or long report. Just as a builder uses blueprints or a traveler consults a map to guide actions, a writer should develop a plan to follow when writing.

   In determining the objective of your written document, analyze the one main idea you are trying to communicate. If you do not identify, ahead of time, the overall purpose of the document, then you are likely to ramble and confuse the reader. You should write out the objective as specifically and as concisely as possible. Then review it often while writing and editing the document. Objectives that are too general provide little direction. For example, writing a letter to a customer to "follow up on a complaint about service" gives little direction about the information, tone, or outcome of the letter. A more specific objective might be to "explain the company's service policy in a way that will retain the customer." Likewise, writing a report to "explore the possibility of drug testing of employees" probably would result in a disorganized, vague document. A more specific objective would be to "examine the legal, financial, and psychological implications of employee drug testing at Company X."

2. *Analyzing the audience.* Another aspect of prewriting involves analyzing the audience so that your document meets their needs. Determine who will read this communication. Are they internal or external to your organization? If internal, what are their job titles or areas of responsibility? If they are external, what is their relation-

ship to the writer and the company? How familiar are the readers with the topic of your communication, or with the field of specialization embodied in the document? What is their attitude to your communication? What do you want readers to do after reading your document?

These are just some of the questions that provide a reader profile. There will be other audience-analysis questions related to specific forms and objectives of written communication. By creating a reader profile, you can select what information to provide, what writing style to use, and what language to include.

The steps of determining the objective and analyzing the audience go hand in hand. They have been separated into two distinct steps here for the sake of clarity. Obviously, the objective of a document must be based on the nature of the reader. For instance, a letter to employees about anticipated layoffs would have a different objective than a letter about layoffs written to the head of personnel.

3. *Gathering information.* After determining both the objective of the communication and the nature of the readers, it is time to gather information to be included in the document. The extent of this step will vary according to the type of document being written. A minimal amount of information may be needed for a memo to announce an upcoming meeting, for example. A substantial amount of information, on the other hand, may be necessary for a formal report on sales volume or minority recruitment.

Whether you are writing a short memo or a detailed report, however, you will have to gather information and check its accuracy before including it in the written communication. If you are writing a memo to announce a meeting, you will need accurate information about the date, time, place, and purpose of the meeting. It may take only a few minutes to gather this information, but you still have completed this step of the prewriting process.

Gathering information for a formal report can take many months. You will need published material from libraries, data from company records, or specialized information from professional associations. You may need to commission market research studies, interview employees or clients, or distribute questionnaires. Depending on the purpose and scope of the report, the manager as writer may launch a comprehensive research investigation before writing the report. Managers who write formal reports must be skilled researchers as well as skilled writers.

One additional point should be made about the information-gathering step. There comes a point where information gathering should stop and writing should begin. This is important because some writers use information gathering as an excuse not to write. You can easily delay writing because of the need to collect more information. The report, which should be written this week, is delayed so next month's sales figures can be included or a few more sources can be checked. Each day, new information becomes available on any topic. Productive writers make sure that their information is thorough and timely, but they do not get caught in the trap of an endless search for complete information. If a report deadline is not imposed on you, make sure that you impose a realistic deadline for completion and cut off information gathering at an appropriate point.

4. *Outlining.* The next step is to arrange the information into an order appropriate for communicating it. You must decide what the best sequencing of information would be, given the nature of the information and the document's purpose and audience. Again, the extent of outlining will vary from one type of written communication to the next. Some reflection on the order of points suffices for a letter. But the writer of a formal report should spend considerable time writing and rearranging an outline to achieve the best organization of information.

Outlining means organizing information by dividing it into smaller parts. There are various ways of dividing information and various orders in which that subdivided information can be presented. You should reflect on your purpose, audience, and body of information to arrive at a logical approach to subdividing and sequencing.

A report on increases in the cost of employee benefits may lend itself to a chronological pattern of organization. You could present information on a year-by-year basis. Or, if the information revealed that certain types of benefits were more costly than others, then a topical pattern of organization might be preferable. You could subdivide the information according to medical, dental, child-care, insurance, and vacation benefits.

Other common approaches to organizing ideas include arrangement by place, quantity, problem solution, and comparison. An example of organization by place is a nonprofit organization's report on fund-raising, divided into eastern, midwestern, southern, and western regional concerns. A report evaluating the success of a quality circles program in a hospital could be divided into sections that deal, in turn, with the medical, nursing, dietary, housekeeping, maintenance, security, and administrative departments.

Examples of the organization of ideas by quantity are a market research report showing consumer purchases by income levels from under $5,000 to over $50,000 and a report from a pharmaceutical company to physicians about a new drug, with research data broken down according to the age of patient. Organization according to a problem-solution pattern would be, for example, a report calling for building renovation that shows the problems (maintenance costs and safety violations) stemming from lack of renovation and the solutions (tax savings and expansion possibilities) stemming from renovation. A comparison method of organization could be used in a report showing the sales of paperback versus hardback books for a publishing company.

Regardless of the method of organizing and sequencing information, there should be a comparable amount of material written for each main idea. If the information is presented for Plants A, B, and C, for example, you should not provide one paragraph of material on Plant A and three pages of material on Plant B. When outlines are included with reports, use proper outline symbols and parallel construction of terms. Consult style manuals for conventional outline symbols. Parallel construction means that you use either complete sentences or noun phrases throughout, but do not mix the two. Likewise, if most entries begin with "-ing verbs," then all entries should be similarly constructed. Finally, writers often create outlines that are too skimpy or too detailed. A good rule is to make the total number of words in an outline less than one third of the number of words in the report.

Writing

Two issues must be considered when writing business documents. They must attract attention and be readable.

Creating Attention-Getting Material Managers and executives in organizations usually receive large amounts of written information. They read some documents in great detail, skim others, and give others little more than a cursory glance. This means that your document, if it is to compete with all the others in the organization, must grab the reader's attention. There are several ways to create attention-getting documents.

First, the format and appearance of the document will create an overall impression. If readers obtain a favorable first impression of the material, then they are more likely to read it. The impression comes not from what the document says, but from how it is packaged. The quality of the paper, the neatness of the typing, the amount of white space, and the visual appeal of charts and graphs all contribute to the reader's impression of the document. A long letter packed with words, with narrow margins and few paragraphs, will seem intimidating. A report without subheadings, summaries, or professional-looking visuals may be impossible to comprehend. Writers of internal memos should devote care even to these brief, informal documents. A sloppy memo without visual appeal may not be taken seriously.

Another way to produce attention-getting documents is to have a powerful opening. The first few sentences of a letter, for example, should immediately convey the document's purpose. Within the first minute of scanning the document, the readers should see how the material relates to them. If the first few lines are confusing, vague, rambling, or irritating, readers may toss the material aside. The opening should compel them to continue.

A final suggestion for producing attention-getting written material is to make the document easy to read. The reader should not have to struggle to process the information in your documents. Of course, ease of reading depends very much on the quality of the writing. But there are devices that can make your documents easy to read. In a memo, you can underline dates for deadlines, meetings, or decisions. You can highlight information in a letter by placing it in a list form with bullets next to each entry in the list. A report ought to have an outline or executive summary to highlight major points.

Creating Readable Material   While there are general guidelines for creating readable material, the question of readability depends on the nature of the audience. A highly technical report that uses specialized jargon, for example, will be readable to experts in that speciality but not to a lay person. What is readable to college graduates may not be readable to people who have not completed high school. Writers must adapt their writing level to fit the identity, education, experience, and knowledge of the readers. When the audience is diverse, it is best to aim for the lowest-level reader.

A major factor in producing readable material is to simplify your writing. Simple sentences with familiar words are always more readable than complex sentences replete with impressive vocabulary. In business writing, sentences should be short and powerful. Aim for an average sentence length of 15 words. This does not mean that all sentences should be fewer than 15 words. An occasional longer sentence provides variety and interest to a document. But a document containing only long sentences with dependent clauses and multiple ideas will be tedious even for the most advanced reader. If you tend to produce long sentences when writing, then try to break each of them into two sentences. After a while, the shorter sentences will come to you more naturally.

Another way to simplify writing is to select the simplest words. In conversation, most people select simple, familiar words. But for some reason, many writers fall into the trap of using stilted, awkward words. If we wrote more similarly to the way we talked, documents would be clearer. Consider the following list of less familiar words found often in business documents and their more familiar counterparts:

Unfamiliar Word	Familiar Word
utilize	use
furnish	give
ascertain	find
accomplish	do
transmit	send
attributable	due
correspondence	letter

Substitute the simpler word for the more complex one not only to make the document easier to read but also to create more powerful writing. Listen to the tone of the following two sentences. The first sounds stiff while the second is more vivid. "In regard to your inquiry regarding damages, this company has ascertained that you will be compensated in the amount of $20." "We will pay you $20 for damages, as you requested."

You can also improve the readability of material by using the active rather than the passive voice. This means that the subject of the sentence should come before the object of the sentence. The following sentences show the difference between active and passive voice:

Passive: "The meeting was arranged by Jane Smith."
Active: "Jane Smith arranged the meeting."

Passive: "Sales reports must be distributed by sales managers each Friday."
Active: "Sales managers must distribute sales reports each Friday."

Sentences using the active voice tend to be more interesting, shorter, and clearer. They immediately call attention to the subject performing the action. By converting sentences from the passive to the active voice, you will eventually learn to compose originally in the active voice.

Next, check your grammar, spelling, and punctuation. It is impossible to cover all the relevant rules here. You can familiarize yourself with common problems in these areas by consulting reference books on writing style. Otherwise, use competent editors and proofreaders.

Using transitions is another way to increase readability. Transitions are words that help the reader make a shift from one idea to

another. They can be words, phrases, or sentences that signal a movement in information. Transitions help readers follow the progression of
ideas and connect points in a document. For example, the word
"conversely" signals a contrast of ideas. The word "thus" signals a
conclusion. "In addition" suggests movement to a similar point.

A final suggestion for increasing readability is to eliminate trite,
cluttered phrases. Over the years, the conventions of business writing
have led us to use some of these tired phrases. Writers should remove
the following expressions from their material:

Enclosed, please find
Deem it advisable
As per your instructions
In accordance with your request
Kindly advise
Thanking you in advance
Pending receipt
Agreeable to your wishes in this matter
Under separate cover
Regarding the aforementioned

Writing readable copy becomes easier with practice. However, you
will see immediate improvement in the readability of your documents
if you follow the six guidelines discussed:

1. Keep sentences short.
2. Use familiar words.
3. Convert sentences from passive to active voice.
4. Use correct grammar, punctuation, and spelling.
5. Use transitions.
6. Avoid cluttered phrases.

Editing

The final phase of the writing process involves editing. Under no
circumstances should a writer consider the first draft of a document to
be the final draft. Even experienced business writers cannot produce
letters and reports in their complete and final form. All writers should
expect to edit and revise written material. The number of drafts of a
document will vary according to the writer's skill and the nature and
importance of the document. A short letter may need only one rewrite
to become excellent copy. When writing a formal report, you may need
five or six drafts before it is in excellent shape.

Editing is a skill that improves with practice. The following
suggestions can guide the editing process and help writers become
skillful editors:

1. *Let the material sit awhile before revising it.* You are less likely to catch errors or to notice confusing information if you are very familiar with the writing. Reading the material "cold" will enable you to look at it from the reader's perspective.

2. *Do not become wedded to the written material.* Some writers have trouble revising their material or accepting editorial suggestions from others because they attach their egos to their writing. They feel the need to defend every idea, sentence, or word; or they reread their copy to bask in the pride of their eloquence. Editing should mean rereading with the goal of changing and improving your writing.

3. *Review the document four separate times with the goals of editing content, organization, style, and appearance.* Editing content means examining the information to see if it is correct, thorough, and understandable. Does the content convey the appropriate tone? When examining your organization, ask yourself if the order of information makes sense, if the ideas progress logically, if the information rambles, and if your reader could outline the information. Stylistic revisions involve enhancing the readability of the material. Are sentences short? Are simple, clear, and vivid words used? Does the document include correct grammar and transitional devices and does it avoid trite expressions? Finally, examine the physical appearance of the document for spelling, punctuation, and typographical errors. Is there enough white space? Are margins appropriate? Is the paper free of smudges, tears, and erasures? Is the print dark enough?

Only after all these areas have been examined and revised and the document is as good as it can get should it be sent to the reader. Clear and credible written communication is imperative in workplace organizations. While the writing process can be time-consuming, you will greatly benefit from going through the steps of prewriting, writing, and editing whenever you create written material.

When to Use the Written Form

Some managers and some organizations opt for the written form of communication when oral communication would be better. Writing a memo rather than talking to someone can be the cowardly or the ineffective choice. Managers who are unsure about the efficacy of written communication should follow these guidelines:

1. Put information in writing if you want a verifiable record. Often, managers need to document actions or need a written record for later use.
2. Put complex or detailed information in writing. Some information cannot be grasped orally or remembered if it is not written down.
3. Create a written document if you want to convey the same information to several people. It is easier and quicker to distribute a written document to many people than to communicate with each one of them individually. You can be sure they each get identical information if it is written, whereas individual conversations would inevitably differ.
4. Use the written form if it is too costly or too inconvenient to meet in person or to talk on the telephone. Sending a letter to someone in another state is usually more logical than traveling to talk. Written communication may be necessary if your repeated attempts to reach a person by telephone have failed.

For Additional Information

Andrews, Deborah C., and William D. Andrews. *Business Communication.* New York: Macmillan Publishing Company, 1988. A textbook aimed at a student audience that also provides substantive information for managers on writing letters, memos, and reports. Additional chapters cover the writing process, writing for international audiences, finding business information, designing documents, and using computers in writing.

Brill, Laura. *Business Writing Quick and Easy.* New York: AMACOM, 1982. How to achieve a natural writing style in short letters, complex reports, or manuals. There is advice on eliminating jargon, putting action into writing, using transitions, focusing on facts, eliminating misunderstanding, and using correct grammar and punctuation.

Cross, Mary. *Persuasive Business Writing.* New York: AMACOM, 1987. A guidebook for creating letters, memos, and reports that get action. Various formats for persuasive writing are suggested and applied to business purposes.

Davies, John. "Teaching Managers to Write." *Personnel Management,* Vol. 19 (1987), No. 1, pp. 26–29. Posits that many managers lack the ability to express themselves logically, clearly, and concisely. The author describes some common failings of managers as writers and offers guidelines for better written communication.

Jones, Barbara Schindler. *Written Communication for Today's Manager.* New York: Lebhar-Friedman Books, 1980. A source of practical information on holding attention, gathering information, organizing ideas, writing for readability, and editing material. The book includes a discussion of special forms of writing such as reports, memos, letters, brochures, and newsletters.

Lesikar, Raymond V. *Report Writing for Business.* Homewood, Ill.: Richard D. Irwin, 1981. Focuses on report writing, but its thorough coverage of the writing process in general makes it a good sourcebook. Lesikar explains the planning process, the information search from primary and library sources, the interpretation and arrangement of information, outlines, layouts, graphic aids, and readability. He includes a primer on punctuation and grammar, a checklist for evaluating reports, sample report problems, and illustrations of types of reports.

Seekings, David. "Effective Writing." *Management Decisions,* Vol. 25 (1987), No. 3, pp. 11–15. Principles and simple rules for achieving effective writing.

Career Development

A CAREER can be defined as an evolving sequence of work experiences over time—the course that you take through your work life. You deal with career issues at two levels: First, you must be concerned with your own career, that is, make choices, accept opportunities, and develop strategies for dealing with it. Second, you must think about the careers of your subordinates; develop, coach, and act as mentors to them; and delight in the career successes that result.

Many organizations are concerned about how employees move through their structure of roles and responsibilities. Their forecasting and long-range planning efforts often involve projecting personnel needs relevant to human resources development activities. Consequently, career-development issues are important to managers whatever their level, function, or organizational type.

The Need for Career Development

Career-development issues are taking on greater importance for individuals and organizations alike. From the individual perspective, people are no longer spending a lifetime in one career or at one job. The day of the loyal employee affiliating with one company and allowing that company to dictate career decisions is clearly over. Employees at all levels are taking greater responsibility for the development of their careers.

Employees are also bringing different motivations to the workplace. Increasingly, they want challenging work and a sense of contribution to the organization. Salary and promotions as motivators compete with other job features such as meaningful work, flexible schedules, and input into decision making. Nor is the work force as

28

homogeneous as it used to be. Women, minorities, handicapped people, foreign-born workers, and older employees add diversity to the traditional population. A different composition of employees means different work attitudes and career patterns. Moreover, family and leisure concerns have taken on more importance to today's workers at all levels. Career decisions are affected by family needs and avocational interests more than by promotional opportunities.

Burgeoning changes in technology, business activity made volatile by mergers and acquisitions, and foreign business competition have all caused workplaces to become more dynamic. Employees in some industries have found that the job they performed yesterday is not there today. Certain job skills and knowledge are rapidly becoming obsolete. Employees are often forced into an awareness of the dynamics of their careers.

In short, individuals are making explicit career decisions and want more control over their careers. Compared to previous generations, they are willing to take more risks, are more geographically mobile, and want to be more self-directed in career matters. And because of societal forces and business activity outside of their control, employees must face more career decisions than they ever had to before.

From the organizational perspective, career-development issues are equally important. Increasingly, companies are realizing the costs associated with low productivity and high turnover. Thus, they see career development as a way to retain talented employees and to motivate them to reach organizational goals. It is more cost-effective to develop existing employees than to recruit, hire, and train new ones. Organizations also emphasize career development as a way of meeting affirmative action and equal employment opportunity (EEO) goals. By providing career-development assistance, they retain and develop the potential of certain underutilized categories of employees.

Finally, companies turn to career development to ensure that personnel will be qualified for future staffing requirements. By assisting current employees with career-development concerns, progressive organizations can match career goals with future organizational needs. Thus, career-development programs become an important human resources planning tool.

Companies that disclaim the need to provide career-development information should realize the many ways that they already provide career information. Managers who think that career guidance is not their responsibility should examine the abundant career advice they give inadvertently to subordinates through their role modeling, performance feedback, and promotion decisions. And through their norms, values, structures, and reward systems, organizations also provide information about career strategies.

Individual Strategies for Career Development

There are many ways that you can plan your own management career, whether your goal is to stay with one organization or to switch organizations. Managers often turn to career-development strategies when they are dissatisfied with the current job situation or are facing a job loss. But strategizing your career should be an ongoing activity and not be neglected until a time of crisis. By being aware of career-development issues as they relate to individual career goals, you can develop a sense of direction and control over your career. Successful managers who are attuned to their career dynamics practice many of these strategies:

Clarifying Your Values

It is important to know how work fits into your life priorities. Is career success your top goal? How do career goals fit in with personal, family, leisure, or spiritual goals? In order to be satisfied and successful, a job must fit your needs and must not contradict your fundamental values. Some people, for example, may find themselves in highly competitive work situations although collaboration or helping others is more important to them than competition. Other people with high needs for affiliation may have jobs that isolate them from others. What do you find important in a job—challenge, excitement, stability, responsibility, freedom, money, titles, chances for advancement?

Obviously the first step in planning a career path is determining the kind of work or job you would like. By clarifying values either before embarking on a career track or while in the midst of a career, you can profile the right kind of career for yourself. A variety of values-clarification books, workshops, or counselors are available to assist with this self-assessment activity.

Determining Your Occupational Aptitudes and Interests

In addition to clarifying values, it is important to know what kinds of jobs you would be good at and interested in. There are numerous standardized tests for measuring vocational aptitudes and interests. These are best administered, scored, and interpreted by qualified career counselors. High school and college guidance counselors often administer these tests before prospective graduates enter the world of work. Industrial psychologists and assessment center evaluators also use these tests relative to hiring and promotion decisions. It would be interesting for all working adults to know if standardized tests reveal an aptitude and a preference for the line of work they are in.

Realizing Your Options

The number of career options that any manager has is enormous. There may be a number of directions you can take within a particular organization. Probably there are numerous employers within a particular industry for whom you could work. Then there are an infinite number of possible job types that you could hold. Indeed, for each of us, career options are more expansive than we realize.

Realizing options means being aware of the opportunities within a company and identifying the market for your skills. Managers should have well-developed networks of company colleagues in order to receive advance information about opportunities, trends, and projects. They should discuss career interests and goals with their superiors and stay abreast of options through job posting, reorganization, relocation, job redesign, or project management. In short, the people who are able to seize opportunities within their organizations are the ones who are tied into the information network of the firm.

Most successful managers stay aware of the job opportunities in their fields even if they are completely satisfied with their current position and current employer. For the sake of career development, it is important to "keep your eyes open." In order to practice self-determination in your career, you should continually, but subtly, job hunt. Network to learn of opportunities at other firms, join placement bureaus of professional associations, circulate your credentials to recruiting firms, and check the classified advertisements. In essence, be acutely aware of the market for your skills and experience.

Creating a Career-Development Plan

In order to realize financial or retirement goals, you must plan early and follow a series of steps along the way. The same is true of career goals. It is wise to have both a short-term and long-range plan for your career. What would you like to be doing one year from now, five years from now, ten years into the future? What skills, experiences, education, or training accomplished now would pave the way for reaching future career goals?

A career-development plan is like a blueprint for putting the pieces of a career together. Of course it is tentative and will be altered as unexpected opportunities or exigencies occur. It seems ironic that while most adults spend at least two thirds of their lives in a career, few adopt a systematic plan for charting the course of that career.

Using Career-Development Resources

A variety of resources are available to assist managers in their career-development activities. You can look to mentor and networking relationships, the human resources department of your company, professional associations, educational institutions, and the public library for career-development assistance. Mentors provide career information and opportunities for protégés. Developing mentor relationships can provide both immediate and long-term career benefits. Likewise, developing a network of professional contacts is a positive career-development strategy.

The human resources function in organizations exists to develop personnel to meet organizational needs. Some have career-development specialists or provide workshops on career dynamics. But even those human resources departments that do not have explicit career-development functions can help you advance your career. Take advantage of all training workshops that could help you develop the skills necessary for reaching your career goals.

Attending seminars or conferences of professional associations is a great way to develop knowledge, to learn trends, and to meet influential people in your field. Many managers have developed leadership, communication, and planning skills by holding office in professional associations. Participation in professional associations can lead to career advantages later.

Local vocational schools, colleges, and universities offer a wealth of courses, materials, and experts to help you plan and advance your career. There you can learn the technical skills, obtain the knowledge, and find career counselors for developing your career in the direction you want it to take. Finally, public libraries offer substantial information about occupational opportunities and outlooks, job hunting, vocational aptitude and preference testing, and values clarification.

Being Realistic About Career Development

It is important to realize that career goals are not reached overnight. Setting unrealistic aspirations or being impatient about career progress will only create dissatisfaction. Careers take years to build. They require nurturing. They require periods of maintenance and reflection. Sometimes the best action is to step back, slow down, or start all over again in something new.

Career-Development Strategies for Organizations

There are many ways in which companies assist their employees with career development that will ultimately benefit the companies themselves. Of course, there must be a match between the employees' career goals and organizational needs. While it is important to retain valuable employees and to reduce turnover, it is counterproductive to try to keep an employee whose career goals would be better served elsewhere. One casualty of career-development assistance is that some employees leave. Nevertheless, the advantages of developing satisfied and productive employees for future personnel needs far outweigh the risk. Some strategies to achieve this include the following:

1. *Encouraging management-employee discussions of career path-ing.*   One of the responsibilities of an organization manager is to help your subordinates with career development. Help them develop realistic career plans by sharing information about organizational career opportunities and help them attain career goals. Managers and executives at all levels should have career-development meetings with their contingent of employees. This activity reduces the number of bored, unproductive, or plateaued employees and channels employees into paths that meet organizational needs.

2. *Practicing job enrichment.*   Typically, there are not enough higher-level positions for all qualified employees who would like to be promoted. This means that some careers must develop other ways. One way to encourage growth and development in employees is to expand or to enrich job responsibilities. By adding new responsibilities that the employees find appealing or by increasing authority, you are helping them to develop their careers without abandoning their current positions. The keys to successful job enrichment are sensing when employees need more challenge and adding duties that are challenging, not just time-consuming. Job enrichment is best negotiated between you and your subordinates.

3. *Practicing job rotation.*   Another avenue for career development is horizontal. Moving to another function or department without a vertical change in position can provide career-development opportunities. Such horizontal moves can offer new challenge, develop new skills, and help you meet career goals. In some organizations, managerial candidates work in various departments to get a perspective on the whole organization and to develop generalist skills.

Job rotation implies a series of lateral moves over time. For the organization, such movement can be a way of testing employees in certain jobs. For the employees, job rotation can be an unthreatening way of experimenting with job moves.

4. *Providing opportunities for project management.* All organizations have ongoing projects as a way of bringing about change in systems and procedures or as a way to implement new programs. Putting key organizational personnel in charge of such projects represents another career-development strategy. By heading a temporary project, a manager can develop technical knowledge, enhance planning and problem-solving abilities, and practice leadership and communication skills. The opportunity to lead or to participate in an exciting, innovative project may be just the catalyst to stimulate an employee whose job has become routine and who was considering leaving the organization.

5. *Providing education and training for career development.* Progressive organizations develop their people so they will stay with the company. Providing employees opportunities to learn about new developments in their field, to retool, to master a new skill, or to branch into a new area keeps the organization vital and competitive. Companies can enhance the careers of their employees by offering tuition assistance for education and by sponsoring training on relevant topics.

6. *Offering career-planning workshops.* Besides offering training on technical and managerial topics, organizations can sponsor career-planning workshops. A sample workshop can help participants clarify their values and goals, pinpoint their aptitudes and interests, and identify organizational options for career development. In addition to teaching individual employees about career dynamics, career planning can help them understand organizational decision making in such areas as personnel selection, appraisal, promotion, and termination.

7. *Providing access to career-counseling specialists.* Managers can assist with career-development issues, but they are not career-development specialists. The training department can provide self-assessment and information resources, but career development is just one of many topics training must address. Organizations that are dedicated to the career development of their staffs will provide them with access to career-development specialists. If organizational size and financial resources cannot justify a full-time career counselor, consider using consultants or providing career counseling in conjunction with an employee-assistance program.

For Additional Information

Arthur, Michael B., Lotte Bailyn, Daniel J. Levinson, and Herbert A. Shepard. *Working with Careers.* New York: Columbia University School of Business, 1984. Intended for specialists in human resource planning, organizational training and development, career advising, and adult development. The authors provide a theoretical and philosophical examination of career issues in your total life situation.

Hall, Douglas T. *Career Development in Organizations.* San Francisco: Jossey-Bass Publishers, 1986. A volume of contributed articles that cover theory, research, and practice in career development. Beginning with an overview of the field of career development, the book examines how careers are affected by cultural and organizational factors, discusses the individual career-development process, looks at career-management programs in organizations, and offers perspectives on the future of career development.

Jackson, Tom, and Alan Vitberg. "Career Development: Challenges for the Individual." *Personnel,* Vol. 64 (1987), No. 4, pp. 54–57. Examines what some organizations are doing to get employees started on individualized, self-directed career management.

Kaye, Beverly L. *Up Is Not the Only Way.* Englewood Cliffs, N.J.: Prentice-Hall, 1982. Information for career-development specialists designing and implementing career-development activities in organizations. Topics include preparing the organization for career-development activities, helping employees identify skills and target opportunities, and evaluating organizational career-development programs.

Coaching Employees

Since the success of an organization depends on the performance of its people, the development of optimum human resources is essential. The task should not be left solely to the human resources specialists within a company, however. Rather, all managers should be committed to this as well. Part of your role as a manager is to correct subordinates' performance problems and to help them grow professionally so that they can contribute to the organization while advancing in their careers. That means all good managers must be coaches. Indeed, many specific managerial job requirements entail coaching, specifically face-to-face techniques for solving employee performance problems and for helping employees develop to their fullest potential on the job. You must employ coaching techniques when giving job instructions, when correcting performance problems, when delegating, when developing work teams, and when encouraging employees' career development. Managers who are good coaches benefit in two ways: They receive quality work from subordinates and they look good in the process; as a consequence, they are recognized and rewarded by their supervisors. Being a good manager-coach means knowing whom to coach, when to coach, and how to coach. It also involves being aware of common coaching problems and developing the characteristics of a good coach.

Deciding to Coach

Ask yourself several questions before selecting coaching as a technique for solving a performance problem. First, is there actually a performance problem? In other words, is the employee not meeting some objective performance standard? Some managers will assume a performance problem in an employee because they do not like the employee or because the employee is not performing as well as someone else. Coaching involves the development of specific behaviors and should not be used to change attitudes or to foster competition in a work group.

After determining that a performance problem exists, the next question is whether the problem is correctable. This may entail your judgment about the subordinate's motivation, past performance, and ability to change, as well as an assessment of the available time and resources for bringing about a change. For example, some employees make it clear that they do not want to change behavior or develop a new skill. Past attempts at improving performance may have failed, or the seriousness of the problem precludes taking the time that coaching involves. Alternatively, instructional resources may not be available to equip the poor performer with the necessary skills for changing behavior. If the performance is not correctable for these or for other reasons, then coaching is not the answer. Other options might include transfer or termination.

Another area to consider in the decision whether to coach involves external obstacles to performance. Are there circumstances beyond the employee's control that are leading to poor performance of a job or impeding employee development? If so, then no amount of coaching will solve the problem or promote career development. Instead, you must remove the obstacles affecting employee performance. Many factors can be involved. The employee who points to external causes for performance problems may not be passing the buck or merely making excuses. Faulty materials, late deliveries, deadlines missed by others, lack of information, equipment failures, confusing instructions, and unrealistic schedules are just a few of the circumstances that can hinder an employee's job performance. Nor will coaching help a subordinate develop if growth opportunities are unavailable or if political or economic deterrents to advancement exist in the workplace.

Yet another consideration in your decision whether to coach involves the pattern of rewards and costs associated with job-related behavior. Ironically, in many organizations, poor performance is rewarded. How many times are poor performers relieved of important tasks and those tasks given to more competent workers? Many employees realize that the less you do, the less you're asked to do. For unmotivated, overworked, or stressed subordinates, performing poorly inadvertently is a way to be relieved of difficult tasks. Therefore, you must ascertain whether negative performance is being rewarded or reinforced in the workplace. Unless the reinforcers of poor performance are removed, no amount of coaching will result in performance improvements.

Finally, it is important to know when to coach subordinates. It is not necessary to wait until there is a performance problem to use coaching techniques. While coaching is often associated with performance problems, you can use it to bring about any change in behavior. For example, when you delegate an important project to a competent subordinate, you may want to coach that person on strategies of successful performance. If you give new job instructions, you should coach the employee on how to do that new job. Training involves not only introducing job skills but helping employees to develop those skills through observation, feedback, and advice, i.e., coaching. Any manager who acts as mentor to a capable subordinate coaches that person to develop professionally. If sufficient coaching is given prior to the observation of problems, fewer job-performance problems will develop. Thus, you should think of coaching as a tool to develop employees as well as a device for correcting performance. Like the athletic coach who equips players with necessary skills and motivation before the game and can relax as the team emerges victorious, if you successfully develop employees you can quietly observe their job success.

Preparing for a Coaching Session

Before communicating with the subordinate in a coaching session, do some advance planning: collect necessary information, structure the message appropriately for a particular subordinate, anticipate possible reactions, and choose a suitable time and location for the discussion. If the session concerns a performance problem, then you should gather written materials such as job descriptions, policy statements, performance records, training history, and prior disciplinary actions or grievances. If the session involves employee development, you should possess all the details of the project to be assigned or the growth opportunity to be offered. As in all formal superior-subordinate communications, you should have enough documentation to be thorough, specific, and objective.

You don't manage the same way with all subordinates. What may work with one employee may not work with another. What may motivate one group may stifle another. This is especially true in coaching employees. As manager-coach, you should analyze the best strategy for dealing with each individual in light of the employee's personality, intelligence, competence, motivation, work experience, and career goals. Then you can structure the message and communicate in a style that is most likely to be effective with a given subordinate. One person may respond to a tough coaching style characterized by challenges, demands, and timetables. Another employee may need praise, encouragement, and instruction to produce new behavior. One work team may welcome competing against other departments; another group may respond better to personal bonus incentives. Adapting a coaching style to an employee means identifying when the person is ready to be developed, knowing how to motivate, or anticipating the best way to discuss a performance problem. Managers who treat each subordinate as a unique individual get the best results from their subordinates.

Likewise, you should anticipate how the subordinate might react to the performance feedback, delegated assignment, or career-advancement opportunity. Examining a message from the receiver's point of view can only improve the coaching session. Has the subordinate responded angrily to prior discussions of performance problems? Does this subordinate underestimate the capabilities for handling new projects? Will the subordinate welcome or feel burdened by your attempts to coach?

Finally, in preparing for a coaching session, you must select an appropriate time and location. The session should be private and the physical surroundings comfortable. Enough time should be allowed to accomplish the coaching objectives. From a psychological standpoint, there may be a best time to coach: An individual may be ready to take on a difficult assignment after a visible success; a work team may need coaching after a project budget cut; the poor performer may profit from feedback immediately after making a mistake.

Conducting a Coaching Session

Because coaching is frequently used to correct performance problems, we will emphasize that aspect of the technique. The steps can be altered slightly for coaching employees while delegating, giving job instructions, or team building.

Basically, there are five steps in the coaching process:

1. *Seek agreement about the need for change.* Presumably, there is a problem or a deficiency in the employee's behavior that makes coaching necessary. You must get the employee to agree that a problem exists. That means discussing the exact nature of the problem, how often the problem occurs, possible causes of the problem, and consequences of the problem. Both you and the employee must perceive the problem similarly if you are to agree on a change.

Typically, managers speak in vague generalities about work-related problems. Employees, who naturally want to end an uncomfortable discussion about their poor performance, may agree to a problem without really understanding it. Then both manager and employee become frustrated when subsequent progress does not occur.

Getting agreement on a specific problem versus vaguely hinting at a problem can be illustrated by the example of a sales manager who says to a subordinate, "You're slipping in customer service." A better approach is to give specific examples of what "slipping in customer service" means. You might say, "Four of your customers this month complained that you didn't return their calls after you closed the sale." Then you can identify the customers and ask whether your subordinate returned the calls. If the subordinate should agree to the problem by indicating a failure to return the calls, then ask for reasons behind the behavior. Such a discussion will reveal whether there was a valid reason for not returning the calls. You should also indicate the consequences of unreturned calls in terms of a loss of customers and profits.

2. *Discuss alternative solutions to the problem.* Again, being specific is important. You and your employee should consider several specific options for solving the problem and not merely agree to the most obvious solution. In our example, the simple solution is for the subordinate to return customers' calls. More specific solutions, however, might include these: the employee could reserve the last hour of each day for returning customer calls, the customer-service department could handle the routine calls, or a pamphlet for handling common customer questions could be prepared. All feasible options should be considered for dealing with the problem. The more thorough and flexible you and your subordinate can be in suggesting solutions, the more likely the problem will be solved permanently.

3. *Agree on the specific action to be taken.* It is not sufficient to get the employee to agree to try harder or to do a better job. That promise, no matter how well intentioned, is still an empty commitment. You and your subordinate should agree on one option as well as a target date by which the problem should be solved. Further, you should agree on how success will be evaluated. In this example, the problem could be considered solved when no more customer complaints about unreturned calls are received.

4. *Follow up to make sure the action was taken.* This might entail, for example, checking with your subordinate to assess progress or calling customers to see that their requests are handled promptly.

5. *Recognize accomplishments.* Praising behavior helps to reinforce that behavior. You should recognize progress that contributes to the solution of a problem as well as subordinates' successful accomplishment of behavioral change. This motivates subordinates in difficult areas of change and makes them more amenable to the coaching process in the future.

If your goal is to develop an individual or a team to succeed at a project, you can alter the five steps in this way: (1) Obtain agreement that a task needs to be accomplished; (2) make sure subordinates know the exact nature of the job; (3) discuss possible approaches to the task; (4) agree on what would comprise successful completion of the project (this includes a discussion of how the project outcome will be evaluated); and (5) follow up to make sure the tasks are accomplished, and then reward the accomplishment.

Common Coaching Problems

The manager as coach should be aware of and try to avoid these four common pitfalls:

1. *Coaching only when there is a problem.* If coaching is to be your tool for developing subordinates, then it cannot be associated only with correction or discipline. If you coach only to correct poor performance, then subordinates will be resentful and not respond to your attempts. Subordinates should regard coaching as an opportunity for growth, not as a punitive measure.

2. *Lecturing the subordinate instead of coaching.* Coaching should involve dialogue and mutual decision making. It is a type of teamwork between supervisors and subordinates. Telling or directing an employee to engage in a certain behavior is not coaching. The employee may not see the need to change or know how to change. Coaching means working with an employee to develop skills and motivation for the competent performance of some behavior.

3. *Dealing in generalities.* Probably, the hardest part of coaching involves being specific. We often think that labeling a behavior is the same as a specific description of that behavior. To avoid generalities, you should provide examples, documentation, quotations, statistics, and dates to illustrate a point.

4. *Making assumptions.* To avoid assumptions, you should explicitly communicate every step of the coaching process to your subordinate. Do not assume that employees realize per-

formance needs or problems, know how to perform compe-
tently, will perform appropriately even when they promise to,
or know when they have done a good job.

Characteristics of a Good Coach

Studies of good coaching practices, regardless of the coaching
context, reveal some common characteristics of successful coaches.
The manager who wants to succeed in developing subordinates:

- Is interested in people.
- Is predictable.
- Is straightforward.
- Lets you know where you stand.
- Gives credit to others.
- Builds confidence.
- Has high standards.
- Is objective.
- Is firm but fair.
- Is a good teacher.
- Makes employees want to do their best.

[See also Feedback; Mentoring]

For Additional Information

Concilio, Richard V. "Will Coaching Pay Off?" Management Solutions,
Vol. 31 (1986), No. 9, pp. 18–21. How, through an effective coaching system geared to developing employees, management can increase productivity and efficiency.

Deegan, Arthur X. II. Coaching: A Management Skill for Improving
Individual Performance. Reading, Mass.: Addison-Wesley Publishing Company, 1979. Though written some time ago, a good discussion of the need for personnel development in organizations and
helping managers to expand their human resources development
skills. The author covers communication techniques, transactional
analysis, and interviewing skills for the manager as coach. Self-
tests, checklists, and practice cases are included.

Fournies, Ferdinand F. Coaching for Improved Work Performance. New
York: Van Nostrand Reinhold Company, 1978. Managerial attitudes
that affect coaching and techniques to solve employee performance
problems. Coaching techniques are demonstrated in dialogue form

and numerous cases are included. The information should prove as useful to today's managers as when it was written.

Peters, Tom, and Nancy Austin. *A Passion for Excellence.* New York: Random House, 1985, chapter 18. The manager as coach, which includes educating, sponsoring, coaching, counseling, and confronting. Chapter 18 of this book includes questions, guidelines, and checklists for each of these roles.

Quick, Thomas L. *The Manager's Motivation Desk Book.* New York: John Wiley and Sons, 1985, chapter 12, pp. 289–317. A case-study discussion of the elements of management coaching, including short-term and long-term coaching, the coaching interview, goal setting and feedback, and informal coaching.

Tyson, Lynne, and Herman Birnbrauer. "Coaching: A Tool for Success." *Training and Development Journal,* Vol. 37 (1983), No. 9, pp. 30–34. The role of the coach, a coaching plan, and coaching rules to follow and pitfalls to avoid.

Conflict Management

INTERPERSONAL CONFLICT is inevitable in the workplace. Because organizations consist of numerous individuals who must coordinate their activities to get work done, there are many opportunities for conflict. Whenever two people or two groups have opposite goals, they are likely to find themselves in conflict. Hardly a day goes by in the workplace when the activities of one person or group are not at odds with others. The sales department may be in conflict with the advertising department, supervisors of different shifts may be at odds, executive officers may disagree with trustees, management and unions may have conflicting goals, customers' needs may oppose company policies, or co-workers may have personality clashes.

Dealing with conflict is a part of every manager's job. You will find yourself in conflict with others and will be called on to settle the disputes of subordinates. Never shy away from conflict; the effective handling of conflict is a necessary part of your managerial duties. Effectively handling conflict means understanding what causes disputes, promoting positive effects of conflict in organizations, encouraging the use of productive styles of communicating, and following guidelines for managing conflict.

Reasons for Conflict in the Workplace

There are many reasons why conflicts develop on the job. Causes can range from basic human nature to workplace structure and policies. A common cause of workplace conflicts is scarce resources. Because resources are needed to get jobs done and because resources are limited, we often compete for them. Managers from two departments may compete for budgetary resources. The larger one manager's budget, the smaller the other's. Resources also include office space, equipment, personnel, and decision-making power.

Conflicts also occur because of basic differences in beliefs. A conflict can develop, for example, if one member of a planning team believes in expanding the company's product line and another team member doesn't agree. The personnel specialists in an organization may believe in the value of employee assistance programs while upper management does not. Because beliefs guide actions, we find ourselves disagreeing with others over the logic or the legitimacy of certain beliefs. Just as there will never be enough resources in an organization to satisfy everybody, there can never be total agreement of beliefs.

Competition or rivalry between individuals or groups in an organization also leads to conflicts. Disputes are likely between two people who must work together when both are in line for one promotion. Two divisions of a company may refuse to cooperate with each other if both are competing for leadership of a key project. Two research colleagues may argue because of their long-standing rivalry over equipment and facilities.

Some conflicts arise because lines of authority are not clearly delineated. Power struggles are particularly difficult, because the power issues usually are not openly discussed. A secretary who has been with a company longer than a junior executive may feel justified in telling the executive how to do things. A consultant to an organization may make decisions that the client organization did not authorize. One department may make changes that affect another department without checking, in advance, with those who will be affected. Anytime that people or groups feel that their power has been usurped or that their authority has been questioned, disputes are likely to result.

Sometimes conflicts occur because people simply cannot get along. People with aggressive, insecure, or defensive personalities frequently clash with others. In some cases, there are no valid reasons for arguments other than the fact that two people do not like each other.

Conflicts Can Be Positive

Some managers are very uncomfortable with interpersonal conflict. As a result, they try to avoid or suppress disagreements. The wise manager, however, realizes that it is futile to try to eliminate conflict from the workplace. Suppressed conflicts fester below the surface and erupt sooner or later. Inevitable and even a necessary aspect of organizations, conflicts are not necessarily bad but can be challenging and enjoyable. Employees who disagree with each other and debate issues care enough about the job to fight for their positions. Where there is no conflict, there usually is apathy. Better decisions often result from a real give-and-take of ideas. Challenging decisions rather than rubber-stamping them makes for better decisions.

Conflicts can stimulate creativity and prevent stagnation. When someone questions your beliefs, you examine them. Differences of opinion challenge the manager who may have become complacent or dogmatic. Rivalry between groups can stimulate motivation and performance. Two departments with opposing goals may work cooperatively to find creative solutions to problems between them.

When conflicts are resolved, the conflicting parties feel more respect for each other. The ability to work together to resolve differences builds a sense of cohesiveness. Working through disputes brings individuals closer together, increases loyalty, and enhances solidarity.

Styles of Communicating in Conflicts

People display many different kinds of behaviors in conflict situations. Some people use a predominant style of dealing with conflict regardless of the nature of the dispute. Other individuals vary their conflict-management style based on the context, the issues, or the conflict partner. If you find yourself involved in conflicts or drawn into others' disputes, you should be equipped to identify conflict styles. Further, you should assess whether a conflict style will resolve a particular dispute and encourage flexibility in conflict-management behavior. Common styles of dealing with conflicts include aggression, withdrawal, surrender, compromise, problem solving, and third-party intervention.

The **aggressive** style of dealing with conflict involves threats, ultimatums, defensiveness, name-calling, and coercion. Rarely does it result in a resolution of the dispute. Through aggression, one person may force the other to "give in." The aggressor has seemingly won, but the conflict usually continues below the surface and will erupt again later. This is the most emotional style of dealing with conflict. Rather than focusing on the issues in a dispute, aggressors aim to win at all costs. They lash out at others with the goal of harming or destroying the opponent. People who are aggressive in conflicts do not follow any rules for civil behavior. They are irrational and would rather escalate the fight than make even small concessions.

Most managers would agree that there is no place for the aggressive style of dealing with conflicts. Organizations may tolerate a rare and mildly aggressive outburst from a valuable employee, but most would consider an aggressive style of communicating as grounds for dismissal. Some companies offer psychological counseling to employees who demonstrate aggression in interpersonal conflicts on the job.

Withdrawal as a style of behavior in conflicts means physically or psychologically removing yourself from the situation. It is an attempt to avoid or to ignore the conflict altogether. "Looking the other way" can be an effective approach if used infrequently. It may be wise to avoid a conflict if the issue is minor or if the potential conflict partner is a formidable opponent, for example. But you should not routinely withdraw from conflicts. The manager who uses withdrawal as a predominant conflict-handling style will appear weak, will have to give up resources, and will get little respect from others.

Realizing that conflicts are inevitable and can be positive can help the withdrawer plunge into disputes with confidence. Other ways to replace withdrawal behaviors with more effective techniques include starting with small disputes and working up to larger confrontations, watching how others successfully handle conflicts, and taking assertiveness training.

People who **surrender** in conflicts are willing to get involved in them but give in prematurely. Rather than trying to fully represent their own position, they accommodate to the partner's position too quickly. When you surrender, you do not actually see the merit of the other position. You merely give in because you are uncomfortable with the conflict. A disadvantage of this style is that good ideas can get lost when you throw in the towel. Like withdrawers, managers who surrender sacrifice their positions and their reputations.

Compromise represents a rational and effective way to deal with conflicts. With this style, the parties agree to partial victory and partial defeat for each. Each person is willing to concede minor points in order to preserve higher priority goals. By trading concessions, both parties win a little and lose a little. The conflict partners stick with the issues, care about an equitable outcome, and are willing to take the time needed to reach a compromise.

Being skilled at the bargaining or negotiating process involved in reaching a compromise is the hallmark of a good manager. Compromise through bargaining is a part of many managerial functions including hiring, salary or contract settlement, budget allocations, purchasing, selling, customer service, and handling grievances or complaints, to name a few.

The **problem-solving** approach to conflict means cooperatively and objectively examining the issues in a dispute to arrive at a solution that represents the best interests of all conflict parties. Rather than examining the positions advocated by the conflicting parties as a starting point for compromise, this approach seeks innovative, creative options not yet considered by the people in conflict. If a new option fully satisfactory to everyone involved can be generated, then trading concessions need not occur. The problem-solving style involves collaboration and mutual decision making. People do not cling to their positions. In fact, positions are not associated with certain individuals. Instead, conflict parties brainstorm, evaluate, and select options together.

While true collaborative problem solving may be difficult to apply to workplace conflicts, this style probably best meets organizational goals. It forces people to work together as allies rather than to argue as adversaries. There are no sides in a dispute, but only mutual problem solvers. Indeed, if you want two adversaries to get along better with each other, you can assign them to work together on a task. Often they will resolve their differences when they have to cooperate to reach a larger goal.

When all other approaches to conflict resolution fail, conflicting parties can seek the help of a third party or have a mediator intervene. Basically, there are two types of external intervention in conflict situations: mediators and arbitrators. A mediator is a **third party** who assists with the conflict process. Mediators have no power to make decisions, but they can help clarify the issues, urge participants to cooperate, establish ground rules for rational interaction, and serve as impartial aids to help the conflicting parties settle their own dispute.

An arbitrator, by contrast, is a third party who intervenes to make a decision. The conflicting parties agree on an arbitrator, who will decide on the issues. The arbitrator hears both sides, evaluates the evidence, and makes a decision to settle the dispute. The conflict participants agree to abide by the arbitrator's decision.

It is preferable for conflicting parties to settle their own disputes rather than resort to third-party intervention. However, in many instances, managers will be called on to serve as mediators or arbitrators of others' conflicts. To maintain the trust and credibility of conflicting participants, arbitrators and mediators must treat each side fairly and equitably. By intervening, the manager seeks not only to help resolve the conflict, but attempts to develop rational, effective conflict-management skills in others.

Guidelines for Managing Conflict

Following these guidelines will help make conflicts constructive, rational, challenging, and manageable activities with positive outcomes for both individuals and organizations:

1. *Take your time in conflicts.* It takes patience to listen, to weigh issues, and to reach equitable outcomes. When you slow down the

communication and avoid interruption, real discussion can occur. It may take several sessions or many months to settle a disagreement. Don't rush it.

2. *Avoid defensiveness.* Try to remain objective and cooperative. This means being open-minded and not forcing predetermined positions or solutions. Avoid manipulations, put-downs, know-it-all attitudes, and stubbornness. Rather than blindly defending your position in the hopes of winning, be willing to consider the merit in others' positions.

3. *Avoid deception.* In an attempt to inflate a position or enhance bargaining power in conflicts, deception is sometimes used. This can impede conflict resolution and destroy credibility. Effective managers of conflict are ethical, straightforward, and honest. Deal directly and assertively with issues rather than misrepresenting or distorting facts.

4. *Be willing to admit mistakes and allow others to graciously admit mistakes.* Dealing effectively with conflict means a willingness to give and take. When presented with opposing evidence, rarely can a conflict participant hold steadfast to all original points. Be willing to accept valid reasoning and evidence. Refrain from ridicule, gloating, or blame if a conflicting party accepts your valid points.

5. *Avoid assumptions.* When situations get heated, we sometimes fail to communicate explicitly. We jump to conclusions, make faulty assumptions, and try to second-guess our partner. It is important to spell out all details, to ask questions, to put agreements in writing, to summarize progress, and to list agenda items for discussion. The more rational, specific, and direct the communication, the more likely the conflict will be resolved fairly.

[*See also* Dispute Resolution; Negotiating]

For Additional Information

Baker, H. Kent, and Philip I. Morgan. "Handling Conflict." *Supervisory Management*, Vol. 31 (1986), No. 2, pp. 24–29. Takes the position that conflict management is a skill that must be learned. The authors present five strategies for effectively handling conflict.

Blake, Robert R., and Jane S. Mouton. *Solving Costly Organizational Conflicts.* San Francisco: Jossey-Bass Publishers, 1984. An interface conflict-solving model, examples of its use, and guidelines for applying it effectively. The authors discuss how to solve line-staff conflict, union-management conflict, conflict between corporate and field operations, and conflict between parent and subsidiary organizations.

Hart, Lois Borland. *Learning from Conflict*. Reading, Mass.: Addison-Wesley Publishing Company, 1981. A handbook for trainers and group leaders to help managers understand the conflict process and develop conflict-management skills in others. Exercises and instruments deal with conflict styles, values, assumptions, problem solving, and goal setting.

Pneumen, Roy, and Margaret Bruehl. *Managing Conflict: A Complete Process-Centered Handbook*. Englewood Cliffs, N.J.: Prentice-Hall, 1982. A problem-solving, pragmatic approach to managing conflict. Through examples, checklists, analysis forms, and reflection questions, the reader can learn a process for managing conflict. Chapters cover sources of conflict, factors influencing conflict, choices of behavioral strategies, and ways to prepare for and communicate during conflicts.

Rahim, M. Afzalur. *Conflict in Organizations*. New York: Praeger, 1986. A design for the management of conflict at the individual, interpersonal, group, and intergroup levels. The thesis of this book is that the management of organizational conflict involves appropriate diagnosis, intervention, and behavioral styles in conflict situations. The book includes two cases and eight exercises for developing conflict-management skills.

Robert, Marc. *Managing Conflict from the Inside Out*. San Diego: University Associates, 1982. An assortment of specific ideas for handling conflict in personal and professional arenas. Topics include identifying conflict styles, handling criticism, avoiding assumptions, coping with anger, using humor, dealing with power and problem solving, and serving as a third party to conflict.

Wilcox, James R., Ethel M. Wilcox, and Karen M. Cowan. "Communicating Creatively in Conflict Situations." *Management Solutions*, Vol. 31 (1986), No. 10, pp. 18–24. How the inability to handle conflict effectively can be a barrier to job satisfaction and success. The authors offer guidelines for communicating creatively in conflicts.

Consultants

THE TERM *CONSULTANT* has come to refer to a broad range of roles, activities, or functions that people perform. Consultants may solve problems, give advice, disseminate information, perform specialized services, or intervene in other ways in organizations. They may be self-employed, may affiliate with large consulting organizations, may be on the payroll of the organization for which they consult, or may be professors, lawyers, doctors, engineers, psychologists, or other professional specialists. Recently terminated managers may call themselves "consultants" as a job-seeking strategy. The term is so frequently used these days that it can create confusion and skepticism. That does not mean that consulting is an activity devoid of integrity and respectability, however. Consultants play an essential role in many organizations. By understanding the role of consultants, the reasons organizations use them, the process of selecting consultants, and the nature of the consultant-client relationship, you can utilize consultants effectively.

What Is a Consultant?

Typically a consultant is a person with specialized knowledge or skills who establishes a temporary relationship with a client to help that client in some way. For internal consultants, the client may be another division, department, or unit in the same organization, and the transfer of money for services may not take place. External consultants provide services to an organization of which they are not a member and receive compensation in return.

In either case, there are some key points in defining the term *consultant*. The relationship is voluntary, temporary, and helping. The

51

nature of the client, the nature of the help, and the duration of the relationship are variable elements. The arenas in which consultants perform are also quite diverse, including accounting, personnel, information systems, law, engineering, finance, safety and health, recruiting, public relations, sales and marketing, labor relations, organizational development, and research. There are many consulting specialities within each of these areas as well.

Why Use Consultants?

The question of why we need consultants can be examined from two perspectives. First, why has the profession of consulting proliferated in society? And second, why should a particular organization use consultants?

There are many reasons why the need for consultants has accelerated in the workplace. Our society, and the workplace in particular, is becoming increasingly complex and technological. Economic and social forces are rapidly changing. Information and technology is expanding at such a rate that many managers can no longer keep pace with the change. Managers can no longer be generalists, possessing the information and skills to handle all problems. Some industries are so dynamic that managers in certain areas need specialists to advise them. Burgeoning technology and information in the engineering, computer, and communications fields, for example, can make the proficiencies of even the most conscientious managers outdated. Rather than restaffing the organization to acquire people with state-of-the-art skills, the organization can hire consultants on a project-by-project basis.

There are several issues to consider when deciding whether your organization should use the services of a consultant. First, you should question whether someone in the organization has the expertise or could easily acquire the expertise to handle the project. Unlike some large organizations, small firms may not have designated internal consultants. This does not necessarily mean that the organization lacks the resources to handle a specialized project or to solve a problem. Many organizations overlook their internal talent and assume that a consultant is the only option.

Second, cost must always be a consideration in hiring a consultant. Can your organization afford the services of a consultant, or would it be more cost-effective to recruit and hire a specialist as a permanent employee? Perhaps your organization could underwrite the education or training to help existing staff stay current in their fields. In some cases, internal personnel may have the necessary expertise to handle projects, but using an external consultant might be the wiser financial decision.

Another reason why organizations use consultants is the credibility factor. While inside people may be able to do the same thing that you would hire a consultant for, the external person might have more credibility with employees. Information provided by an outsider may be seen as more valid, or a change recommended by a consultant may be more readily accepted. Situations addressed by outsiders are sometimes taken more seriously than if handled by insiders.

An organization may also prefer a consultant for certain sensitive tasks that are more difficult for an insider to accomplish or for unpopular tasks that could destroy the insider's career. For example, a consultant will get more honest responses to an employee-opinion survey than an insider would. It is also less awkward for consultants to handle reorganization or retrenchment decisions, since they can leave the organization after unpopular decisions are implemented.

The Process of Selecting a Consultant

Once the decision has been made to hire a consultant, there are certain steps to follow in selecting the right one. The decision is crucial, because poor performance by a consultant is often the result of hiring the wrong person or the wrong firm. Managers may blame consultants for lack of effectiveness and fail to see how their selection of the consultant for the task has contributed to the outcome. In selecting consultants, you must identify your needs, locate consultant possibilities, and screen applicants to make a selection decision.

Identifying Needs

Someone in the organization must perceive a problem or realize a need in order for the question of a consultant to arise in the first place. The more specifically you can define your need or problem, the greater the chances of selecting a qualified consultant to address it. There is a dilemma, though, in the attempt to match your needs with a consultant's services. Your organization may not be able to accurately or objectively perceive its own needs or problems. In the process of identifying the need for a consultant, your organization can also fall into the trap of dictating a solution to the consultant.

So you must identify a problem in enough detail to target the kind of consultant you need, but not misdiagnose the problem or settle on a particular solution. At the very least, you must decide what you want from the consultant.

Locating Possible Consultants

Once key people in your organization identify the type of consultant they need and the goal the consultant is to accomplish, it is time to search for possible specialists to assume the consultant role. This step involves detective work. If the need is quite specialized, it may mean a national or international search for the handful of qualified people who are capable of meeting your needs. If the task is somewhat routine, there may be plenty of talent in your local area.

There are various sources to check to locate a pool of potential consultants. The professional associations affiliated with the speciality area are a good place to start. Libraries have directories of associations. Rest assured that there are numerous professional associations for every narrow speciality. Professional and technical associations can serve as clearinghouses for information you need and will be able to recommend specialists within their fields who serve as consultants. The faculty of your local university represents another pool of talent that is abreast of the latest developments in many fields. Professors often have the time, the desire, and the expertise to consult for organizations. There are also directories of consulting organizations and associations for consultants in various specialities. Other sources for consultants include the business-to-business yellow pages, the chamber of commerce, and the network of colleagues in your industry or profession.

Screening Potential Consultants

The various specialists who are capable of and interested in doing the job usually submit proposals. After meeting with their organizational contacts, and in some cases doing some needs-assessment research, consultants prepare a proposal outlining the proposed project, their qualifications, a tentative schedule, and expected costs. The proposal is an important device for evaluating a consultant. Its length, formality, and information will vary according to organizational needs and consultant specialities. But, in any case, the proposal allows the client organization to see sample work of the consultant and to make some judgments about a consultant's problem-solving style, writing ability, fee structure, and professionalism.

Consultant proposals serve another function in addition to being a screening device: they allow organizations to see the various approaches to their problem that different consultants would take. Through proposals, you obtain information about your problem from different perspectives. In other words, proposals serve as marketing devices for consultants and provide free information to clients. Submitting proposals without compensation to apply for a consulting project is a standard and legitimate practice in the profession. Naturally, consultants make the proposal general enough so as not to give away their services. You should be reluctant to retain the services of consultants who do not submit proposals or who charge for the proposals.

One aspect of a proposal that is often difficult to evaluate is the fee structure. There are no standard rates for consulting services. Even within a particular consulting speciality, rates vary. This is problematic for both consultants who are not sure what to charge and for clients who do not know what to expect.

Some relatively standard practices can serve as guidelines, however. Most consultants charge daily fees ranging from $500 to $1,500 per day. The more sophisticated the project, the more unique your need, and the fewer specialists there are capable of performing the service, the higher the rate will be. Most consultants will negotiate their fee downward for long-range projects, and some will adjust rates according to the size (and budget) of the client.

Some consultants charge by the project and not by the day. Whatever the fee structure, it is advisable to know what can be billed and what cannot. Some consultants will not charge for preliminary or follow-up work and others will charge for telephone calls. You should determine the maximum amount that a project can exceed cost estimates and realize that almost all proposals are negotiable. Rather than rejecting an applicant because of one feature of the proposal, for example, cost, discuss objections with the consultant and invite a revised proposal.

Proposals represent just one, albeit important, source of information for screening consultants. Other sources include testimonials, work samples, and trial projects. Reputable consultants should be able to provide names of clients as endorsements or actual letters of recommendation. Obviously, a testimonial from a respected colleague or from someone in a prestigious organization should carry more weight than endorsements from anonymous or unknown clients. Some client organizations ask for names of former clients to call to ask specific questions about the consultant's work.

Some consultants will invite you to examine samples of their prior work through portfolios, videotapes, or site visits. Whatever the consulting speciality and nature of the prior work experience, the consultant should be able to provide pictures, models, diagrams, slides, manuals, or workbooks to document their work quality.

Another way to evaluate potential consultants is to hire them for small projects. Allowing them to do a pilot project or some small aspect of the job will allow them to demonstrate their skills and will allow you to make an objective decision about their capabilities in meeting your needs. This trial project also provides information to both parties about the nature of their working relationship. Many consultants, especially the excellent ones, will delight in this opportunity to show their stuff. Some large, prestigious consulting organizations, on the other hand, will not be willing to take anything other than the entire project.

Though it will take time, it is wise to get as much information as possible to use in screening consultants. Information from proposals, recommendations, background qualifications, work samples, or trial projects will help you to make the best decision about which consultant to hire.

The Client-Consultant Relationship

After evaluating possible consultants and hiring one for your project, you still have some important roles to perform. Three areas of concern in the initial client-consultant relationship include the working agreement or contract, the identity of the client, and the nature of the client-consultant relationship.

The Working Agreement or Contract

The working agreement or contract is a written statement that specifies the expectations of both parties: who will do what, to whom, how, by when, and for how much. The written agreement varies in detail and explicitness, but early dealings between consultants and organizations should probably be characterized by explicit statements. Long-term relationships between clients and consultants may involve no more than oral agreements.

But whether the agreement involves a formal contract or an oral understanding, both parties must agree to the objectives of the project, their roles and responsibilities, the physical and personnel resources devoted to the project, the tentative schedule, and the costs of the project.

Consider a specific consulting project to see how assumptions in each of these areas should be identified and negotiated in the early part of the relationship. Imagine that a consulting firm has been hired to do a team-building project in an organization. First, each party should discuss why the project is being launched. What expectations do you and the consultant have about what will be accomplished by the project? Do you expect your employees to become better problem solvers, better communicators, more motivated, more loyal to the organization, and more productive as a result of the team-building project? Suppose the consultant assumes that the outcome of the project is to have employees understand group dynamics and solve group problems. With such divergent views about the objective of the project, the client-consultant relationship is bound to end in disappointment. The consultant who accomplishes the objective will see the project as successful, whereas you will think the consultant fell far short of honoring agreements.

Next, what are both the consultant and your organization expected to do during this project? Will the consultant collect data to determine team-building needs? Will the consultant do follow-up evaluations after the project? Will you give the consultant access to employees at all levels in the organization? Will you make recommended policy or structural changes to support the team-building effort? The more both parties know their respective roles and responsibilities, the less misunderstanding during the project and the more chance of a mutually satisfactory outcome.

You and your consultant should also reach agreement about the resources each will devote to the project. Will the experienced and prestigious owner of the consulting firm who landed the project actually do the team building or will a junior assistant be assigned to the project? Will you or the consultant be responsible for preparing written instructional materials, for supplying videotape equipment to record meetings, for providing meeting rooms or secretarial assistance?

Finally, both parties should agree to a tentative schedule and cost estimates for the project. Typically, you will want the project completed sooner and at a lower cost than the consultant expects.

Identity of the Client

While this seems like an obvious point, the actual identity of the client can be elusive. Is the consultant working for the contact person in your organization, the unit or department that perceives the problem or need for the consultant, top management of your organization, your entire organization, the larger social system such as the customers of your organization or its stockholders or financial supporters?

Anyone who has served as a consultant knows how difficult it is to identify the client. This question is important because it determines who the consultant reports to, who has decision-making authority, who the consultant has access to, and who evaluates the success of the project. There may be many clients with different perspectives about the project making simultaneous demands on a consultant. The client and consultant should try to reach agreements about the client's identity before the project begins.

Nature of the Relationship

The relationship developed between you and your consultant probably has as much to do with the success of the project as the competence of the consultant does. But organizations usually put more effort into selecting a consultant than into building the client-consultant relationship. Several relationship factors such as power, collaboration, trust, and integrity should be considered.

Some consulting projects fail because of the perceived power differences in the relationship. The best client-consultant relationship is a partnership. Neither party makes all the decisions or is totally dependent on the other. You should know enough about the project speciality area to participate in the project. Decisions should be mutual. However, in many consulting projects, one party feels superior to the other and tries to take charge. For example, a renowned consultant with a large ego dictates decisions and intimidates you, or a prestigious, international corporation controls the consultant and hence cripples the project's effectiveness.

Before the project begins, the parties should discuss the nature of authority and decision-making power in the relationship. While power is not an easy issue to discuss in initial interactions, it is important to bring the underlying power issues to the surface so that both parties can determine if they can work with each other.

The client and the consultant may want to include mechanisms for collaboration in the working agreement. Perhaps an individual from the consulting organization should work with someone from the client organization as project codirectors. At the very least, both parties should realize the collaborative nature of their relationship. They should get in the habit of exchanging information and opinions and making mutual decisions.

The factors of trust and integrity are essential to the success of the client-consultant relationship. Neither party should withhold information from the other. You have to be honest and open with each other. Sometimes your organization will distort information to present itself in a good light to the consultant. Likewise, consultants may be reluctant to disclose their shortcomings or uncertainties to your organization. Each party must have confidence in the other. You and your consultant are a team working together to solve a problem. Your relationship certainly should not be characterized by antagonism, deception, or distrust. Following are some guidelines for using consultants:

1. *Avoid consultants who do more selling than helping.* While consultants must market their services, their primary role is to be a consultant. Be wary of the consultants who spend more time pushing services than listening to your needs. They are more concerned

with obtaining clients and making money than with working closely with clients to help solve problems.

2. *Beware of crippling the consultant's effectiveness.* Some organizations hire competent consultants and then put too many restraints on them. As sensitive as some information can be, the consultant needs access to all people and all information in the organization to be effective.

3. *The client should not become dependent on the consultant.* Some consultants create procedures or systems to foster client dependency on them. Some organizations cling to consultants. Remember, the relationship should be temporary. Both parties should work toward completing the project and ending the relationship.

4. *Beware of consultants who apply the same solution to all problems.* Some consultants rely on one mode or approach for all clients, all needs, and all situations. Consultants who push certain solutions or approaches during initial meetings are likely to have canned answers before they even know your needs. Solutions should emerge in collaborations between clients and consultants over time after the problem or need has been fully identified.

5. *Do not put unrealistic expectations on consultants.* Consultants help organizations solve problems. They are not magicians. They do not work miracles. Most organizations would be well advised to set their expectations a bit lower when working with consultants. Realize that change in organizations comes slowly. It may take several attempts at the same problem before it is solved effectively.

6. *Do not make decisions on the basis of cost alone.* Cost should be just one consideration in selecting consultants. Some organizations opt for the lowest bid and get nothing more than a quick fix. Most organizational problems are complex and multifaceted, requiring interventions from several perspectives. Good solutions take time. Some problems are never completely solved. Your organization may have to spend more money than it anticipated to obtain the results it expects.

For Additional Information

Blake, Robert R., and Jane Srygley Mouton. *Consultation.* Reading, Mass.: Addison-Wesley Publishing Company, 1976. A classic examination of the dynamics of the interaction between consultant and client that discusses the techniques involved in various approaches to consulting including acceptant, catalytic, confrontational, prescriptive, and theory-principle interventions. For each approach, Blake and Mouton discuss the power/authority, morale/ cohesion, norms/standards and goals/objectives implications for the organization.

Holtz, Herman. *Utilizing Consultants Successfully*. Westport, Conn.: Quorum Books, 1986. Ways for managers to select and utilize consultants. Topics cover how to analyze problems to determine whether you need a consultant, where to find consultants, how to evaluate them, how to determine what you should be paying for consulting services, and how to develop proper working relationships with consultants.

Laporte, Michel. "Choosing a Consultant." *Optimum*, Vol. 16 (1985), No. 3, pp. 58–63. Guidelines for the selection of a consultant, factors to be used as a selection guide, principles, methods, and procedures of selection, elements of a model statement of qualifications, and a consultant's evaluation grid.

Preedy, Jeremy. "What You Should Expect from Consultants." *Personnel Management*, Vol. 19 (1987), No. 1, pp. 20–25. The premise: many organizations are spending ever-increasing sums on using consultants, yet few are completely happy with the results. The author warns of the pitfalls and suggests how a better working relationship can be achieved.

Steele, Fritz. *The Role of the Internal Consultant*. Boston: CBI Publishing Company, 1982. Written from the perspective of the internal consultant, but Steele's explanation of the process of internal consulting and consulting in general can help managers who utilize consultants. Steele explains steps in the consulting process, consulting roles, the client-consultant relationship, and typical dilemmas of consulting. The book examines the advantages and disadvantages of internal and external consultants.

Corporate Social Responsibility

IF THEY ARE TO SURVIVE AND THRIVE, CONTEMPORARY ORGANIZATIONS must respond to the expectations that society puts on them. In exchange for using community resources, companies increasingly are expected to contribute to the social environment in which they operate. Corporate social responsibility takes many forms including philanthropy, urban planning, fair employment policies, consumer protection, and environmental safeguards. No longer are these issues considered corporate frills. Indeed, they are an integral and expected part of corporate conduct. Rather than reacting defensively to societal standards of appropriate business behavior, progressive organizations should anticipate social demands and plan policies to meet emerging areas of social responsibility. In addition to positioning an organization as a "good citizen," this business stance can give a company a competitive edge in the marketplace. Managing corporate social responsibility entails identifying areas of social performance that an organization can meet, realizing the benefits of accepting social responsibility, understanding the managerial implications of the issue, and establishing mechanisms for implementing a program of corporate social responsibility.

Identifying Areas of Social Performance

The areas of social responsibility for which an organization will be held accountable vary according to company type, size, and geographic location. A large firm located in the inner city will be expected to contribute to urban renewal and job-training efforts in the community while a small suburban company will be asked to sponsor athletic programs for the local school district. A manufacturing firm may have to concern itself with environmental-pollution issues while a service organization is evaluated according to levels of consumer satisfaction. A multinational corporation may face limits on how it can change the host society for the sake of doing business.

Essentially, all companies must not harm society while doing business and will be expected to contribute, based on unique resources and expertise, to the improvement of society. The following are areas of social responsibility addressed by contemporary organizations. You should assess your company's performance on each issue. Should the company be concerned with that issue? What is the company doing to ensure appropriate action on that issue? What policies or programs could be instituted to deal more responsibly with the issue? Here are some suggestions:

- Respect for environmental resources
- Product safety and quality
- Fair employment policies and working conditions
- Assistance in solving community problems
- Contributions to philanthropic, educational, and artistic organizations
- Employee education, training, and career development
- Involvement in civic organizations
- Fair and inoffensive advertising
- Respect for the norms and customs of a culture or subculture

Benefits of Corporate Social Responsibility

While social goals seem incompatible with the economic mission of business, they need not be. Doing business in a responsible and ethical manner is not a societal obstacle to overcome. Organizations that willingly embrace reasonable standards of business conduct can realize many benefits. Some of these include:

1. *An improved business environment.* Improving the community, providing safe working conditions, and educating workers, for example, means a better environment for doing business. Such improvements result in a better-quality labor force, fewer accidents, less vandalism or sabotage, and a reduction in employee turnover, all of which clearly translate into cost savings.
2. *An improved public image.* Organizations that contribute to society in visible ways enhance employee, customer, and community goodwill. Innovative social programs can bring local and national recognition to an organization. Through public

credibility, you can gain more customers, a higher quality work force, and improved financial standing in the community.

3. *Fewer government restrictions.* When business avoids its social responsibility, government inevitably intervenes to make it accountable for environmental, safety, employment, and consumer standards. Organizations that anticipate social demands and behave proactively can preempt such intervention. Thus, rather than responding to external pressures that result in rigidly restrictive legislation, executives with foresight can participate in shaping rules for business conduct.

4. *Profitability in the long run.* Companies that anticipate social trends and create innovative responses to societal demands gain competitive advantages in the marketplace. For example, meeting consumer demands for product ingredient labeling or guidelines for advertisements aimed at children rather than ignoring consumer discontent might place a company ahead of the competition. Progressive employment policies such as child care or retirement counseling could improve employee morale and productivity. The need to reduce environmental pollution may lead to the development of commercial products from industrial wastes.

5. *The opportunity to shape public policy.* By early action rather than defensive reaction, progressive organizations can have valuable input into the legislative and regulatory processes in society. Smart business executives take responsibility for helping to formulate public policy. In this way, they can contribute their expertise to society in matters affecting business as well as ensure decisions amenable to the business enterprise system.

Some people believe that even if no tangible benefits result from corporate social responsibility, businesses still have an ethical imperative to concern themselves with social issues. The very fact that organizations function within a social system makes them accountable to it. A sense of fair play dictates that organizations repay the community for its hospitality. "With power comes responsibility" is an additional argument in favor of business responsibility. Businesses wield a great deal of power, and business decisions and actions affect all aspects of social experience. Thus, organizations have an inherent social responsibility.

Implications for Management

By incorporating social responsibility goals, you create implications for all levels of management. Active pursuit of these goals inevitably affects the very character of your organization. Executives must include social-performance considerations into planning and resource-allocation processes. Managers must deal with issues of business ethics within training programs and job responsibilities. Personnel and public relations functions, for example, must embrace new requirements stemming from corporate social-responsibility concerns. In short, all levels of an organization, from board members to first-line supervisors, must understand and demonstrate a consistent philosophy and behavior regarding social aspects of business. The following represent typical considerations that you face when embracing social-responsibility goals:

1. *Including social responsibility in long-range planning.* Most business planning focuses on economic considerations. It will take a change of philosophy and a broader orientation to plan to include social goals as well. Senior-level executives may want to solicit advisers with sociological and ethical expertise. Effective planning must include information about social attitudes and forces and predictions about their effect on future business decisions and behavior.

2. *Enlarging management responsibilities to include social issues.* Managers must understand corporate social goals. You must embrace social considerations as necessary corequisites of business success. In effect, you must be motivated and trained to execute an organization's social policies. Whether the goals concern working conditions, employment policies, quality assurance, or community involvement, you must behave in ways that encourage rather than discourage such objectives. Management training programs on fair employment practices, workplace safety, environmental concerns, consumerism, or business ethics should become standard practices of socially aware organizations.

3. *Conveying social-performance expectations throughout the organization.* Management will have to develop ways to discuss social-policy implications with supervisors, workers, and unions. Non-management personnel must become aware of new policies or programs stemming from social-responsibility objectives. Companies must be able to demonstrate sincere commitment and credibility in these areas. Through open communication, employee questions, concerns, or objections to perceived changes in the workplace can be met. Indeed, employee and union input when the company is first developing corporate social goals is a wise practice.

4. *Using corporate expertise.* Certain departments such as personnel, public relations, or research and development face special chal-

lenges because of organizational social goals. The personnel department should develop innovative policies regarding appointment, promotion, dismissal, or retirement decisions. Personnel specialists need to update themselves in areas of affirmative action, age discrimination, employee-assistance programs, child care options, or employee drug testing. The public relations (PR) department has an increased responsibility to advise senior management of emerging and projected business concerns in areas of government, customer, community, or employee relations. The PR function will likely suggest and help develop corporate social programs. In addition, PR departments will be charged with creating communication programs for conveying a company's social commitment to the public. Research and development departments will be called on to design safer, better-quality products or to develop manufacturing processes that protect environmental and human resources. A commitment to social responsibility means more than a philosophical statement of business ethics in a company handbook. It entails a change of motivation, action, and communication among every member of the organization.

Implementing Corporate Social Responsibility

All organizations cannot concern themselves with the gamut of social concerns. No matter how important social expectations are for business, they still are not its primary mission. Naturally, organizations must weigh the ethical imperative against the financial feasibility of taking on a particular social goal. Corporate social response can take several forms including single company programs, cooperative efforts by industry type or community, and joint ventures by private-public liaison. For example, one company realistically may not be able to make an impact on inner-city unemployment in the community without overburdening its own resources. But many companies in the community working cooperatively will be able to combine resources to create job-training programs and employment opportunities for a significant portion of the community's unemployed population. Likewise, all the hospitals in any area can combine talents to develop a wellness program for senior citizens in the community. Government grants combined with contributions from the private sector can fund local arts, recreational, or educational services.

The process of developing social-performance expectations for business is essentially the same whatever the organization or social goal. First, the organization must be able to forecast social trends. What attitudes or forces will affect business in the future? When will social changes occur? With what probability will social changes occur? While strategic planning has always involved economic predictions, it must now include sociological predictions as well. Second, the organization must be able to identify the implications of social trends on business. How will business policies and practices be affected by social trends? What expectations will society place on business in the future? Finally, organizations must be able to develop feasible policies and programs that respond to social trends and expectations. That is, business must change in ways that successfully deal with, indeed exploit, social forces of the future.

One device for achieving a sense of social responsibility in an organization is the social-responsibility audit. Just as you can audit any other aspect of a company's performance, a systematic assessment of corporate social responsibility is possible. Although it is difficult to put dollar figures on ethical actions of a business, costs and benefits of social-ethical actions can be evaluated. Organizations should ask themselves a number of questions regarding existing or planned programs: How much does it cost? Who is affected positively or negatively? Are there criticisms of the program? Are they justified? How can they be avoided? Does the program violate or protect anyone's rights? Is the organization ashamed or proud to publicize the program? Why?

An organization that wants to implement programs or policies in response to social concerns must realize the widespread commitment necessary for successful action. Boards of directors, CEOs, senior and middle management, as well as supervisors and workers must take responsibility for achieving standards of social action. The organization must make a philosophical and financial commitment to social goals. Lip service is not enough. Organizations must develop creative ways to achieve social goals. In many ways, ensuring corporate social responsibility means instilling a sense of individual ethics in everyone associated with the organization. Social responsibility should become an integral part of strategic planning, management training, and performance evaluation systems of the organization.

[See also Public Relations]

For Additional Information

Anderson, Jerry W. "Social Responsibility and the Corporation." *Business Horizons*, Vol. 29 (1986), No. 4, pp. 22–27. Claims that a company's social responsibility program should have three major areas: complying with laws, setting and abiding by moral and ethical standards, and philanthropy. Anderson offers guidelines by which firms can evaluate themselves in these areas.

Anshen, Melvin. *Corporate Strategies for Social Performance.* New York: Macmillan Publishing Company, 1980. Practical problems of managing corporate social performance, including offensive and defensive strategies, strategic planning, and measuring social performance. Anshen suggests ways to create responsible boards of directors, where to place responsibility for social performance, and ways to deal with employees, the government, and the public.

Evans, William A. *Management Ethics.* Boston: Martinus Nijhoff Publishing, 1981. Problems of ethical and moral behavior in management from an intercultural perspective. Through many situational examples, the book examines options for individual social conscience in the organization.

Freudberg, David. *The Corporate Conscience: Innovations in Responsible Business.* New York: AMACOM, 1986. Thirty interviews with business leaders. This book looks at the conflict between morality and the bottom line. It examines such issues as public safety, the environment, the work force, loyalty to suppliers, and questionable advertising as they relate to the profit motive.

Solomon, Robert C., and Kristine R. Hanson. *It's Good Business.* New York: Atheneum, 1985. Drawn from the authors' experience, and business seminars in strategic ethical thinking. The authors examine the relationship between financial prosperity and personal and corporate integrity. The book contains questionnaires, survey results, and case studies covering a variety of issues in business ethics.

Werhane, Patricia H. *Persons, Rights, and Corporations.* Englewood Cliffs, N.J.: Prentice-Hall, 1985. The moral relationships between corporations and their employees. Werhane covers such issues as employment at will, freedom, privacy, safety, fair pay, participation, and meaningful work. The book includes examples of specific programs and policy statements.

Customer Service

ALL ORGANIZATIONS, NOT JUST SALES-ORIENTED BUSI-NESSES, have customers. Increasingly, medical, educational, and governmental organizations also are focusing on their customer service functions. While customer service used to be narrowly defined as handling customer complaints, it is now regarded as a philosophy as well as an activity. That is, progressive organizations of any type make sure that concern for the customer, or end user of their product or service, permeates the entire culture of the organization. When the whole organization is customer-oriented, fewer customer complaints occur. And when they do occur, they are handled swiftly and appropriately.

How often you deal directly with customers obviously depends on the particular function or the nature of your organization. Nevertheless, all managers should be aware of the basics of customer service. We are in an era when customer service is being emphasized as a way to enhance productivity and profits. Perhaps because the quality of service has deteriorated to abysmal levels in some spheres, customers are demanding better service. Stiff levels of competition in many industries are forcing managers to pay more attention to service. Indeed, you may find yourself immersed in customer service issues, which the business environment will no longer allow you to ignore.

What Is Customer Service?

There are various views of customer service ranging from all-encompassing philosophies to specific actions. Which definition best reflects your organization's view of customer service?

- Meeting customers' expectations
- Providing customers with what they want, when they want it, in good condition, at a fair price
- A philosophy that affects every organizational decision and policy
- An opportunity to retain and build business
- Behavior to ensure a long-term vendor-customer relationship
- Handling customer complaints satisfactorily
- Sacrificing short-term costs for long-term customer loyalty
- Providing consistent, quality products or service
- All events related to keeping customers
- All communication between an organization and its customers

You may favor one definition over another. Though they seem to be encompassing different aspects, each view is a necessary component of customer service. Customer service means all those things! Once you realize the extent of customer service, you can help your organization provide improved service.

Why Emphasize Customer Service?

There are many reasons, besides the current popularity of the concept, to emphasize customer service in organizations. It makes good business sense to give high priority to customer needs. The many advantages of a customer-focused orientation include:

1. *Customers are the livelihood of any business.* They are the very reason why organizations exist. Whether they are patrons of the arts, patients in a hospital, students in a school, guests in a hotel, residents using city services, wholesale distributors, or retail shoppers, people using products and services keep organizations alive. Employees who do not come into regular contact with customers may forget the pivotal role customers play. We must all remind ourselves that our jobs and our livelihood depend on someone else using the services we perform or purchasing the products we make. For some managers in advertising or industrial organizations, for example, losing an important account may mean losing your job. Even people in support functions in organizations should realize that they contribute to the organization's production of goods and services and that they have jobs only as long as there are users of those goods and services.

2. *Customer service gives organizations a competitive edge.* Often there are negligible differences between the products or services

that organizations provide. Some carry identical stock. Department Store A carries the same five brands of lawn mowers as Department Store B. Airline X has the same number of flights to the same cities at the same prices as Airlines Y or Z. So on what basis does the customer select between vendors? One company will be favored over another on the basis of the nature and quality of the service provided by each. Some customers will go out of their way and will pay higher prices to obtain better service. That is how important service is to customers!

3. *Losing customers costs a company money.* Not only is revenue lost, but finding a new customer to replace the former one is costly. Some companies project that it costs at least twice the annual business of the original customer to find a new customer. Therefore an accounting company that loses a corporate client of $50,000 per year not only loses that revenue, but will have to spend at least $100,000 to woo a replacement customer. The costs of sales, advertising, and marketing to attract new customers far exceed the costs of good service to maintain that customer.

   Calculating the lost revenue from just one angry customer who decides to boycott your business should convince you of the financial importance of customer service. A person who spends $60 a month on gasoline and defects to a competitor will give that competitor over $7,000 in business over a ten-year period. Imagine the staggering amounts of lost revenue from industrial and corporate customers.

4. *Quality of service may be what the customer is buying.* In some situations, the customer is purchasing a relationship with an organization rather than a specific product or service. A patient may be loyal to a physician or a customer may use a certain dry cleaner not because of the competence of the physician or the quality of the cleaning, but because of the nature of the relationships each provides. Customers may care more whether the service providers know them by name and make them feel special than they do about the actual service provided. Managers and organizations should determine just what their customers are buying. It may be that customers select you over a competitor because of the personal relationships or reliable service you provide.

5. *Customers remember poor service.* A customer is more likely to remember one incident of poor service than 100 incidents of good service. Organizations receive little feedback about what they do well, but their problems are noticed. Indeed, organizations should provide ways for customers to communicate problems to the orga-

nization. A customer who complains always is preferable to the customer who silently disappears. In either case, dissatisfied customers will tell their friends about the poor service they received from your organization. So one incident of poor service can have a multiplying negative effect. Some customers have long memories and are quite unforgiving. If mistreated, they may refuse to do business with your organization for the rest of their lives!

6. *Customers provide information about product or service operations and improvements.* Customers are the major source of information about the quality of your products or service. If one location is losing customers or receiving more complaints, this tells you something about the operation of that location. If one product needs more repair than another product in your line, you may eliminate or redesign that product. Customers who complain or praise one employee more than they do others provide valuable feedback about employee performance.

Some organizations solicit customer reactions before they encounter customer complaints. At the very least, they should regard customer complaints as valid sources of feedback. Information from customers can help organizations improve products, develop new products, or enhance services.

Who Are Your Customers?

When we think of customers, we tend to think of people external to the organization who interact with the organization and provide money either directly or indirectly to it. In addition, groups of employees within an organization serve as suppliers and customers to each other. Production may need the services of research and development, physicians need the services of laboratory technicians to make diagnoses, educators need the maintenance staff for the upkeep of classrooms, and salespeople need warehouse personnel to supply merchandise. The list is endless.

The service that a company provides to external customers will be a direct reflection of the service that various departments within an organization provide to each other. We can carry the analogy even further. The way that employees treat each other and the way they treat customers is directly associated with the way they are treated by their supervisors and managers. So for good customer service to exist, there must be quality relationships throughout the organization. Consider anyone who interacts in or with the organization (employees, vendors, suppliers, distributors, contractors, etc.) as customers. They do not have to provide money to your organization to be considered a customer. If you depend on them in any way for the existence or success of your business, they should be treated as valuable customers.

It may be overwhelming to think that all aspects of the workplace affect the organization's ability to provide customer service, but a mistreated, underpaid, stressed, or underappreciated employee cannot be responsive to customers' needs. An employee who gets little cooperation from supervisors, co-workers, or other departments in the company is not likely to cooperate with others.

Caring about internal customers as well as external customers affects all organizational decisions and systems, including hiring practices, orientation and training, compensation and benefits, working conditions, job security, supervisory and management styles, performance-review practices, motivation and reward systems, and career-development opportunities.

Providing Customer Service

Attention to every detail of organizational life is necessary for maintaining high standards of customer service. But this is such a broad caveat that it may paralyze you in your attempts to develop customer service orientations in your company. A step-by-step process for developing or enhancing customer service in an organization follows:

1. *Hire the right people.* If you want to develop a customer service focus, then you must remember, when hiring employees, that some people are more pleasant, more motivated, more cooperative, and better communicators than others. Even if a job description does not involve customer contact, an employee who is skilled at interacting with others will contribute to the overall customer service philosophy.

2. *Provide orientation and training.* The employee should receive information about the company, its history, its mission, its leaders, and its policies. It is important that employees know how their jobs both fit into the overall mission and coordinate with other jobs. Training can equip employees with customer-relations skills and can emphasize the importance of customers to the organization.

3. *Set standards for customer service.* For each job, there should be clear standards for performance. What is the maximum allowable time between receiving an order and shipping the goods? How long should a restaurant patron wait before placing an order and receiv-

ing the food? What is the maximum number of rings before the telephone is answered? Such standards enable you to establish, monitor, and control quality. Jobholders benefit from knowing what is expected of them, supervisors know when to intervene to develop improved performance, and customers know what to expect in terms of quality and consistency.

4. *Improve communication throughout the organization.* Good customer service depends on several basic communication skills. Whether it is for dealing with client departments internally or for retaining paying customers externally, employees need to listen, to be patient, to coordinate information, to ask and answer questions, to avoid being defensive, and to handle conflicts.

5. *Develop shared accountability.* A sign of poor customer service in an organization is passing the buck. Nothing angers a customer more than hearing such remarks as "It's not my job," "I just work here," or "I don't know what to do." Shared accountability means several things. First, the organization must develop in its employees a sense of shared responsibility for customers. Customers are not the concern of just sales, service, or delivery personnel. Everyone in the company from the boardroom to the shop floor must keep customer service in mind.

   Second, organizations must empower their employees at all levels to make decisions that benefit the customer. Customers with a problem do not want to hear that the person dealing with them does not have any authority to act. Making them wait until a supervisor or manager can intervene is not good customer service. Organizations that encourage their employees to make decisions, to bend rules, or to act immediately to satisfy customers' needs are well on their way to having exemplary customer service.

6. *Audit customer service.* Organizations with excellent customer service records collect information about their performance in this area. Ways to collect such information include the full range of research and evaluation methods. Some companies use computer systems to record all information about product movement such as order entry, processing, shipping, billing, and repair. Other companies use customer service questionnaires to measure satisfaction with such transaction elements as pricing, convenience, reliability, friendliness, and quality. At the very least, organizations should log and track customer complaints to identify and solve problems.

7. *Put as many employees as possible in contact with customers.* Some progressive companies have a system of job rotation so non-customer-contact employees can interact with customers from

time to time. Perhaps employees from all functions can rotate through the customer service department and deal with customers' questions in person or via the telephone. Engineers, quality-control experts, or operations people can accompany the sales staff on customer calls. Educational administrators can teach courses occasionally, and the management staff of a hospital can visit patients. Whatever the method, organizations can improve their service to customers by putting more of their people in contact with more of their customers more often.

8. *Recognize and reward quality service.* Organizations can develop creative ways to foster customer service. Incentive programs, contests, awards, banquets, recognition letters, bonuses, publicity, or something as simple as verbal praise can recognize and reward excellence in customer service. Such devices can motivate employees and reinforce the organization's customer service goals.

[*See also* Quality]

For Additional Information

Albrecht, Karl, and Ron Zemke. *Service America.* New York: Dow Jones, 1985. The importance of service quality as a competitive tool, key factors of service, and organizational examples of excellent and poor-quality service.

Desatnick, Robert L. *Managing to Keep the Customer.* San Francisco: Jossey-Bass Publishers, 1987. Proposes a total organizational commitment to service and provides suggestions and examples for developing customer service through employee relations, selection and training, and managerial behavior. Desatnick discusses the need for customer service, the role of top management, and ways to measure customer service results.

Fine, Seymour, and Raymond Dreyfack. *Customers: How To Get Them, How To Serve Them, How To Keep Them.* New York: Dartnell, 1986. A management workbook that includes advice, questionnaires, checklists, and case examples of various aspects of customer service such as developing customer awareness among employees, handling complaints, staying ahead of the competition, upgrading field service, improving customer service in small and big companies, handling public relations, and measuring and improving customer satisfaction.

Heskett, James L. "Lessons in the Service Sector." *Harvard Business Review*, Vol. 87 (1987), No. 2, pp. 118–26. Asserts that a total service strategy includes the identification of a target market segment, the development of a service concept to address the targeted customers' needs, construction of an operating strategy to support the service concept, and the design of a delivery system. Companies must also focus on the employees who deliver the service and on a close relationship with customers.

Kurman, Marsha. "Customer Relations: The Personnel Angle." *Personnel*, Vol. 64 (1987), No. 9, pp. 38–41. How an organization's hiring, orientation, and personnel policies can make or break its customer relations program.

Delegation

DELEGATION involves the assignment of a job as well as the accompanying authority and responsibility for doing that job to a subordinate who is held accountable for the performance of the job. Quite simply, it is getting things done through others. Effective delegation means clearly communicating the specific results expected, empowering and motivating the subordinate to achieve the results, monitoring the subordinate's progress, and evaluating the subordinate's performance when the task is completed. Delegation is an essential part of any manager's job. Understanding the advantages, process, problems, and ground rules of delegation can make this role more comfortable and more effective for you.

Why Delegate?

There are many reasons why you should delegate. The major advantage is that delegation makes the job of managing easier. It frees you from some time-consuming, repetitive, or detailed tasks and allows you to concentrate on other important activities such as long-range planning or new-project development. Managers who try to do everything themselves are burdened unnecessarily and fail to make effective use of their human resources. Some management experts believe that delegation is the key ingredient distinguishing good from bad managers.

Delegating is the best way to develop subordinates. While subordinates can learn from observing managers as role models, as well as from training and coaching, delegated assignments give them hands-on experience. You can develop your subordinates by giving them challenging but not too difficult assignments and the authority to make decisions about those assignments. Through effective delegation, subordinates have the opportunity for guided practice of their own management skills.

Delegation allows for the best use of human resources in an organization. Employees at lower levels who are closer to a work unit are often in a better position to perform tasks and make decisions related to the unit. Many of these people have good ideas and would welcome the responsibility and power to implement them. A manager comfortable with the process of delegation gains brainpower and manpower by encouraging subordinates to handle projects themselves. Besides utilizing employees fully, delegating frees your own time for more efficient use of your own managerial talent. The organization benefits by challenging more of its people and using more of its human resources.

When done properly, delegation motivates subordinates. Most employees enjoy greater responsibility. Surely there are exceptions, and you must identify those individuals who fear or resent additional responsibility. But for subordinates who like to be challenged, delegated assignments can be a real boost to morale.

Delegating Effectively

There are several key elements to successful delegation:

1. *Select appropriate subordinates for a task.* A good manager is keenly aware of subordinates' strengths and limitations and delegates projects accordingly. Work cannot be effectively delegated unless the subordinate is capable of handling the task. Managers who do their jobs of training, coaching, and developing subordinates will know when subordinates are ready to handle certain kinds of projects. This is the first step in promoting successful delegation.

2. *Trust the subordinate.* The delegator must believe in, support, and help the subordinate succeed with the delegated task. Effective delegators realize that they look good when their subordinates succeed. You must trust subordinates to select them for delegated projects in the first place. That trust then enables you to share authority and allows the subordinate enough freedom to make independent decisions.

3. *Clearly communicate the task to be accomplished.* You must fully understand all that is involved in the work to be assigned. Only then can you communicate the objectives and anticipated outcomes of the project to your subordinate. Too often, managers make general

and vague delegations. When the subordinate is not given enough direction, especially on initial delegations, work performance rarely meets your expectations. A personnel manager, for example, who asks a subordinate to "work on finding a new benefits plan for employees" has omitted much essential information. A more thorough communication would be "We'd like to find a new insurer that's customer-oriented but provides comprehensive coverage at a lower rate. See if you can get at least three bids on benefits packages that would reduce our cost by at least 3 percent from last year's budget while maintaining the same level of coverage in all areas."

4. *Indicate what the subordinate is accountable for and how performance will be judged.* Frequently, subordinates accept a delegated task without clearly understanding what exactly they are expected to do or what criteria will be used to evaluate their performance on the task. It is your responsibility to make these issues clear, to encourage the subordinate to ask questions, and to check the subordinate's understanding of the delegated project.

5. *Give the subordinate enough authority to complete the task.* The subordinate must have free rein on the task. That means defining an approach to the project, obtaining information, utilizing other people, and making decisions. An essential element of delegation is granting power to the subordinate. The subordinate must have the resources necessary to complete the task and the freedom to operate fairly independently. If you ask a subordinate to get permission for small details of a project, you are violating the principle of delegation.

6. *Establish a schedule for progress reports and task completion.* The manager who delegates must maintain some control over the project in terms of periodic checks to see progress and to detect problems. Delegation does not mean abdication. A good delegator gives subordinates freedom while establishing a system to determine whether satisfactory progress is being made toward the accomplishment of the objective. This reduces some of the risk for the delegator. The subordinate benefits also by having a clear schedule and the opportunity for periodic feedback on performance.

7. *Be accessible but not meddlesome.* You should let the subordinate know that you are available if the subordinate wants to consult with you. This is not to encourage dependence, but to promote dialogue and teamwork. Nor does this mean that the subordinate has to check with you. A confident, competent subordinate working on an assignment that develops no snags will not consult with you except for prearranged progress reports. An accessible delegator provides

some security to subordinates on new projects. On the other hand, you should refrain from repeatedly asking about the project or needing to be familiar with all details. Accessibility means letting subordinates come to you.

8. *Give credit for tasks well done.* An effective delegator acknowledges the subordinate's successes and gives public recognition as well as private praise. You always look good when a delegated project turns out well. Thus, it is not necessary to take any of the credit. By letting subordinates shine, everyone benefits.

Why Managers Fail to Delegate

There are many reasons why managers are reluctant to delegate tasks to subordinates. Being aware of some of the common excuses for the failure to delegate may help reluctant managers feel more comfortable with the process.

- *Perfectionism.* The perfectionist has the attitude that "no one can do the job as well as I can." Included in this excuse is the view that "I want the job done my way."
- *Fear.* This excuse includes fear of looking bad if the subordinate performs badly, as well as a fear that the subordinate might do too well and outshine the delegator.
- *Lack of trust.* Some managers do not have enough trust in subordinates to delegate projects to them. These managers may not perceive that any subordinate is qualified to assume the project, or perhaps they have suffered in the past because of an irresponsible subordinate.
- *Workaholism.* Some managers want to do every task themselves. They thrive on hectic schedules and working around the clock and need to have their personal stamp on all projects.
- *Need for control.* A fear of losing control or giving up power keeps some managers from delegating. The delegator does have to give up some authority and control when delegating to subordinates. Managers who cannot tolerate any loss of power or control avoid delegating.
- *Guilt.* Some managers feel that they should do all the work rather than burden subordinates with it. This excuse also involves a fear of being caught with nothing to do or guilt about accepting a salary without working hard enough for it.
- *Waste of time.* The view that delegation takes more time than it saves keeps some managers from delegating. Some reluctant delegators claim that "the project is too complicated to explain

to someone else," "I don't have enough time to train an assistant," or "I can do it more quickly myself."

- *Organizational norm of nondelegation.* Some companies have a "do it yourself" philosophy. In this setting delegation is not encouraged or supported. Instead, managers are expected to "roll up their sleeves and get their hands dirty."

Why Delegation May Fail

It is rare that all delegated assignments turn out well. Mistakes do occur. Managers just beginning the process of delegation should be aware of these common mistakes:

- The subordinate did not understand the task.
- Too much was expected of the subordinate.
- The schedule for the project was unrealistic.
- The subordinate did not feel free to ask questions.
- The subordinate did not have enough authority on the task.
- The manager did not monitor progress on the task.
- Problems were not anticipated.

Guidelines for Effective Delegation

Experienced delegators offer these additional tips to make the process of delegation smooth and effective:

- *Make sure that delegators function as role models.* Subordinates learn how to organize, manage time, and make decisions by observing their managers.
- *Delegate total projects, not parts of projects.* Subordinates learn better when they can handle entire tasks themselves rather than merely doing detail work. Also, it is too difficult for you to coordinate a project when several people are in charge of many small pieces of the project.
- *Allow subordinates to make mistakes.* An effective way to develop subordinates is to let them make mistakes on their own. You must resist the temptation to jump in to keep subordinates from making a mistake.
- *Realize there is no best way to handle a project.* You must allow subordinates to use methods different from your own. Resist the tendency to become upset if things aren't done "your way." By allowing subordinates enough freedom, you will discover better ways to solve old problems.

- *Delegate good and bad projects.* Resist the tendency to keep exciting projects for yourself while delegating boring or distasteful projects to others. A motivated subordinate will soon turn sour if given only "grunt work" to do.

[*See also* Coaching Employees; Motivation; Time Management]

For Additional Information

Cummings, Paul W. *Open Management.* New York: AMACOM, 1980, chapter 5, pp. 77–92. A discussion of delegation as a management investment, including information on preparing subordinates, selecting jobs to delegate, and avoiding excuses for not delegating. This chapter also offers a twenty-item survey to assess delegation skills.

Engel, Herbert M. *How to Delegate: A Guide to Getting Things Done.* Houston: Gulf Publishing Company, 1983. An examination of the concepts of delegation, authority, and trust to provide a foundation for techniques of delegation. The book includes examples, case studies, and questionnaires as well as guidelines for communicating in delegation. It covers the process from the perspectives of both manager and subordinate.

McConkey, Dale D. *No-Nonsense Delegation.* New York: AMACOM, 1986. Covers such topics as deciding when and what to delegate to whom, knowing what you should not delegate, and using effective control techniques.

Steinmetz, Lawrence L. *The Art and Skill of Delegation.* Reading, Mass.: Addison-Wesley Publishing Company, 1976. A guide for supervisors, middle managers, and executives on how to practice delegation at these various organizational levels. Chapter 10 includes exercises for developing delegation skills or for use in training programs on the topic. Chapter 10 examines delegation in staff, technical, and professional environments.

Disciplining Employees

DISCIPLINED EMPLOYEES VOLUNTARILY meet work standards and follow workplace rules. They know what is expected of them and willingly comply. Employees find it comfortable to be a part of a disciplined work force where expectations are clear, behavior is predictable, and supervisors are fair and consistent in their treatment of employees. Certainly employers benefit from developing a disciplined work force. There are fewer performance and behavior problems; there is higher morale and productivity; and the rate of discharge, with its associated financial and psychological costs, is reduced.

While discipline often carries a negative connotation, a disciplined work force is an organizational asset. Reexamine your attitudes toward employee discipline and strive for corrective rather than punitive discipline. Developing employee discipline means training, coaching, and molding employees to exhibit appropriate behavior on the job. Indeed, it is the responsibility of management to develop disciplined employees. An effective and equitable system of employee discipline should include a set of clear rules, a set of progressive actions for rule infractions, well-trained supervisors, and an understanding of documentation procedures, legal constraints, and employee rights of appeal.

Communicating Workplace Rules

If employees are to meet organizational standards of behavior and performance, they must know the standards. It is ironic that in some organizations employees learn that a rule exists only by being punished for violating it! You cannot assume that they know the rules. Many problems can be prevented merely by making employees fully aware of the rules, policies, and regulations to which they should adhere.

All new employees should receive an employment handbook that includes, among other things, the rules they are to follow. Orientation training should explain the rules, the reasons for them, and the specific consequences for rule violations. You should be able to explain workplace regulations to new and existing employees. In short, there should be no surprises about how employees are expected to act. By providing a written statement of expectations for conduct, by explaining the rules, and by answering employees' questions about rules, you are helping them meet organizational expectations. Most employees are reasonable and will gladly comply with rules, if they know what the rules are. By making expectations clear, you need not accept ignorance as an excuse for breaking a rule.

Policy statements about appropriate behavior often include specific requirements in the areas of attendance, use of sick leave, tardiness, leaving the work area without permission, adhering to work schedules, unauthorized visitors, insubordination, use of alcohol or drugs, fighting, disruptive behavior, safety regulations, smoking, theft or destruction of property, sabotage, failure to meet job performance standards, and falsification of records. Include all rules that are relevant and reasonable. In each area, there should be an explanation of what is expected, what constitutes a violation of the rule, and what disciplinary action occurs with each successive violation of the rule.

For example, how is tardiness defined? Is the employee considered late after one minute, five minutes, or ten minutes? What action will be taken the first time the employee is late? The second time? The third time? Some employee-conduct statements are quite detailed in terms of defining the nature and severity of rule violations and quantifying how violations result in certain disciplinary actions.

Establishing Progressive Discipline

Progressive discipline is a series of disciplinary actions that progress in severity as rule violations increase in frequency or seriousness. A system of progressive discipline gives employees plenty of time and assistance in correcting their behavior. It becomes punitive only after various approaches to correction have been used and the employee still refuses to follow a rule. A system of progressive discipline increases communication between you and your employees and ensures that they are treated fairly. Likewise, progressive discipline helps you solve problems, retain employees, and develop documentation necessary to justify personnel decisions.

Typically, the sequence of disciplinary actions in a progressive system of discipline includes counseling, oral warning, written warning, reprimand, suspension, and discharge. This means that for minor or first offenses, the immediate supervisor begins by counseling and coaching the employee to help alter problem behavior. In many cases, this is successful in bringing the employee's behavior into compliance with workplace rules. If the particular problem continues, however, the supervisor goes to the next step in the disciplinary sequence—an oral warning. Here, you indicate that the employee has failed to correct the problem, reiterate the specific change required, and warn the employee that noncompliance will result in a more severe disciplinary action. Finally, maintain a written record of the interaction.

If the misconduct continues or if the initial transgression was severe, the next step in the progressive discipline process is a written warning, which provides the employee with a written statement of the rule violation, the desired change in behavior, and the next consequence for noncompliance. The employee receives a copy, you retain a copy, and a third copy is placed in the employee's file.

A reprimand is an official notification produced by a higher level of management such as a department head. Again, the employee receives written notification of the problem and desired change of behavior, as well as a warning that termination may occur if the problem is not corrected.

If the problem persists, a suspension may be necessary. This means that the employee is relieved of job duties for a certain length of time without pay. A written notice of suspension, authorized by the department head or a higher authority, is provided to the employee, maintained by the supervisor and manager, and placed in the employee's file. At this point, the employee is notified, in writing, that the next step for noncompliance is termination.

Should discharge need to be used as the final step in the progressive-discipline process, the manager must adhere to various personnel and legal guidelines for conducting a termination.

The progressive-discipline system is fair in that it encourages supervisors and managers to work with employees to help them correct problems. It gives employees ample opportunity to change problematic behavior and plenty of warning about ensuing disciplinary actions. Indeed, in this system, the employee is included in at least five separate communications about the problem. The employer has accumulated a thorough record of documentation and can demonstrate just cause for a discharge.

Training Supervisors in Corrective-Discipline Methods

The key to developing a disciplined work force is the supervisor, who has the most contact with employees and is the first in the line of authority in the organizational structure. The supervisor is the person aware of rule violations who administers the steps in the progressive-discipline sequence. How the supervisor handles problems affects whether the discipline is corrective versus punitive. Well-trained supervisors are essential for progressive discipline to be effective. It is the responsibility of management to develop supervisors' skills in the area of employee discipline.

1. *Supervisors should be helpful.* View your role as collaborative, not antagonistic, with employees. The goal is to help the employee correct problem behavior. By noticing the problem early and bringing it to the person's attention immediately, you improve the chances for solving a problem. Effective supervisors are direct and specific with feedback and coach the employee toward improvement. Both parties benefit when performance or behavior problems are corrected. The employee is no longer in jeopardy and is more secure and productive at work, and you no longer have the hassle of dealing with a problem and can devote time to other tasks.

2. *Supervisors should be objective.* It is important to view employee behavior in an unbiased way. Stay in the realm of facts and consider the employee's explanation for a problem. In some instances, the rule violation is due to a misunderstanding, uncontrollable circumstances, or unintentional behavior. Do not jump to conclusions or let your attitudes toward employees prejudice your perception of situations.

3. *Supervisors should show consistent behavior.* The same behavior should receive the same response no matter who violates the rule. Showing favoritism is a sure way to destroy morale and expose yourself to legal liability. Employees become confused and resentful when discipline is applied selectively. The consequence for violating a particular rule should be clear and predictable throughout the workplace.

4. *Supervisors should be good communicators.* You must be skilled in giving feedback, coaching for improved performance, asking questions, and listening. You must be able to remain calm and avoid being defensive when dealing with the emotional behavior of subordinates. Work cooperatively with employees to motivate them to improve while simultaneously indicating the consequences of noncompliance with organizational rules.

Developing Adequate Documentation

Thorough record keeping is an essential ingredient in an effective employee-discipline system. Written records serve to maintain objectivity and to protect the rights of both employers and employees. They eliminate problems of recall and distortion of information. Whenever you communicate with an employee about a performance or a behavior problem, document the discussion. The elements of the discussion to be documented include the following:

- *The nature of the rule violation or performance problem.* Indicate the specific rule or performance standard and the way(s) that the employee's behavior fell short. Use quantifiable terms whenever possible.
- *The date, time, and location of the problem.* When and where did the problem incident occur?
- *The nature of the discussion with the employee about the problem.* Indicate what you said to the employee about the performance or behavior problem.
- *The nature of the employee's reaction to the indication of a problem.* Did the employee agree that a problem exists? What reasons were given for the problem? What was said during the discussion?
- *The date, time, and location of the discussion about the problem.* When and where did the disciplinary discussion between you and your subordinate occur?
- *The nature of any agreements reached.* What did the employee promise to do in the future? What did you promise to do in the future? What did you indicate would be the next consequence for noncompliance? Were any time frames for behavioral change indicated?
- *The tone of the discussion.* Was the atmosphere of discussion rational, emotional, professional, hostile, or defensive? Did the subordinate cry, shout, or threaten?

In addition to recording these areas of content, be aware of the process of maintaining documentation. Document the incident immediately after it occurs. Recall is most accurate at this point. Waiting even a few hours will mean losing valuable information.

You should be as objective as possible when keeping written records. Record only facts and clearly observable behavior. Refrain from indicating motives, assumptions, or personal impressions of the employee. Maintaining objectivity may be difficult if you dislike the employee or if the discussion was heated. Nevertheless, for documentation to be credible, it must be factual and not emotional.

It is important to document the positive and negative performance and behavior of all employees. Recording the problems of one subordinate and ignoring the problems of another is tantamount to discrimination. Selective record keeping is perceived as building a case against an individual rather than letting the facts speak for themselves. While it is time-consuming, maintaining documentation (good and bad) for all subordinates allows you to make objective assessments of your staff.

Legal Constraints

Employers should be aware of the body of laws regulating employee discipline and employ personnel specialists who are knowledgeable about state-of-the-art legal guidelines affecting personnel decisions. Additionally, retain legal counsel for advice and representation in the areas of personnel record keeping, discipline, and discharge. While printed sources of information in the area are helpful, they should never supplant expert personnel and legal help.

There are a host of restrictions affecting your actions regarding employee discipline and discharge. Some of these include state laws, union contracts, civil service regulations, federal discrimination laws, case law, and statements in employee handbooks. Make sure that disciplinary procedures and actions, from the first incident of a problem through termination actions, comply with these various regulations.

Rights of Appeal

Where there is a system of employee discipline, there must be a system of appeals to protect the rights of employees. The right of appeal is a way for employees who believe they have been disciplined without just cause to have their case heard. There are various ways to provide employee rights of appeal. Many organizations set up mediation teams where employees and management listen to the facts of a disciplinary case and make a judgment about its fairness and adherence to organizational procedures. Union contracts specify grievance procedures for employees to follow when they believe they have been disciplined without just cause. Civil service boards, arbitration proceedings, and court hearings are other vehicles for employees to appeal disciplinary actions.

Whatever the process of appeal, you should be prepared to answer the following questions about the employee-discipline process:

- *Was the employment rule or performance standard reasonable?* As part of the examination about the employee's alleged infraction, the original rule will be scrutinized. You cannot hold employees accountable for unreasonable or harmful rules, standards, or procedures.

- *Was the employee aware of the rule or standard?* Employees cannot be held accountable for rules of which they are unaware. It is your responsibility to provide written statements of rules and performance standards, to explain those rules, and to make sure that employees understand the consequences of noncompliance.
- *Was the employee confronted in a timely and specific manner about the rule violation?* It is your responsibility to discuss the problem with the employee immediately after its occurrence and to explain the problem in a direct and specific manner. The employee must understand the nature of the problem and the consequences of noncompliance.
- *Was the employee given sufficient opportunity to solve the problem?* This means that you should have indicated ways the employee could solve the problem, assisted the employee in solving the problem, and provided a reasonable time frame for change.
- *Was a system of progressive discipline followed?* The employee should have been given several warnings with progressively more severe disciplinary actions along the way.
- *Were the disciplinary actions appropriate to the offense?* The nature of the disciplinary action must be commensurate with the severity or frequency of the problem.
- *Was the rule or standard applied consistently to all employees?* It must be clear that this one employee was not singled out for disciplinary action.
- *Does thorough, objective, and convincing documentation exist to show that the employee committed an offense and that the disciplinary procedures were followed appropriately?*

Documentation is the key to answering all of the previous questions.

[*See also* Coaching Employees; Feedback; Terminating Employees]

For Additional Information

Hill, Norman C. "The Need for Positive Reinforcement in Corrective Counseling." *Supervisory Management*, Vol. 29 (1984), No. 12, pp. 10–14. Correcting, coaching, and consulting as three forms of positive discipline.

Imundo, Louis V. *Employee Discipline*. Belmont, Calif.: Wadsworth Publishing Company, 1985. Intended to help supervisors, managers, executives, and staff specialists develop productive, meaningful employee relations and use discipline as a constructive management tool. Topics include developing an effective discipline program, determining just cause for discipline, conducting a disciplinary interview, handling difficult employees, conducting a termination, and handling typical disciplinary situations such as absenteeism, incompetence, drug or alcohol abuse, sexual harassment, fighting, and theft. The book includes summaries, outlines of key points, discussion questions, and case studies.

Spitz, John A., ed. *Employee Discipline*. Los Angeles: UCLA Institute of Industrial Relations, 1978. A manual of policies and practices regarding employee discipline and disciplinary action. The focus is on correcting employee problems rather than punitive action. Sections cover such issues as progressive discipline, types of discipline problems, the role of the supervisor, the counseling interview, documentation, legal constraints, and the appeals process.

Dispute Resolution

AN IMPORTANT PART OF YOUR ROLE AS SUPERVISOR OR MANAGER is the ability to handle disputes. A dispute is any type of problem or complaint in which two people disagree. In many workplace organizations, especially in unionized firms, the complaint can take the form of a grievance, in which an employee makes a formal complaint about the actions of management. Whatever the terminology and whatever the process for handling complaints, disputes between employers and employees are inevitable.

All supervisors and managers, whether they work in the public or the private sector, in unionized or nonunionized environments, must be knowledgeable about resolving disputes. Such knowledge means identifying the factors that lead to disputes, being aware of options and methods of handling disputes, and knowing how to prevent the escalation of disputes. You are typically the frontline people in organizations who initially receive complaints from employees and/or union representatives. How you handle initial complaints will affect the severity and outcome of the problem situation.

It is common for labor contracts to include procedures for handling grievances. During the negotiation of the contract, labor and management can develop and specify procedures to be followed regarding disputes. Both sides agree to an orderly and amicable way of resolving disputes with as little disruption as possible in the typical work routine. The contract-mandated procedures will outline a series of grievance-handling steps that increase in formality and end with a mediation or arbitration option. Such a grievance-arbitration procedure represents both a protection and a risk for each party. Labor gives up the right to strike, while management gives up the right to unilateral decision making about and authority over employees. But each side in the dispute gains as well. You gain stability in knowing that work will not be interrupted by a strike and your employees benefit from a procedure that seriously considers their rights and ensures fair treatment.

A formal system of handling disputes is not restricted to unionized workplaces. Many types of organizations are realizing the benefits of having systematic procedures for dealing with employees' complaints. Appeals committees, peer-review boards, personnel-policy committees, mediators, and arbitrators are being used increasingly on a voluntary basis in nonunion organizations. An equitable system for resolving disputes can prevent unionization, enhance employee morale, improve employee relations, and eliminate the need for litigation. Since disputes between employees and employers are inevitable, all organizations should have some way of effectively resolving disputes before they escalate into costly, long-term problems.

Causes for Disputes

Supervisors and managers who are aware of the typical factors leading to disputes or grievances will be in a position to understand and improve employee relations. Many factors inherent in the work environment spawn disputes. Let us examine a nonunion work organization first.

First, conflict is part of human nature. Whenever people interact, they will disagree. The employer-employee relationship is no different in this respect from the relationship between friends, family, neighbors, or countries. When people are concerned about their own self-interests, those interests are bound to clash. By realizing the inevitability of disputes, you can learn not to take complaints or grievances personally.

The fact that employers have power over employees can lead to disputes. The manager-subordinate relationship is not characterized by equality. You hire, fire, make rules, and enforce those rules. Granted, a large body of legal restrictions limit your authority, but you still have it. Complaints and grievances are one means of challenging authority in the workplace. Just as children challenge the authority of parents and citizens challenge the authority of governments, employees will challenge the authority of management.

Another factor tied to complaints and grievances is communication. Obviously, communication is the means for resolving disputes, but it can also be a catalyst for producing grievances. A workplace organization characterized by poor communication, a lack of listening to employees, the withholding of information, and rampant rumors is likely to provoke large numbers of grievances. If employees feel they have no other recourse to communicate their needs and concerns, then disputes and grievances emerge as the only option.

Complaints are likely to emerge from ineffective supervisory and management practices. Hostile supervisors and managers, arbitrary decisions and actions, unfair discipline, favoritism, and inconsistent treatment will all produce grievances.

Obviously all of these causes for disputes can exist in a union organization as well. Additionally, there are some factors unique to union situations that can create grievances. Grievances may be filed because of perceived violations of the terms of a contract. If management and labor negotiate an employment contract, then unions on behalf of their members have the legitimate right to file a grievance if they believe the contractual agreement has been violated.

Disputes arise over the meaning of certain language in the contract. In the stressful and exhausting process of negotiating a contract, the parties often cannot decide on the specific meaning of all words in the agreement. Both parties may compromise on certain words that may be ambiguous. Later, events may test management's and labor's understanding of those words in the contract. A dispute can result from each side's different definition of a given clause in the contract.

Disputes also emerge as political strategies in union organizations. Union officials may encourage grievances as visible signs to the membership that the union is working on their behalf. Management may refuse to deal with minor complaints and encourage grievances as a show of strength and a challenge to union power.

Ways to Resolve Disputes

There are many ways to resolve disputes between employees and managers, though the most typical mechanisms include formalized grievance procedures, mediation, arbitration, and an innovative alternative called "med-arb," which combines elements of both mediation and arbitration.

Grievance Procedures

Most systems of handling grievances follow a similar sequence of steps. Management does something that an employee or several employees deem unfair. The first step is for the employee, or the union representative, to communicate orally the nature of the complaint to the appropriate supervisor or manager. In many organizations, this informal step does not constitute an actual grievance. The problem may be resolved at this point by management changing its action or by clarification of a misunderstanding to the satisfaction of the complaining employee. Even if the problem is not resolved, the employee (or the union) may decide not to pursue the complaint any further.

But if the employee or union was not satisfied with the outcome of the complaint, a written statement of the complaint is provided to the department head or next level of authority. In many organizations, this formal notification of a dispute constitutes an actual grievance. Most grievance procedures stipulate a time in which a formal grievance must be filed. Here both parties begin an investigation of the facts. Each side accumulates documentation and develops its view of the situation. The disputants discuss and debate the problem, present the facts to each other, and try to reach resolution.

If the dispute is not resolved, then the employee must either withdraw the grievance or opt for the next step within a specified period of time. The next step will probably involve a meeting between the union and management leadership. The chief union steward and the labor-relations manager (or other comparable titles) become involved. Together they review the facts and opinions about the case as they relate to labor-relations principles and contractual agreements, and together they try to arrive at a decision.

If the dispute cannot be resolved at this level, then the case will go to arbitration where a neutral third person will examine the facts and make a decision that both sides in the dispute must accept.

Mediation

This method involves the intervention of a third party for the purpose of helping the disputants reach their own agreement. Unlike an arbitrator, a mediator does not make a decision but assists the conflicting parties to resolve their differences voluntarily. The mediator can make suggestions but cannot impose solutions.

The stage at which a mediator intervenes in the dispute will vary. Obviously, the earlier the intervention, the less rigid the positions and the better the chance of helping the parties reach agreement. Also, the method for selecting a mediator will vary. Any neutral third person whom the disputants agree to can serve as a mediator. More formal approaches involve obtaining a list of qualified mediators from mediation agencies such as the Federal Mediation and Conciliation Service or from industry-maintained mediator lists.

Examining specific methods used and functions served by mediators can pinpoint the value of this method of resolving disputes.

Mediation Methods   To be effective, mediators must be impartial. The mediator cannot be perceived initially or during the discussions as favoring one side over another. Mediators of management-labor disputes must be knowledgeable about labor relations as well as human psychology. They must be good listeners and demonstrate to both parties a knowledge and appreciation of each of the positions. Through the use of questions, restatement of positions, and reiteration of the facts, the mediator tries to get each side to question its position. When the parties begin to doubt their entrenched positions, they are more likely to move from those positions toward a compromise. Finally, the mediator suggests options or alternatives that the disputants may not have considered. By subtly suggesting creative options and not pushing any one solution, the mediator helps the conflicting parties to arrive at a mutually agreeable solution.

Functions of Mediators   The many roles filled by mediators show the benefits of this method of resolving disputes. The mere presence of a mediator can be a catalyst to agreement because both sides try to be more logical and reasonable. This alone can facilitate resolution of the dispute. Because of their knowledge and training in labor relations, mediators are valuable information resources. They possess technical knowledge about collective bargaining or labor law, as well as examples of how other parties resolved similar disputes. Mediators are a communication resource helping the parties to listen, to entertain each other's position, to reduce defensiveness and dogmatism, and to reestablish open dialogue. Finally, both parties are less likely to reject each other's proposals when a mediator is present. If only to save face, both parties become less stubborn about their original positions. The presence of a mediator typically eliminates deadlocks.

Arbitration

Arbitration involves turning the dispute over to a third party who makes a judgment about how it will be resolved. If the parties cannot settle the dispute through any other means, they submit the problem to one or more neutral persons who evaluate the evidence and testimony to make a binding decision. The disputants realize that they must abide by the decision of the arbitrator(s).

Selecting Arbitrators   Both disputants must agree on the selection of a certain arbitrator or arbitration team. Management and labor will often review a list of qualified arbitrators developed by the Federal Mediation and Conciliation Service, private groups such as the American Arbitration Association, or professional associations unique to certain industries. Management or labor may reject certain people from the list because they have a reputation for making certain decisions favorable to one side or the other. When there are unfamiliar names on the list of arbitrators, the disputants can check published reports of arbitration decisions or check with other companies or unions that may have used the services of a particular arbitrator. If the arbitration process is to be a satisfactory option for both disputants, they must feel comfortable with the arbitrator selected.

In some cases, particularly in organizations represented by unions, a permanent arbitrator has been appointed. In large unionized companies where many grievances result in arbitration, it is practical to have one arbitrator selected for the entire term of the contract. The same criteria for selecting a permanent arbitrator apply. Naturally, the permanent arbitrator serves at the will of both management and labor and can be discharged at any time.

The qualifications and requirements of arbitrators are similar to those of mediators. Because they render binding decisions, arbitrators must be completely impartial, must have a reputation for integrity and fairness, and must be knowledgeable about labor relations and human behavior and be skillful communicators. Because they act as judges, arbitrators must have sufficient status and credibility.

Arbitration Formats Arbitration can take many different forms. Arbitrators can be selected on a case-by-case basis or be permanent. An individual arbitrator or a team of arbitrators can be used. Using an individual arbitrator saves time and money, but it is risky to give a single individual the authority to make a binding decision in a case. Arbitration teams can increase the level of expertise. There are two basic types of arbitration teams: neutral and tripartite. A neutral team consists of several neutral individuals. A tripartite team consists of one neutral individual, a member from the ranks of management, and a member representing the perspective of employees or unions. Such an approach can provide more knowledge of the specific case or industry. Sometimes the disputants trust the arbitration team more and are more likely to accept decisions if the team includes someone representing their perspectives. But the team approach (neutral or tripartite), while offering more expertise and perspectives, can be costly and time-consuming.

Med-Arb

Med-Arb is an innovative method of dispute resolution that combines elements of both mediation and arbitration. Here, the third party serves as a mediator to help the disputants reach their own settlement. However, this individual does have the authority to make a binding decision should attempts at mediation fail. Essentially, the arbitrator makes one last attempt at mediation. Another way of explaining med-arb is that a mediator becomes an arbitrator as a last resort. The individual or team using med-arb is skilled in the procedures of both mediation and arbitration.

Preventing the Escalation of Disputes

While formalized grievance procedures, mediation, arbitration, and med-arb are useful methods for resolving disputes, each one is a reactive measure. Supervisors and managers would be well advised to develop strategies for preventing disputes. While workplace disputes cannot be eliminated completely, they can be solved in the initial stages before they escalate. A variety of organizational factors contribute to the prevention or de-escalation of disputes:

1. *Improve communication.*   There must be a communication environment in which individuals feel comfortable talking over problems together. It is always preferable to have disagreeing parties settle their own problems without involving supervisors or union representatives. If representatives from management or labor do become involved, then their communication ability will affect the outcome of the dispute. The number of disputes will decline as employees are given input into decisions, are encouraged to ask questions, and are listened to by management.

2. *Make sure that rules and behavior are consistent and fair.*   Employees will complain if they see people being treated differently. Grievances will develop from arbitrary or unnecessary rules. Virtually all employees will follow rules that are reasonable and applied consistently across the board. They will start complaining if rules are unreasonable or if favoritism is allowed. You should examine policies and procedures to see that they are fair and consistently applied.

3. *Recognize discontent.*   There will be warning signs in a workplace where disputes are rampant. People talk about their discontent, show low morale, and work less productively when they are involved in disputes. Do not ignore these early warning signs of trouble in your unit. By recognizing discontent and intervening early, you can settle disputes before formalized grievance procedures, mediation, or arbitration is necessary. Managers who ignore discontent invite disputes.

4. *Conduct employee training.*   Employees, supervisors, and managers throughout an organization can be given guidance in effectively handling disputes. Providing training in listening, conflict manage-

ment, problem solving, and effective communication can go a long way toward preventing disputes. The cost of such training usually is substantially less than the cost of mediation, arbitration, or litigation.

[See also Conflict Management]

For Additional Information

Baer, Walter E. *Winning in Labor Arbitration*. Chicago: Crain Books, 1982. Typical issues leading to arbitration, the relationship of discipline and arbitration, the selection of an arbitrator, and principles and practices of conducting an arbitration.

Gladstone, Alan. *Voluntary Arbitration of Interest Disputes*. Geneva, Switzerland: International Labour Organisation, 1984. A guide for governments, employers, and labor organizations on how to set up arbitration machinery. Chapters cover the relationship of arbitration to other methods of dispute resolution, formats for arbitration, arbitrator qualifications, preparing for and conducting arbitration hearings, the nature of awards, and innovations in arbitration.

Keltner, John W. *Mediation: Toward a Civilized System of Dispute Resolution*. Annandale, Va.: Speech Communication Association, 1987. Author uses personal experiences, cases, and simulations to examine mediation in the context of managing struggle, looks at the characteristics and ethics of mediators, and offers techniques of good mediation.

McPherson, Donald S. *Resolving Grievances: A Practical Approach*. Reston, Va.: Reston Publishing Company, 1983. Information and case simulations on the grievance-arbitration process. Part I covers the nature of grievances, procedures for dealing with grievances, and arbitration. Part II includes case studies on such grievance issues as absenteeism, insubordination, just cause, misconduct, contracting out, seniority, and wages.

Maggiolo, Walter A. *Techniques of Mediation*. New York: Oceana Publications, 1985. The role and practice of mediation not only in labor-management disputes, but in a variety of areas. This comprehensive volume examines dispute-resolution procedures in the private and federal sectors; discusses the legal framework surrounding dispute resolution; provides a profile of the Federal Mediation and Conciliation Service; and discusses mediation issues such as mediator qualifications, types of mediation, confidentiality, timing, techniques, advantages, pitfalls, press relations, and ethical considerations.

Salem, Richard A. "The Alternative Dispute Resolution Movement: An Overview." *Arbitration Journal*, Vol. 40 (1985), No. 3, pp. 3–11. The options being used to resolve disputes and make litigation unnecessary.

Employee Assistance Programs

An EMPLOYEE ASSISTANCE PROGRAM (EAP) is a method of intervention in the workplace that focuses on a decline in an employee's job performance to restore to full productivity. The EAP provides a tool for the early identification of performance problems and a positive mechanism rather than a punitive measure for the solution of those problems. EAPs are designed to deal with a variety of problems affecting productivity, including alcohol and drug dependency, emotional or psychological health, and marital, family, financial, medical, legal, and career problems. The EAP concept stems from occupational alcoholism programs begun in the workplace in the 1940s and is based on the assumption that workers' personal problems affect job performance.

Employers face substantial costs for impaired employees, including higher rates of absenteeism, sick leave, accidents, workers' compensation, and health-benefit claims. In addition, there are the hidden costs of poor decisions, morale of co-workers, threats to public safety, corporate theft, turnover, and training of replacements.

Developing and Implementing an EAP

Clearly, it is both cost-effective and humanitarian for companies to identify employees with performance problems resulting from personal difficulties and to offer qualified assistance for solving those problems rather than prematurely or routinely terminating troubled workers. The following sections discuss some of the key ingredients in developing and implementing an EAP in any type of organization.

Planning

Before an EAP can be developed, the concept must have top-level support shown by commitments in attitude, funding, personnel, and time. Conceptually, there are two models of EAPs: in-house and out-of-house. The in-house approach uses an EAP staff employed by the organization. In the out-of-house approach, the company contracts with an outside provider of EAP services. Some programs use a combination of these two methods.

Management at all levels, as well as union representatives, should coordinate the development of the EAP. Input from a variety of internal people in the planning process will help ensure widespread company support of the EAP. Make sure current personnel policies and practices as well as union contracts and benefits do not adversely affect the EAP. Small companies should decide whether to set up an independent program or to join an EAP consortium available in the community.

At this stage, the planning group should assess the organization's needs, formulate program objectives, and examine options for program type, staffing, and physical location. One way to see program options is to visit other organizations with established EAPs to learn from their models. Companies without an EAP specialist on staff may want to hire an EAP consultant to assist the project from the planning phase through the program evaluation.

Companies can also elect to use an EAP-provider organization, which establishes and maintains all aspects of the EAP for a company on a contract basis. When investigating EAP-provider organizations, you should assess their philosophies, delivery systems, costs, and capabilities in meeting the specific needs of your company.

Assessment and Referral

The organization must provide a qualified counselor who diagnoses the nature of an employee's problem, gives the employee short-term guidance, and makes a referral to an accessible and effective treatment resource. Assessment-and-referral positions are best staffed with mental health professionals who have industrial-counseling experience, strong administrative skills, and the ability to work with managers, supervisors, and unions.

Essentially, the assessment-and-referral counselor meets privately with the troubled employee for an intake interview, makes a determination about the nature of the employee's problem, and makes a referral for treatment. To make an appropriate recommendation for treatment, the assessment-and-referral counselor must be part of a well-developed community network of human services professionals and agencies. In addition, the assessment-and-referral counselor must keep thorough confidential records, coordinate the company's benefits package, provide follow-up care to troubled employees, help educate employees and their families about the EAP, and help train managers, supervisors, and union representatives for their roles in the referral of workers. Companies typically place the assessment-and-referral counselor in an inconspicuous office in the personnel, medical, or industrial-relations department.

The Community Resource Network

A successful EAP depends on a diverse network of community treatment resources. Because it is a rare treatment agency that can handle all types of problems, a diversity of treatment resources is necessary. The EAP staff should be familiar with the major care-giving agencies in the community, their philosophies, the specialized populations they serve, and their effectiveness. A company's EAP staff should establish a liaison with the key personnel at each agency to ensure smooth coordination of referrals and follow-up activities. All treatment resources should be located near the workplace and available at no cost to the employee.

Employee Education

Publicizing the EAP effectively means making employees and their families aware of the program, allaying fears and stigmas about the program, and encouraging its use. The first step is to develop a written policy statement that spells out such issues as the purpose of the program, the relationship of the program to the organizational structure, who is eligible for participation (for example, employees and their families), the confidentiality for participants, the location of the program, staff responsibilities, and step-by-step procedures for using the EAP. Notify all employees directly about the program through a letter, brochure, or copy of the policy statement. Inform families about the program, emphasizing their eligibility, indicating that they may refer other family members, and explaining methods for easy access to the program.

The EAP can be explained in a special orientation and should be part of all new-employee orientation training. Use posters, films, videotapes, and articles in house organs or union periodicals to announce, explain, and offer reminders about the program. To encourage full use of EAP services by all employees who need help, you should emphasize that (1) the company is concerned about poor job performance caused by personal problems, (2) personal problems can hinder anyone's job performance, and (3) use of the EAP is confidential and will not hinder the employee's future with the company.

Companies with EAPs sometimes provide, as a related component, ongoing education for employees and their families on preventive topics such as wellness, nutrition, exercise, stress management, financial management, and communication. This can be done through speakers, workshops, or flyers.

The Role of Supervisors and Managers

Supervisors and managers play a crucial role in identifying job-performance difficulties caused by personal problems. You must be skilled in identifying such problems without diagnosing them or counseling the employee in any way about them. Familiarize yourself thoroughly with EAP policies and procedures and work closely with the EAP staff to learn how to identify performance problems, refer an employee to the EAP, and document each step of the process.

Essentially, your role is to discuss and document unsatisfactory job performance, recommend use of EAP services in the event of personal problems, advise the union representative of this action (if applicable), and stress concern, open-mindedness, confidentiality, and the goal of performance improvement to the employee. Even in programs where self-, peer, union, and family referrals are common, you still play the primary role in referring employees to the EAP. You are, after all, the key individual evaluating job performance. It is important that managers at all levels, not just first-line supervisors, monitor performance of their staff and make referrals to the EAP when employees' personal problems affect productivity. Successful EAPs are used by all employees from executive to hourly level. When referrals come from many sources and employees throughout the hierarchy use the EAP, the fears and stigmas initially associated with the program will disappear.

Confidentiality and Legal Issues

Confidentiality is an important factor in the legality, acceptance, and use of the EAP. Federal confidentiality regulations and data-privacy acts of various states set forth guidelines that a company's EAP and legal staff should consult. Most companies with in-house EAPs locate the EAP staff within a larger personnel or medical function to maintain privacy and confidentiality. All EAP files should be coded rather than identified with an employee's name or social security number. Both to encourage use and to maintain confidentiality, most companies opt for a flat-fee arrangement with community treatment agencies. For the same reasons, most EAP-provider organizations charge a set monthly fee for companies using their services. With a fee-for-service approach, the company receives separate billings for employees who use treatment services and confidentiality is very difficult to maintain.

There are a number of legal issues affecting EAPs such as malpractice and employee and company liability, in addition to questions of disclosure of records and rights of privacy. Therefore, all EAPs should have legal counsel as early as the planning phase and on a continuing basis during program use.

Cost Analysis

Companies planning an EAP must consider both the cost of implementing a new program as well as the cost of operating the program over a period of years. While there is no universal formula, the following factors should be considered:

- Salary of an assessment-and-referral counselor
- Materials to publicize the EAP to employees and families
- Orientation sessions to introduce the program
- Training for supervisors and managers
- Costs of counseling and treatment (beyond health-insurance coverage limitations)
- Program evaluation costs
- EAP specialist/legal consultant fees (optional)
- Ongoing wellness education for employees (optional)

Not all of these aspects require a new allocation of funds. Salaries to supervisors, for example, are paid whether or not they participate in EAP referrals. The EAP can be publicized through ongoing new-employee orientations, supervisory training programs, and existing house publications. Also, most group health-insurance policies cover from half to all of the costs of treatment for most problems dealt with by an EAP. Experience shows that EAPs, in the long run, decrease insurance premiums as health, disability, sick leave, and workers' compensation claims decline.

Program Evaluation

Valid and objective methods for assessing the effectiveness of an EAP should be a part of the program. Criteria for evaluating the program should be tied into initial program objectives. Have an impartial evaluation team rather than the EAP staff or the original planning group conduct the follow-up assessment. It is important that confidentiality be maintained in this phase also. Typical criteria used to evaluate EAPs include these questions:

- How does the actual number of referrals compare to the expected number of referrals (based on statistical estimates of impaired employees per company size)?
- What is the recovery rate of those served?

- Have there been measurable improvements in job performance of those served?
- Have health insurance claims and costs declined with EAP implementation?

Consortium Approach

A consortium is a cooperative agreement among companies and agencies that do not have enough employees to warrant their own EAP. Typically, they pool resources to obtain a single assessment-and-referral source. This person should be located at a neutral site rather than in one of the consortium companies. Companies and the agencies involved should have a steering committee consisting of representatives from each company to develop the consortium (if one does not already exist in the community), to coordinate its operation, and to evaluate the cooperative venture. Experience shows that consortiums work best for companies with less than 2,000 employees.

The company representative to the consortium should work with key people internally to develop a company policy statement, make employees aware of the EAP, and train supervisors and managers for their roles. While it is cost-effective for small companies to use a single assessment-and-referral counselor, many support functions should be separate and tailored to meet the needs of individual companies. In many cases confidentiality is easier to maintain and employees use the EAP more readily when all EAP services (assessment-and-referral counselor as well as community treatment resources) are located outside of the company.

For Additional Information

Brumback, Cathy J. "EAPs—Bringing Health and Productivity to the Workplace." *Business—The Magazine of Managerial Thought and Action*, Vol. 37 (1987), No. 2, pp. 42–45. An updated view of EAPs considering the corporate interests and discussing how to develop an EAP.

Dickman, J. Fred, William G. Emener, Jr., and William S. Hutchinson, Jr., eds. *Counseling the Troubled Person in Industry*. Springfield, Ill.: Charles C. Thomas Publisher, 1985. A collection of readings on understanding, developing, implementing, and evaluating EAPs. Topics include the historical background, ingredients, administrative aspects, typical clientele, evaluation, and future issues of EAPs.

Lyons, Paul V. "EAPs: The Only Real Cure for Substance Abuse." *Management Review*, Vol. 76 (1987), No. 3, pp. 38–41. The goals and effects of EAPs, the characteristics of a few prominently successful corporate programs, and some legal issues.

Masi, Dale A. *Designing Employee Assistance Programs*. New York: AMACOM, 1984. In addition to general information, chapters on alcoholism, drug abuse counseling, mental health counseling, wellness, working women, and counseling minorities, the handicapped, and international employees.

Wrich, James T. *The Employee Assistance Program*. Center City, MN: Hazelden, 1980. Contains information on developing and implementing EAPs, and sample materials such as policy statements, brochures, letters to employees, record-keeping forms, evaluation instruments, and a directory of resources including the EAP Consultant Organization Hazelden Foundation, P.O. Box 176, Center City, Minn. 55012; (800) 328-9288.

Feedback

ALMOST ALL ASPECTS OF A MANAGER'S JOB involve feedback—giving and getting information about work-related performance. You must give feedback to your employees and receive information from your supervisors about your own managerial performance. Customers give feedback to organizations about products and service. Employees give feedback through various means to their bosses. Smart managers solicit feedback about their own behavior, new ideas, and organizational procedures and programs. In essence, feedback or information about workplace performance permeates the entire communication system of an organization. Despite its inevitability, prevalence, and importance, feedback is an aspect of the job that few managers enjoy or perform effectively.

We will examine the prevalence of feedback in organizational life, the advantages to managers of enhancing feedback skills, and guidelines for giving and receiving work-related feedback.

Why Consider Feedback?

Though you may not use the term "feedback" to describe sharing information about work performance, hardly a day goes by when you do not evaluate others' work and communicate your reactions to it. For example, a colleague presents a report and you give your reaction to it. You discuss a performance problem with a subordinate. You write a congratulatory note to an associate for a recent career accomplishment. In a meeting, you are asked to present your assessment of another department's proposal. You must explain to a consulting firm why you awarded the contract to another company. You must terminate an employee. Your junior associate wants your advice on a few matters. It is time to do performance reviews with your people. The quality-control figures are due. The list of feedback activities continues.

Anytime managers give reactions to other people's work, they are engaged in the process of giving feedback. Raising your eyebrow or critically scowling constitutes feedback. It can be subtle and fleeting or explicit and thorough. Because feedback is inextricably tied to the managerial role, you should be acutely conscious of the feedback process. Become aware of unintentional displays of feedback and realize the advantages of developing feedback skills. By becoming skilled in conveying reactions to job performance, you will dread the feedback process less and take this important role more seriously.

What Are the Benefits of Giving Feedback?

By being direct and clear with feedback to others, managers, employees, and the entire organization will benefit. Here are some of the advantages of developing feedback skills:

1. *Feedback reduces uncertainty.*   Most people crave reactions to their work. We look for subtle signs from others and then try to guess what they think of our performance. Not knowing how supervisors, in particular, perceive our work can be quite stressful. All employees need to know where they stand on the job. Seldom will they ask, but they will always want to know how their performance measures up to standards.

2. *Feedback solves problems.*   If a subordinate has a performance problem, then early feedback about that problem can solve it before it magnifies or becomes ingrained. A manager who has a problem relationship with another manager can use feedback to attempt to resolve their differences. Withholding information or reactions will not make the problem disappear. Only through direct, clear feedback about the problem and a discussion of alternative courses of action will problems be solved.

3. *Feedback can build trust.*   Trust means being comfortable in your predictions of others' behavior. You are in a much better position to predict others' behavior if they have been up front with you in the past. By directly communicating with others, you can help reduce suspicions and fears among work colleagues. Managers who regularly give feedback to subordinates, for example, are predictable managers. Subordinates know what to expect, appreciate that predictability, and show less defensiveness.

4. *Feedback can strengthen relationships.* People who can be honest in their reactions to each other tend to have stronger relationships. While the feedback process can be painful, the ability to communicate openly leads ultimately to more commitment in relationships. Managers who care about their subordinates' success will give them lots of performance feedback and will coach them to greater achievements.

5. *Feedback improves work quality.* Employees cannot be expected to improve their work quality unless they have a clear understanding of what quality is and how their work compares to quality standards. Likewise, praise for performance excellence creates incentives for even more quality. You can build quality and productivity by continually giving your employees feedback about their performance and working with them to meet higher performance goals.

Giving Feedback to Others

There are some managerial guidelines for giving both solicited and unsolicited feedback about the work performance of others, whether they be subordinates, colleagues, or independent contractors to your organization.

1. *Feedback should be specific.* Give examples of the behavior or performance at hand. The more specific you can be with examples and complete descriptions of behavior, the more the other person will understand your feedback. Telling someone to take more initiative, use more common sense, or change a negative attitude are meaningless generalities. To be more specific with the feedback, you must provide examples of when the person should have but did not take initiative. Explain what is meant by common sense. Show how the so-called negative attitude manifested itself in specific, problematic job-related behavior.

2. *Be descriptive, not evaluative, with feedback.* This means describing behavior in observable terms rather than using judgmental words. Notice the difference between feedback that calls a subordinate irresponsible with deadlines and feedback that describes the three times in the last month when the person missed work deadlines. Referring to observable behavior deals in the realm of fact—either the employee missed the deadlines or did not. Using evaluative labels and character attacks moves the feedback into the emotional arena and deals with opinions. It is merely opinion whether someone is irresponsible or not.

3. *Use appropriate timing with feedback.* Feedback usually is most effective if you give it right after the work performance occurs or immediately after it is solicited. Delayed feedback is not as effective as immediate feedback. Timing also means giving feedback privately and when there is enough time for a discussion.

4. *Feedback should be ongoing.* Giving feedback should not be a sporadic event in a work relationship, but an ongoing, natural part of the manager-subordinate relationship. Feedback offered only once a year at the formal performance-review time is insufficient and will have little impact on performance. If feedback becomes a regular part of the work relationship and you comment at least weekly on the positive and negative features of subordinates' performance, the feedback process will be less traumatic and more effective.

Soliciting Feedback From Others

Feedback should be a reciprocal process. Not only do you give feedback to others, but you should solicit it from others as well. Subordinates' feedback on employee programs, for example, can serve as a barometer of the effectiveness of those programs. Participants in orientation sessions, training programs, assessment centers, employee assistance programs, quality circles, teleconferences, or career-development, outplacement, or retirement counseling sessions always should have opportunities to evaluate the programs. These are but a few of the places where employees can give feedback to management.

Additionally, employees can provide their reactions to your behavior in such routine areas as performance reviews, delegated projects, disciplinary procedures, meetings, and decisions. Certain features of the workplace, such as employee-involvement programs, exit interviews, and suggestion boxes, exist for the very purpose of soliciting employee feedback. Indeed, there are few areas of organizational life in which employees cannot provide feedback, and many managers are surprised at the insight and professionalism of employee feedback to them.

If you solicit feedback from others, follow these guidelines in obtaining and reacting to others' evaluations of your performance or programs:

1. *Try to get as much specific information as possible.* The more specific the feedback, the more useful it is. Whether you informally ask for a colleagues' reaction or structure a questionnaire to solicit

program participants' reviews, make sure your questions are specific. Ask follow-up questions to get more detail.

People tend to be vague and general with reactions. They probably will provide global evaluations such as good or bad, effective or ineffective, workable or unworkable. Such evaluations do not have enough substance to elicit the reasons for the reaction. It is up to the recipient of feedback to probe for enough detail to make the information useful. If you intend to use the feedback to make changes in your performance or program, it must be sufficiently detailed so you know what to change.

2. *Do not become defensive when receiving negative feedback.*   The automatic tendency when receiving critical evaluations is to become defensive. We want to deny the evaluation and to provide refutation. Sometimes we resent the person who provides the negative feedback. Managers who receive negative reactions from subordinates regarding a new program or procedure may consider the employees ungrateful or uninformed. In some cases, you discount others' feedback by calling it wrong or incorrect. Such defensive responses defeat the purpose of obtaining others' feedback.

3. *Use feedback.*   It is worse to solicit others' feedback and not use it than to ask for no feedback at all. Employees feel manipulated, for example, when they are asked to provide input to management and their reactions are not taken seriously or used in any way. Ignoring employee suggestions has been the downfall of many employee-input programs.

The feedback we receive from others is often very valid. We should welcome feedback, study it, and use it to make improvements in managerial performance, procedures, and programs. This is not to say that every comment that others make should be accepted, but nor should others' comments be discounted. Sometimes the most unlikely people can give the best advice. Successful managers seriously entertain the feedback they receive, no matter whom it comes from. They appreciate others' evaluations, use feedback to make improvements, and offer explanations to others when they cannot implement their suggestions.

4. *Conduct employee-opinion surveys.*   Employee-opinion surveys are a great way of receiving candid, anonymous reactions from employees. They can monitor discontent or pinpoint problems among employees. By structuring a series of questions on any number of issues and having an outsider administer the survey and summarize results, you can receive substantial feedback from employees. If done regularly with findings disclosed and deficiencies

corrected, the opinion survey can be a valuable feedback tool. The method can be applied to customers, the public, or other groups whose feedback is important to the organization.

For Additional Information

Davidson, Jeffery P. "Giving and Receiving Criticism." *Supervisory Management*, Vol. 30 (1985), No. 5, pp. 10–12. Steps in giving and receiving criticism.

Haynes, Marion E. *Managing Performance*. Belmont, Calif.: Lifetime Learning Publications, 1984, Chapter 6, "Providing Feedback on Performance." The differences between neutral, positive, and negative feedback. This chapter provides practical guidelines for giving positive feedback to enhance motivation and negative feedback to correct problems while preserving self-esteem. Haynes also discusses how to use feedback in formal performance reviews and how to receive feedback from supervisors, peers, and subordinates.

Losoncy, Lewis. *The Motivating Leader*. Englewood Cliffs, N.J.: Prentice-Hall, 1985, Chapter 7. Confronting others with information in order to educate them. The author examines the elements of constructive versus destructive feedback; presents problems that leaders face when they avoid confrontation/feedback; and presents guidelines for assertiveness, discipline, and dehiring (discharge) in organizations.

Smith, Michael. "Feedback as a Performance Management Technique." *Management Solutions*, Vol. 32 (1987), No. 4, pp. 20–29. Feedback is a critical part of the performance improvement and performance review process, benefiting both managers and subordinates. In order to influence performance, feedback must be ongoing. Guidelines for giving feedback and potential pitfalls of using it for performance management.

Intercultural Communication

MANAGERS operate in a global business economy. Many large corporations are international, with branches or offices in other countries. Many American-owned companies use foreign labor or materials. Clearly, the market for products and services spans the world. The number of foreign-owned companies operating in the United States is growing. Indeed, the concept of jointly managed firms, with Japanese and American partnerships, for example, is increasing in popularity. Nor is international exchange limited to the corporate environment. The scientific, medical, educational, and artistic communities are global in scope and cooperation also.

The global workplace requires managers to travel internationally. Some relocate to work in other countries. You may be asked to entertain foreign visitors. Marketing managers may be called on to develop plans for doing business in other countries. Supervisors or managers in the United States work with a largely immigrant labor force.

Thus, to enhance your international success, you must understand intercultural communication—the customs, etiquette, and methods of communication in other countries. Organizations with the best international agreements and relationships are those that understand the nuances of international behavior and can avoid offending business leaders in a host country because of ignorance of that country's culture. A rudimentary knowledge of cultural variations in values and work attitudes helps in the supervision of a culturally diverse work force. Knowing the rules for intercultural communication enhances the image of individual managers, as well as that of their organizations and the nation as a whole. Because of the importance of intercultural awareness, organizations are spending large sums of money on courses in international customs and etiquette.

Intercultural communication is a very broad concept. Books are available on the culture of most every country. Obviously, you will want to familiarize yourself with the intricacies of the particular culture with which you will be involved. You must be aware of the various categories of typical cultural differences and have some general guidelines for developing competence in communicating in another culture.

Areas of Cultural Differences

Almost any aspect of behavior may have cultural variations. However, some categories of behavior related to international business may have wide variations across cultures. Learn the target culture's norms in each of the areas described in the following sections.

Greetings and Terms of Address

First impressions will be formed about the appropriateness of your behavior when you are introduced to a colleague from another country. What greeting behavior is considered polite? By what term or title should you address the other person? What degree of formality is expected?

You may have to learn the phonetic pronunciations of certain names and practice saying them. Some Spanish-speaking cultures use double surnames; the first name is the surname in China. In some cultures, the nonverbal greeting gesture is a handshake; in others, it is a bow or a kiss on each cheek. There can be variation within such greeting gestures as well. How one shakes hands or how low one bows may convey meaning. Of course, the rules become even more complicated for a woman manager in another culture. In certain cultures, appropriate behaviors for women differ from the norms for men.

In regard to greetings and terms of address, it is always better to use the more formal style until invited to become more familiar or informal.

Dining Etiquette

Host colleagues will surely present the international traveler with food and drink as a sign of hospitality. Knowing how to behave while dining is crucial to intercultural success. You may be expected to eat unusual foods. To decline a food offering may offend the host. You may be expected to engage in such rituals as offering toasts or making elaborate welcome speeches. Who is expected to sample the food first, host or visitor? Food may be presented on individual plates, served by the host, or eaten from a common serving dish. There may be norms about whether food should be passed or received with the left or the right hand. Lunch may consist of a five-course meal spanning two hours. There may be obligatory drinking and dancing until the early morning hours.

Knowing how to entertain foreign visitors in your country is equally as important. Among other considerations, it is imperative that you not serve guests foods that are prohibited in their cultures.

Gift Giving

The protocol of giving and receiving gifts is another important area of intercultural awareness. International business often begins with the exchange of gifts. Visiting the host's home means bringing an appropriate gift. Consider the nature of appropriate gifts, how to present them, when to present them, how to receive a gift, and how to communicate appreciation for a gift.

An appropriate gift for an international host can be an item that represents your own culture or something appropriate for doing business, like a pen or an office decoration. Flowers, candy, or toys for the host's children may be appropriate when you visit the home of your host. Sometimes, gifts with the organizational logo are presented. However, personal or intimate items should never be given.

Learn the items that are considered offensive gifts in certain cultures. For example, leather is inappropriate in India, liquor is taboo in Islamic regions, and even the color of presents may have negative connotations!

There may be cultural expectations about whether a gift is presented initially in the relationship, before doing business, after deals are negotiated, or at the time of departure. Cultural norms govern whether to present it publicly or privately. The appropriate value or expense of the present varies across cultures. Always send prompt written thank-you notes for gifts received.

Since gift exchange is a symbol of relationship development and appreciation for hospitality, make yourself aware of cultural norms so that you do not inadvertently destroy the goodwill associated with this behavior.

Dress and Appearance

Styles of clothing differ worldwide. Clothing is an obvious sign of a foreign visitor, although managers worldwide are increasingly adopting Western styles of business attire. It is advisable to wear conservative business dress, appropriate to the weather of the host country, when you travel internationally. Local attire you are expected to wear should be provided for you, since it may be offensive to mimic local appearance customs without first being invited to do so. Certain cultures may have rigid dress codes for businesswomen. You may be expected to remove your shoes in buildings in Eastern cultures. In casual dress when touring a country, certain colors may be considered offensive. For example, white (not black) is associated with death in many Asian countries; green may symbolize freshness in the United States but disease in jungle areas.

Time Consciousness

People regard and use time differently in various cultures. Americans tend to be very schedule-conscious and may be perceived as rushing by others. When doing business in another culture, you should know the meaning of time in that culture and adjust to the host country's time values.

Will a meeting start at the scheduled time? Will there even be a scheduled meeting time? In some cultures, you may be kept waiting for hours or for days until the host is ready to see you. Arriving early for a meeting may be evaluated negatively. You may be expected to arrive promptly even though the host is not subject to the same rule.

In some cultures, procrastination is a virtue and punctuality is not. Deadlines and agendas may be regarded as a sign of efficiency or as a sign of impatience. Each culture emphasizes one time orientation (past, present, or future) or another. Knowing this can affect your approach to business. Appealing to tradition in some cultures may be a more appropriate negotiation tactic than a reference to future progress.

Communication and Language

Language obviously is a distinctive feature of nations and regions within nations. Other aspects of oral communication vary culturally. You would be wise to learn some aspects of the host country's language and to consider becoming conversationally fluent in that language. Americans may be perceived as arrogant when they expect the rest of the business world to speak English. Surely there are business advantages to knowing the language of the area in which you are conducting business.

Even if the business transaction occurs in English, there are other communication features to consider. Avoid using jargon and slang expressions as well as certain topics of conversation. Politics, religion, and personal issues are topics that probably should be avoided in all foreign countries.

People have different styles of communicating in various cultures. These are often subtle difference that can make the uninformed businessperson seem impolite. For example, Americans communicate directly and assertively. In some other cultures, people may hint at what they mean or soften the impact of messages. Americans may come across as rude or pushy in such cultures. American business leaders may develop impatience with foreign colleagues who will not give a direct answer to a question. In some cultures, people will not communicate rejection or bad news. They may tell you what they think you want to hear rather than what they actually believe. Emotion and conflict in conversations may be appropriate in some cultures, but not in others.

Nonverbal Behavior

The meaning attached to gestures, eye contact, and the use of space is not universal. Nonverbal behavior is very culturally specific. So the manager doing business in another country must be aware of the norms for nonverbal behavior as well as the norms for oral communication. This way you will not offend your host nor take offense at the nonverbal styles of others.

People from Latin cultures use many gestures while speaking; the British are more subdued. You may want to adjust your own level of gesturing to approximate that of the host country so that you do not come across as listless or flamboyant. Certain standard gestures have very different meanings internationally. For example, in some countries, the thumbs-up gesture or "A-OK" sign is considered obscene.

Making eye contact shows respect in the United States, while in many Asian cultures, it is considered disrespectful. Staring or pointing may also be considered either appropriate or offensive.

Space is another nonverbal cultural variable. Japanese work environments are open while Americans prefer separate offices or cubicles. Arab and South American people stand close and touch while talking, which is considered crowding by people from cultures with larger space zones. An Arab colleague may perceive an American manager who feels an invasion of personal space and who backs away as rude.

Work Attitudes

There are cultural differences in people's attitudes toward work. What motivates a person from one cultural background may not motivate someone from a different culture. The priority given to work, family, or leisure time is culturally determined. Competition is valued in some cultures, whereas others prefer collaboration. Some cultures are individualistic, and others value group loyalty. Dignity and face-saving is paramount in some cultures; harsh criticism has little effect in others.

Such essential features of cultural identity, values, and habits affect all aspects of international business. Cultural work attitudes affect hiring, supervising, motivating, disciplining, selling, and marketing strategies, among other things. Cultural identity runs deep. An employer will have little success when encouraging workers to behave in ways that contradict cultural conditioning. Likewise, when doing business outside of your own country, you must adjust your work attitudes and behavior appropriately.

Developing Intercultural Communication Competence

One way to become aware of variations in cultural traditions is to examine your own assumptions about greetings, hospitality, appearance, work attitudes, communication, and nonverbal behavior in order to recognize your own habits and how they might be perceived by others. Self-awareness will make you more attuned to the customs of others.

Also, learn as much as possible about the target country. Become familiar with the country's politics, economic system, religions, history, social structure, educational system, business customs, food, sports, music, art, and daily life. Such information can be obtained through libraries, by taking courses at local colleges or universities, by watching travel videotapes, or by contacting consulates, embassies, cultural organizations, or experienced travelers.

Finally, learn the language. Take a language course, hire an individual tutor, or use self-study foreign-language tapes. With an understanding of some of the basics of the language, you will be surprised at how rapidly you develop your proficiency once you are in the target country.

Another suggestion is to get a cultural go-between. This could be someone in your organization or country who can coach you or call ahead to make introductions and arrangements for you—an American expatriate living in the foreign country or an interpreter who can travel with you.

If your company or industry frequently does business in other countries, you might request cultural-awareness training sponsored by your company or professional association. Such an investment in training could have far-reaching business benefits.

To develop intercultural communication competence, you must be willing to learn, adapt, and adjust. You cannot expect the culture to adapt to you, nor should you label another culture's traditions as alien or inferior. Remember, you are the foreigner. With open-mindedness, flexibility, some knowledge about the culture, and support people, you

will find that international business travel or relocation is a valuable
and exciting experience.

For Additional Information

Axtell, Roger E., ed. *Do's and Taboos Around the World*. New York:
John Wiley and Sons, 1985. A practical guide to human behavior
around the world. Chapters cover etiquette, body language, gift
exchange, and American jargon and idioms. A special section
provides suggestions for general protocol, greetings, punctuality,
hospitality, dress, and conversation in approximately ninety countries.

Chesanow, Neil. *The World-Class Executive*. New York: Rawson Associates, 1985. A practical guide for U.S.-based business travelers or
for American business expatriates living in other countries. Each
chapter includes special guidelines for international businesswomen. A potpourri of business and behavioral topics are addressed.

Copeland, Lennie, and Lewis Griggs. *Going International*. New York:
Random House, 1985. For international travelers, employees and
their families living abroad, and anyone who has direct contact
with people of foreign cultures. The authors cover such functions
as marketing, negotiating, communicating, teaching, and managing
in other cultures. Other topics include business and social etiquette, dealing with headquarters, managing personal and family
life, and women in international business.

Harris, Philip R., and Robert T. Moran. *Managing Cultural Differences*.
Houston: Gulf Publishing Company, 1979. The role of the multinational manager as an intercultural communicator and change
agent. This book will help managers understand cultural differences, deal with cultural shock, and manage organizational culture. The role of cultural training and cultural specifics for various
countries are also discussed.

Otsubo, Mayumi. "A Guide to Japanese Business Practices." *California
Management Review*, Vol. 28 (1986), No. 3, pp. 28–42. A guide for
what to do and what to expect when you meet Japanese people
and deal with their business organizations. Specifically, it examines the Japanese customs regarding the business card, bowing, gift
giving, corporate titles, the decision-making process, and the types
and conduct of business meetings.

Rowland, Diana. *Japanese Business Etiquette*. New York: Warner Books,
1985. Greeting customs, uniquely Japanese cultural concepts, com-

munication (verbal and nonverbal), negotiating, making presentations, social aspects of business, Japanese corporate culture, and general information about Japan.

Tucker, Michael F., Vicki E. Baier, and Stephen H. Rhinesmith. "Before Takeoff: What Your Overseas People Need to Know." *Personnel*, Vol. 62 (1985), No. 12, pp. 60–65. To help their employees adapt to life and work in a foreign culture, many international human resources divisions have begun providing cross-cultural training. The results of an eleven-year research effort conducted to answer the question "What is overseas effectiveness?"

Interviewing

INTERVIEWING SKILLS are essential to the managerial role. In the course of doing your job, you must perform several types of interviews. You interview job candidates in order to make selection decisions. You conduct performance-appraisal interviews with your subordinates to give feedback about job performance. In many cases, you must conduct counseling interviews with troubled employees to seek behavioral change. Whenever an employee is discharged or resigns, you should conduct an exit interview to get the employee's reactions to various aspects of the workplace and to discuss severance issues.

There may be other types of interviews in which you are also involved. You may interview consultants before using their services; you may interview your staff members before giving them delegated assignments, leadership roles, or promotions. Managers in charge of new projects typically conduct needs assessments and follow-up evaluations through an interview method. Then there are the situations in which managers are interviewed by others—the media, the public, regulatory agencies, or students.

In order to acquaint you with the interviewing process, let us look at selection, performance-appraisal, counseling, and exit interviews as typical interview types. Then we will examine interviewing as an information-exchange process and present common pitfalls encountered in all types of interviews.

Selection Interviews

Selection interviews are especially important because of the cost and frustration of wrong hiring decisions. The goal in a selection interview is to obtain relevant and detailed information about job

120

candidates in order to make the best match between an individual and an organization. The interviewer of job applicants functions like a detective uncovering clues about performance and personality in order to make a prediction about how well each candidate would perform the job. The interviewer must dig out information because candidates naturally will distort and hide information to put themselves in a good light. While doing the detective work, the interviewer must develop rapport, facilitate a smooth conversation, and present an accurate picture of the job and the organization. Selection interviewing is no easy task.

Once applications have been screened according to job-related criteria and a few candidates emerge as finalists, the interviewing process begins. First, you should develop a set of questions around certain categories relevant to the job. For example, areas for questions might include past job performance; accomplishments; education and experience; least and most preferred job duties; personality; relationship with superiors, subordinates, and co-workers; work motivation; communication ability; and future goals. Equal Employment Opportunity (EEO) guidelines prohibit questions about marital status, children, age, national origin, birthplace, religion, sex, race, ownership of a house or car, credit rating, or type of military discharge. Interviewers should become familiar with EEO requirements for wording questions in permissible areas of inquiry.

The interviewer should plan the question sequence, balance question categories with time limitations, know how to probe for more information, become familiar with the candidate's written materials, and plan a note-taking method. Through planning you obtain substantial information unavailable through other means during a relatively short interview period. The goal is not to amass a great deal of facts from an interview, but to get at intangible information such as how a candidate thinks, reasons for work-related decisions, priorities and values, maturity, temperament, shortcomings, and aspirations.

The interviewer must carefully structure the interview, direct it, focus on relevant areas, probe beneath the surface, and keep track of time. Yet the interview should not resemble an interrogation. Questions should flow easily. Probes should not be threatening. The format should resemble a spontaneous and lively conversation rather than a question-and-answer-session.

Probing below the surface answer is a key to effective selection interviewing. First responses to a question typically are well-thought-out answers that put the candidate in the best light. The candidate can often tell from the question what the expected or desirable answer would be. It is important to seek the "why" or the "how" behind responses. Ask candidates to elaborate, to go into more detail, or to explain their reasoning. Use devices to get them to talk at length about a subject. Patient listening, nonverbal signs of encouragement, silent pauses, paraphrasing, and requests for elaboration will get the candidate talking. The less talking the interviewer does, the more the candidate will talk.

Novice interviewers waste time asking questions about facts that have already been obtained through résumés and applications. They may orally review job history or educational background with the person. Becoming familiar with factual information on written materials lets the interviewer move immediately to substantive, new information.

Take notes to record the wealth of information disclosed in an interview. It is impossible to recall information after the interview, and details become muddled if more than one candidate is being interviewed. Applicants expect you to take notes and they become accustomed to note taking early on in the interview. If you take notes continuously rather than sporadically, the act of note taking will fade into the background. Of course, you must also be skilled in giving enough eye contact while recording information.

Performance-Appraisal Interviews

The purpose of performance-appraisal interviews is to give subordinates feedback about how their performance measures up to job standards and to set future performance goals. When performance appraisals are performed poorly, they do not resemble interviews. The employee receives a written evaluation with no elaboration and no opportunity for discussion. Correct performance appraisals follow the question-asking and question-answering formats of a smooth conversational style.

Just as in selection interviews, you must review written materials, plan the interview, know how to probe, use time wisely, answer questions and provide information, and record information. Prior to conducting a performance appraisal, review the subordinate's job description, reread the last performance evaluation, and consult documentation accumulated on the employee's job performance. Interview time should not be wasted in becoming familiar with written materials.

You should also plan the series of questions and statements to structure the interview. That way, you will be sure that all points are covered and that specific information is discussed. Communicate ratings on the various criteria, discuss the subordinate's perceptions of performance in various areas, uncover reasons for performance problems, and coordinate with the subordinate objectives for the next work period. Do all of this in a professional manner while supporting the subordinate and reducing defensiveness.

Probing is an important ingredient of the communication process in performance appraisal interviews. You must question employee behavior and discover reasons for it. Probe to see if subordinates understand job standards and are capable of and motivated to meet job-performance expectations. Try to learn what motivates employees so you can use appropriate incentives when coaching them. Discover what resources would help them perform the job better.

More often than not, managers rush through performance-appraisal interviews. As a rule of thumb, you should plan to spend at least one hour in each performance-appraisal interview. This allows time to provide examples of good and poor performance rather than merely indicating a rating. There should be time to discuss, from both the manager's and the subordinate's perspective, performance on each job criterion. Time should be set aside to establish goals for the next performance period.

Finally, you must record information during and after the performance-appraisal interview. During the discussion, subordinates typically will provide information that helps you understand their work performance, motivation, constraints, and goals. Record agreements you reached during the interview, that is, what does the employee agree to do during the next work period and how will you support the employee? After the interview, elaborate on notes taken during the performance appraisal and record the tone of the discussion. Comprehensive documentation of performance is necessary to support discharge, demotion, or promotion decisions.

Counseling Interviews

In some cases, poor employee performance is due to personal problems such as alcohol and drug dependency, emotional or psychological difficulties, or marital or family concerns. When personal problems impair work performance, conduct a counseling interview. This does not mean that you conduct psychological counseling. In a counseling interview, you attempt to get the subordinate to recognize inappropriate behaviors and to commit to change. You need not diagnose the personal problem that allegedly affects work performance.

The counseling interview presents a difficult communication situation. You must confront problems while maintaining the subordinate's dignity; you must indicate that personal problems may be affecting performance without labeling the employee as alcoholic, drug-dependent, or psychologically unstable; and you must recommend strategies for change without assuming the therapist role.

The best approach in a counseling interview is to indicate the exact nature of the poor work performance and to ask the subordinate for explanations of the poor performance. If the subordinate discloses a personal problem, then you can recommend professional assistance, preferably through an employer-paid benefit such as medical insurance or an employee-assistance program. If the employee does not disclose a personal problem, you can suggest professional referral options in case the employee has personal problems that may be impairing work productivity.

Like other types of interviews, the counseling interview presents similar challenges of reviewing written materials, planning, probing, using time wisely, providing information, and taking notes. This type of interview also calls for assertiveness and empathy skills. You must be assertive in confronting the performance problem and suggesting professional help while simultaneously showing a caring and supportive attitude toward the troubled employee.

Exit Interviews

Whenever an employee leaves the organization willingly or through termination, the manager should conduct an exit interview. Organizations should establish the procedure of routinely scheduling exit interviews with employees who have resigned or who have been dismissed. This allows managers and employees to discuss the reasons for separation and to make separation agreements. You can learn a great deal from terminated employees about how to restructure the job for the next person hired. In the case of a termination, you must explain to the employee the reasons for dismissal and discuss both the cover story that others will be told and severance benefits.

Provide plenty of time for exit interviews, which can be uncomfortable, especially in the case of termination or a disgruntled resignation. Allowing the employee to disclose feelings, however, can reduce the hostility and negative messages communicated about the organization.

Whether the separation be through resignation or through termination, you should try to create a conversation to give and get information. Plan initial questions and become skilled at using follow-up probes. You must provide information about the details of separation from the organization—paperwork to be completed, benefits to be continued for a certain length of time, and the organizational policy regarding references. Notes should be taken about the content and tone of the exit interview, as well any separation agreements.

The Interviewing Process

There are certain elements of the interview process that cross all types of workplace interviews. Whether you conduct selection, performance-appraisal, counseling, or exit interviews, you must know how to set the appropriate climate, ask and answer questions, control the interview so objectives will be achieved, and take notes and maintain documentation.

Setting the Climate

Selection, performance-appraisal, counseling, and exit interviews present a certain degree of tension for both the interviewer and the interviewee. Despite this tension, thorough and accurate information must be exchanged. In order to reduce tension and to enhance the quality of information shared, you must be skilled in creating rapport. A pleasant but businesslike tone must be established if conversation is to flow smoothly and spontaneously.

Create an appropriate climate by selecting a comfortable, private place for the interview. There should be no interruptions or distractions. You can develop rapport through some initial small talk and then state the purpose of the interview. By making smooth transitions between answers and subsequent questions and by listening more than talking, you reduce threat and build a comfortable climate. Nonverbal signs of encouragement, such as eye contact, head nods, and vocal feedback (uh-hmn) will make the other person feel comfortable. As much as possible, make interviewees feel important. Their information should be regarded as valuable.

Certain interviews, such as counseling discussions with highly emotional people or exit interviews with very defensive individuals, never develop a pleasant climate. But it is your responsibility to develop and maintain a professional climate, however the other person behaves. If the interviewee is emotional, it is important to be patient, nondefensive, and calm. Sometimes sitting quietly while the other person vents emotions is the best course of action. The interview should not appear rushed. You should be confident and prepared. Treat the interviewee with respect.

You should close the discussion with a professional tone by summarizing, thanking the interviewee, and indicating what the next step is.

Asking and Answering Questions

Questioning is the heart of the interviewing process and the most important feature of all interviews. In order to obtain substantive, candid information, you must know what questions to ask, how to ask them, and how to use follow-up probes. Ask questions in such a way that they are hardly apparent.

The best type of interview questions are open-ended, neutral questions. Open-ended questions call for broad, lengthy responses. They cannot be answered with one-word or short replies. Neutral questions do not cue the respondent to the correct answer to lead to an obvious response. Consider the difference between these open-ended, neutral questions and their closed, leading counterparts:

Good: "What job duties do you prefer the most and the least?"
Bad: "Do you like typing? Filing? Making appointments?

Good: "Where do you want to be in your career five years from now?"
Bad: "Do you have any goals of moving into management?"

Notice that the closed questions inevitably call for a "yes" answer and little elaboration. The open-ended questions do not provide clues about what you are seeking and they require longer answers.

You can create open-ended questions by beginning the question with the word "What," "Why," "How did you," "To what extent," and "What would you do if." Practice wording your prepared interview questions into one of these forms.

Prepared questions are just one type of question used in interviews, however. Some people believe that the more important type of question is the follow-up probe, that is, the question you should ask spontaneously after the interviewee has provided a response. You should probe all answers to get more detailed, more accurate, and less rehearsed responses. So, for example, after the job applicant has indicated that working with people is a positive feature of the job, you should probe, "What is it about you that makes you like working with people?" Here is where insightful information about the person can replace a trite, typical response.

To be effective, probes must be smooth, relevant, and conversational. Interrogating probes will create defensiveness and hinder spontaneity. This means that interviewers must be skilled listeners so they can ask logical follow-up questions. Obviously, the person's answers determine the nature of the follow-up probes. An interviewer who is not listening carefully will miss the logical probe. Inexperienced interviewers often spend more time focusing on the questions they will ask than on listening to the interviewee's answers.

Vary the types of follow-up probes you use. An occasional "why" will not threaten people, but following every answer with a "why" question will sound interrogating. An excellent device for getting an interviewee to elaborate is to ask no question at all. Instead, a comment on the previous answer, a paraphrase of the answer, or a silent pause likely will produce elaboration.

Your job is not only to ask questions but to answer them as well. Thus, you must know how to encourage interviewees' questions, be skilled at understanding questions, and be able to provide information. Managers in all types of interviews must encourage the other person to ask questions. It is essential that job applicants get information about the job and the company. Employees must be able to ask questions about the rating of their performance and about performance-evaluation criteria. Employees in counseling interviews may need to ask questions about their options for help. Finally, in exit interviews, questions provide closure and severance information for the person leaving the organization.

A pleasant climate, sufficient time for the interview, and the manager's encouraging style will help the interviewee to feel comfortable about asking questions. Periodically throughout the discussion, indicate a willingness to answer questions. Imply that questions from the interviewee are natural and expected and that all questions are acceptable.

When presented with a question, you should paraphrase it to check understanding. People often provide answers to different questions than the ones they are asked. It is not always easy to know what someone is asking with a particular question. After paraphrasing the question, provide an answer, and then check back with the questioner to see if the response was satisfactory.

It is important that you provide information at a level that the questioner can understand. You probably have much more information on the issue than the questioner needs. By considering the interviewee's perspective, you can provide a sufficient depth of information.

Controlling the Interview to Achieve Objectives

Managers typically have a great deal to accomplish in an interview lasting an hour or less. This means that you must be skilled in controlling the interview without appearing directive or overbearing. Learn to guide the discussion to uncover relevant information and to discourage tangents. It is your job to keep the disucssion focused predominantly on areas of your choosing rather than on aspects the interviewee wants to discuss. While the interviewee should be able to get questions answered and provide input to the interview, the direction and the objectives of the interview rest with you. Managers are often so busy that they cannot afford to let interviewees ramble and prolong discussions. Instead, managers who are skillful interviewers follow careful pacing and provide balance so that all important areas are covered.

There are several techniques for controlling an interview. First, plan categories of questions with a tentative schedule. In a performance-appraisal interview, for example, you could divide the interview into three parts: in the first third of the interview, you could rate and provide examples of the employee's performance on appraisal criteria; the middle part of the interview could solicit the employee's perceptions of and reasons for positive and negative past performance; and the final third of the interview time could be spent in a collaborative development of goals for the next performance period.

In addition to planning an interview schedule, you must watch the time closely and keep the pace moving. Interviewees often ramble and take the interview in a direction you do not want it to go. They may also try to make certain prepared statements. Troubled employees may try to maneuver the subject away from their problems in a counseling interview. Disgruntled employees may try to spread rumors about supervisors or colleagues. While each type of interviewee should have plenty of air time, it is you who controls the direction of the conversation.

Effective interviewers learn to tactfully and unobtrusively interrupt statements to steer the direction of the conversation. You can interrupt at logical points such as during pauses or during transitions. If your interruptions are enthusiastic, friendly, and accompanied by relevant probes, the employee may not even notice them.

Novice interviewers often allow the other person to make lengthy statements that contain little relevant information. As a result, time runs out with little information exchanged. With careful planning, attention to time during the discussion, and skillful, professional interruption, you can direct the conversation to achieve your objectives in a short period of time.

Taking Notes and Documenting Information

Another feature crossing all types of interviews is the need to take notes during the discussion and to maintain documentation following the interview. In all effective interviews, much substantive information is disclosed and must be recorded thoroughly and accurately. Likewise, you must keep detailed documentation of interview conversations, climate, and tone. Such documentation can support your decisions and may be necessary if subordinates appeal them.

Note-taking during the interview must be unobtrusive, a background activity that does not hinder the communication or call attention to itself. With practice, you can develop your own shorthand methods for recording information. Some interviewers develop checklists or forms to facilitate their recording of pertinent information. Whatever the method, you must jot down information while the other person is talking. You will forget information or record it inaccurately if you try to rely on your memory.

After the interview is complete, spend some time elaborating on sketchy notes, writing down additional information and impressions, and summarizing the interview. Do this immediately after the interview, while impressions are fresh. The more detail you record during and after the interview, the more informed and more justifiable your position or decision will be. Notes should be maintained in a file as supportive documentation. In this age of litigation against employers, it is wise to maintain records on all selection, performance appraisal, counseling, and exit interviews.

[See also Performance Appraisals; Recruiting and Selecting New Employees; Terminating Employees]

For Additional Information

Drake, John D. *Interviewing for Managers.* New York: AMACOM, 1982. Interviewing techniques for overcoming defensive behavior, asking the right questions, pinpointing motivators, and ensuring equal employment opportunity (EEO) compliance. Interviewing charts, questionnaires, and forms are included.

Drost, Donald A., Fabius P. O'Brien, and Steve Marsh. "Exit Interviews: Master the Possibilities." *The Personnel Administrator,* Vol. 32 (1987), No. 2, pp. 104ff. Reviews techniques for improving exit interview programs, examines a number of exit interview programs, and presents a prescription for improving them.

Fear, Richard A. *The Evaluation Interview.* New York: McGraw Hill Book Company, 1984. A practical book of procedures for dealing with job applicants. Topics include EEO guidelines, handling job applicants coached in the interview process, interpreting information, writing interview reports, and training interviewers.

King, Alice Gore. "How To Interview Job Applicants." *Supervisory Management,* Vol. 31 (1986), No. 4, pp. 37–43. A look at three stages of selection interviewing: before, during, and after the interview.

Intrapreneuring

INTRAPRENEURING is a process within an organization that encourages, supports, and rewards innovation. The innovation may result in new ideas, processes, products, or services. While many organizations encourage the development of new methods or inventions, few include mechanisms for readily accepting and implementing them. Intrapreneurial organizations develop structures and practices for encouraging innovation and thereby become well equipped to adapt to the future. The term *intrapreneur* is a permutation of the word *entrepreneur* and implies the same personality traits, motivations, and behaviors of self-starters who create independent enterprises. Unlike entrepreneurs, however, who are self-employed, intrapreneurs bring about change and start new business ventures inside organizations.

Reasons for Intrapreneuring

Intrapreneurship is more than just a new, progressive organizational philosophy. There are some compelling reasons why companies should promote an intrapreneurial culture as well as some tangible benefits realized by intrapreneurial organizations. In many ways, intrapreneurship capitalizes on the inherently independent American personality. Workers often question authority, are less willing to conform, and care more about job satisfaction than job security. An intrapreneurial organization can nurture such attitudes rather than fight them. By exploiting independence and creativity, the corporation as well as the employee can benefit. Rather than frustrating the needs of its work force or trying to indoctrinate traditional corporate values, the progressive and ultimately successful organization adapts its structure, culture, and management practices to incorporate the changing values and motivations of its people.

130

Another benefit of cultivating a spirit of innovation in an organization is the retention of entrepreneurial talent. Many would-be innovators report leaving established organizations to start their own businesses because they felt frustrated and suppressed when trying to turn their ideas into action. Such talented individuals had creative visions of better ways to do things but were not allowed to implement their ideas. Frequently, frustrated intrapreneurs start their own ventures, which become direct and often serious competitors of the companies they left. The phenomenon is not unique to large corporations either. The talented individual with a better idea whose insights are routinely ignored by supervisors in a small company can take those ideas to a competitor or establish a new enterprise to implement the idea.

Intrapreneuring is one of the means by which American businesses survive in periods of rapid societal, informational, and technological change. The capacity to foster innovation keeps organizations competitive and adaptive. The inability to foresee, value, and embrace change in any area will lead to obsolescence. Albeit indirectly, an innovative spirit in an organization may be tied to its bottom line. Because the ability to establish new products, markets, processes, or services is what brings growth and profits to a company, intrapreneurship works with rather than against predominant employee attitudes, allows an organization to retain rather than to lose its entrepreneurial talent, and fosters growth rather than decline.

Characteristics of Intrapreneurs

Organizations interested in implementing strategies of intrapreneurship should first understand the personality and motivations of intrapreneurial employees. Some organizational behavior specialists challenge the notion of a dominant entrepreneurial/intrapreneurial personality type. They contend, instead, that anybody can be innovative given the right organizational environment. Nevertheless, case studies of successful and well-known innovators (internal or external to corporations) reveal these characteristics:

- Leadership abilities
- Ability to make rapid decisions with little information
- Capacity to take risks
- Defiance of authority
- Refusal to take no for an answer
- Action orientation
- Well-developed imagination and sense of visualization
- Strong need for achievement

- Drive and dedication
- Opinion that failure is a learning experience

An examination of some of these characteristics reveals why many traditional, large, hierarchically oriented companies, by their very nature, suppress intrapreneurial spirit. Most companies emphasize research-based decisions, which slows action. The defiance of authority and the inability to accept no for an answer have not been tolerated by American business. Rather than being tolerated as traits of creativity and innovation, such behaviors have been grounds for dismissal in most organizations.

Organizational Practices Suppressing Intrapreneurship

Many current organizational structures and practices inhibit innovation. Some of these inhibitors include:

1. *Emphasis on hierarchy and chain of command.* When people are positioned in a steep vertical structure in the organization, power becomes concentrated rather than shared. Change is bogged down in processes such as approval seeking, reporting, and record keeping. Both formal rules and regulations and the informal political system favor the traditional rather than the innovative. Innovation is sabotaged by the organizational structure, nay sayers, and the desire to maintain the status quo.

2. *Segmented functions and departments.* When people are isolated into small units to work on parochial tasks, both lateral communication and cooperation necessary for innovation do not exist. People are caught up in their own routines and cannot see the larger perspective, and units become strongly embattled in turfism issues. Because there is little perception of the need for change, the cooperation needed to fuel innovation is missing.

3. *The need to move ideas upward for implementation.* In most organizations, talented managers who propose changes do not possess the authority or the resources to act on them. The proposal moves upward for approval and resource allocation. Unfortunately, no one will be as enthusiastic about and dedicated to the idea as the person who proposed it. Unless intrapreneurs are empowered with some authority and resources to put their ideas into action themselves, innovation will not occur in organizations.

4. *Committed time and funds.* Organizational budgets and workers' time are allocated to existing projects. There is often no time or

money to work on creative, new ideas, which occur spontaneously, and are not planned into budgets or work schedules. Thus, long-range innovation becomes secondary to immediate maintenance concerns and innovators have little opportunitity to act on their creative ideas.

5. *Intolerance of risk and failure.* Innovation is inherently risky, unplanned, and unpredictable. Intrapreneurs often begin their projects on gut-level instincts and make intuitive rather than research-based decisions. Few companies tolerate this style or encourage it. Yet many of the most successful innovations throughout the history of American business were steeped in risk or emerged as accidents. Few new attempts at anything succeed on the first try. The corporate tradition of abandoning failed attempts and expelling leaders of unsuccessful projects makes intrapreneuring almost impossible.

Organizational Practices Fostering Intrapreneurship

An organization interested in cultivating innovation must examine its structure, culture, and management practices. Some strategies to enhance intrapreneurial activity include:

1. *Decentralization of control.* The fewer lines of authority required to approve a new project, the more likely innovation will occur. Intrapreneurial organizations put more emphasis on the individual than on the hierarchy. They throw out organizational charts or create structures to spread power through fewer levels of management.

2. *Establishment of cross-functional teams.* This promotes cooperation and communication laterally and vertically and gives some of the advantages of smallness to a large organization. Because cross-functional teams consist of members from various functions in an organization, they promote organization-wide support for a project. Each function, through its representative, already has "bought into" the idea from the start. Such teams combine to produce a holistic perspective in the organization and can move quickly to get things done.

3. *A strong sense of organizational community.* Employees of innovative companies are proud. Regardless of their level, they want their company to succeed and have strong loyalties to it. Their sense of community results from a more participative orientation and a greater sharing of power throughout the organization. Such identifi-

cation and cohesiveness fosters innovation at all levels of the company.

4. *Sufficient capital for new projects.* Some innovative companies designate a fund for use by a specific intrapreneur to start new projects. It is important that intrapreneurs have a great deal of financial discretion. The project leader who can spend money without asking for permission is empowered to act quickly and strategically.

5. *Less structured job descriptions.* Rigid, detailed job descriptions do not leave room for creativity. Intrapreneurs can function better with broad job responsibilities. This way, they do not have to step out of the boundaries of their role or infringe on others' territories to spawn innovation. Innovative companies will give talented employees the broad responsibility and accompanying support to make sweeping changes.

6. *Focusing on opportunities, not only problems.* The amount of time that organizations spend reacting to problems prevents them from anticipating and seizing opportunities. Some innovative companies schedule time for creative idea-sharing sessions and the discussion of future trends and opportunities. Real intrapreneurial organizations then act on those ideas.

7. *Spotlighting creativity and success.* If an organization wants to cultivate an innovative philosophy, it must demonstrate support and commitment to intrapreneurial efforts. It should focus on its innovative people, projects, and teams and give them organization-wide visibility, which provides recognition to the innovators and stimulates further innovation from others in the company.

8. *Creating appropriate career pathing for intrapreneurs.* The typical career path in organizations, moving up the hierarchy to greater levels of responsibility, may be a disincentive for intrapreneurs who prefer to be hands-on doers rather than managers and delegators. Perhaps giving successful intrapreneurs the opportunity to lead a series of start-ups would better meet their career-development needs. Rewards such as larger capital allocations for projects, personal bonuses or stock options, and more autonomy on projects can accompany each subsequent success in lieu of traditional promotions.

[*See also* Organizational Culture]

For Additional Information

Brandt, Steven C. *Entrepreneuring in Established Companies.* Homewood, Ill: Dow-Jones-Irwin, 1986. A look at old and new management practices regarding organizing, planning, and controlling and strategies to help established businesses become more entrepreneurial. Some of these include managing by consent, creating variable structures in organizations, experimenting with human resources practices, funding entrepreneurial projects, and creating an entrepreneurial culture.

Dechambeau, Frank A., and Fredericka Mackenzia. "Intrapreneurship." *Personnel Journal*, Vol. 65 (1986), No. 7. pp. 40ff. How companies can encourage creativity and leadership, thereby intrapreneurship.

Drucker, Peter F. *Innovation and Entrepreneurship*. New York: Harper and Row Publishers, 1985. An examination in some detail of sources of innovative opportunities and the practice of entrepreneurial management in businesses, public service organizations, and new ventures. Drucker relates entrepreneurship to the economy, provides strategies for marketing an innovation, and presents numerous examples of entrepreneurial individuals and organizations.

Harris, Philip R. *Management in Transition*. San Francisco: Jossey-Bass Publishers, 1985, chapter 3, "Venturing in Entrepreneurialism and Innovation." How to nourish the entrepreneurial spirit, how to encourage the female entrepreneur, and how to manage innovation. In addition, there is a case study on entrepreneurialism.

Kanter, Rosabeth Moss. *The Change Masters: Innovation and Entrepreneurship in the American Corporation*. New York: Simon & Schuster, 1983. An examination of ten companies to build a theory of organizational innovation. Through data-based research, Kanter compares the differences in culture, structure, and performance of innovative and noninnovative companies and draws conclusions about the conditions encouraging change in American business.

Pinchot, Gifford III. *Intrapreneuring*. New York: Harper and Row Publishers, 1985. How managers can create an environment supportive of innovation and intrapreneuring. In addition, there is advice to intrapreneurs on choosing ideas, planning projects, and identifying sponsors. Pinchot offers profiles of numerous intrapreneurs as well as a twenty-eight–page project-planning guide for intrapreneurs.

Listing

LISTENING is a communication activity required of all managers at any function or level. According to some estimates, about half the total time a person spends communicating is devoted to listening. While listening is a process that many of us take for granted, poor listening can be costly and can result in production errors, disgruntled employees, conflicts, rumors, workplace accidents, and lost sales. Listening mistakes waste time, anger others, affect productivity, and hurt a company's reputation. Many organizations realize the importance of effective listening on the job and, consequently, spend large sums of money training employees to be better listeners. The following information can help you identify poor listening habits in yourself and in others and can provide the basis for improvement.

The Listening Process

Listening involves more than just hearing a message. When we listen, we receive a stimulus, convert it to words, attach meaning to the words, relate the message to our past experiences in order to comprehend it, and choose a response. Because we do all this in a matter of seconds, there is room for error.

Let us examine each element in the process of listening to understand where mistakes are likely to occur. Listening can be divided into four major steps: sensing, interpreting, evaluating, and responding. First, we must receive a signal through the sense of hearing. That means that we must be paying attention and must have good hearing skills. If we have hearing problems or are not paying attention, then listening efficiency will be hindered in this first stage.

After sensing the stimulus, we interpret it in a way that makes sense to us. We take sounds that we hear, translate those sounds into words, and attach meaning to the total message. What meaning we attach to the message is a matter of individual interpretation. Our backgrounds, experiences, attitudes, self-concepts, and moods will affect how we interpret another person's words. Because we differ, our interpretations of each other's messages differ. Correctly interpreting another person's words entails some negotiating and checking until our understanding matches the other person's original meaning.

Once we feel that we understand the other person, we usually have an evaluative reaction to the message. We decide if the information is good, accurate, useful, important, and so on. While listening, we tend to judge the message: what is evidence and what is opinion? Is the speaker believable or not? Do we agree or disagree with the message? Do we need the information or not? Sometimes our judgments are premature or erroneous. There is the tendency to evaluate before completely comprehending.

Finally, in the listening process, we respond. The response is based on what we have heard, how we have interpreted it, and the judgments we have made about the message. Any errors along the way will lead to an inappropriate response. The response is the only external element of the listening process. Sensing, interpretation, and evaluation occur in our heads. How we respond, then, becomes the measure of our listening success. Until we make a concrete response, the speaker does not know if the point was made and understood.

Common Listening Problems

Managers who want to improve their own listening efficiency or develop subordinates' listening skills should try to eliminate these poor listening habits:

- *Tolerating or creating distractions.* Noise interferes with hearing. External noise in the physical environment as well as internal distractions (lack of concentration) will impede listening.
- *Faking listening.* Poor listeners pretend to be paying attention when they are not. They fake facial expressions, eye contact, and head nods to signal interest while they actually daydream or go off on a mental tangent.
- *Tuning out dry subjects.* Poor listeners quickly declare a message boring, develop a "who cares" attitude, and refuse to put forth listening effort. If the message is not captivating or entertaining, poor listeners become lazy and give up.

- *Mentally disagreeing.* Some listeners cannot remain objective enough to understand a message before evaluating it. They let their emotions take charge and internally refute or argue all the points they hear.
- *Focusing on the speaker's delivery.* Poor listeners pay more attention to the speaker's voice and appearance than they do to the message. They have trouble paying attention to content and instead focus on the speaker's mannerisms.
- *Daydreaming.* Many of us fall into the trap of daydreaming because we can think faster than anyone can talk. The average person speaks about 175 words per minute but can think at a rate of over 400 words per minute. Poor listeners do not use this extra thought speed productively. They think about unrelated topics and tune into the speaker only occasionally.

Ways to Improve Listening

You can improve your own or your subordinates' listening efficiency by developing these good listening habits:

1. *Develop powers of concentration.* Good listeners can ignore distractions in the environment and seem to will themselves into listening. Also, they actively reduce controllable noise by closing doors, holding calls, and clearing their minds. The more we work at concentrating while listening, the more our powers of concentration develop and the easier listening becomes.

2. *Generate interest in information.* Good listeners can find areas of interest in most any message. They are receptive to information and try to find ways to apply or use the information, which builds tolerance and patience into listening. Rather than declaring a subject boring and tuning out, good listeners develop an inquiring mind.

3. *Overlook speaker's mannerisms.* If we focus on the content of a message, the style in which the message is delivered becomes secondary. Good listeners do not prejudge the value of a message on the basis of a speaker's delivery or appearance. Important information can be obtained from an unimpressive messenger. The content of the message is much more important than the way it is packaged.

4. *Focus on central ideas.* Learning to identify the major points of a message improves listening efficiency. Central ideas and subpoints anchor the facts and details of a message. It is difficult to grasp detailed information without organizing it into a few major points. Good listeners are concept listeners rather than fact listeners.

5. *Hold your fire.* Good listeners separate the tasks of interpreting and evaluating messages. They make sure comprehension is complete before judging the message and resist the temptation to mentally debate instead of listening. It is wise to slow down the listening process. Ask questions to check your understanding before agreeing or disagreeing with the information. Holding your fire also means paying total attention to the speaker without mentally framing a response.

6. *Work at listening.* Listening is not a passive activity. Active listening is hard work. It involves an expenditure of energy characterized by a rise in body temperature, increased heartbeat, and higher levels of adrenalin. Good listeners realize that listening entails work, not relaxation.

7. *Pay attention to body language.* Visual cues can help us more accurately interpret the meaning of a person's words. When communicating face-to-face, we can look to the speaker's facial expressions, posture, and gestures to give added meaning to the message. A good listener observes as well as hears.

8. *Capitalize on thought speed.* Our capacity to think faster than we can speak should not be a drawback to communication. Rather than daydreaming, we can use our thought speed to mentally summarize information, anticipate the next point, and listen between the lines to the tone of voice.

9. *Paraphrase remarks.* Good listeners practice the skill of paraphrasing what they hear. This entails summarizing a speaker's point back to the speaker to check understanding and seeking feedback. This way misunderstandings or faulty assumptions can be discovered early and corrected.

Eliminating any bad habit takes motivation, determination, and support. Replacing bad listening habits with effective listening techniques takes time and commitment. Managers who want to improve their listening skills should work one at a time on each suggestion provided until mastering it. Trying to accomplish all of the suggestions at once would be overwhelming. Through self-discipline and practice, you can realize the benefits of listening efficiency. Good listening is good business.

For Additional Information

Glatthorn, A. A., and H. R. Adams. *Listening Your Way to Management Success.* Glenview, Ill.: Scott, Foresman and Company, 1983. Instructs managers how to better comprehend information; how to listen critically, analytically, and creatively; and how to respond empathically. The book provides tools for managers to evaluate their own listening effectiveness.

Maidment, Robert. "Listening—The Overlooked and Underdeveloped Half of Talking." *Supervisory Management*, Vol. 30 (1985), No. 8, pp. 10–12. Steps to help managers become better listeners.

Morgan, Phillip, and H. Kent Baker. "Building a Professional Image: Improving Listening Behavior." *Supervisory Management*, Vol. 30 (1985), No. 11, pp. 34–36. How to improve listening skills.

Steil, Lyman K., Larry L. Barker, and Kittie W. Watson. *Effective Listening*. Reading, Mass.: Addison-Wesley Publishing Company, 1983. A guide for listening improvement for professionals in business and industry. Chapters include information on identifying listening strengths and weaknesses, dealing with distractions and emotions, note taking, evaluating messages, and responding. Each chapter includes references.

Wolff, Florence I., Nadine C. Marsnik, William S. Tacey, and Ralph G. Nichols. *Perceptive Listening*. New York: Holt, Rinehart and Winston, 1983. Combines listening theory with practical principles for improvement. Topics include misconceptions about listening, types of listening, skills for developing listening, listening as a means of conflict resolution, and the importance of listening for professionals in business settings. Each chapter includes a summary, exercises, and references.

Meetings

SUPERVISORS, MANAGERS, EXECUTIVES, AND ADMINIS-
TRATORS ALIKE spend an inordinate amount of time in meetings.
In addition to the usual staff, department, sales, or team meetings, we
have special committees, task forces, or projects that require us to work
together in groups. The increased emphases on teamwork, employee
involvement, and participatory management create the need for more
meetings. Business meetings can be very useful tools for communicating ideas, disseminating information, solving problems, and making
decisions. They are an important and necessary part of getting the job
done. Unfortunately, few meetings are as effective as they could be.
While we cannot do away with meetings, we can work to make them
more productive and efficient. By realizing common problems, understanding the legitimate functions, and following guidelines for leading
and participating in meetings, we can eliminate all the wasted time
and make meetings useful and enjoyable. They should facilitate our
work, not interfere with it.

Common Problems With Meetings

We complain about spending too much time in meetings because
many are disorganized, poorly run, and seem to produce few results.
The following are some common pitfalls of business meetings:

1. *We are not informed of the purpose of the meeting.* Little work can
   be accomplished if members do not know why the meeting was
   called or what the outcome of the meeting should be. In this
   situation, the group spends the entire time trying to figure out its
   task. Members become frustrated as they argue over what they are
   supposed to do.

2. *We are not given a detailed agenda ahead of time.* Participants should know exactly what issues will be discussed, what items will be covered, or what reports will be given. Without a specific agenda in advance, we come to meetings unprepared. We do not have the necessary information with us; nor have we given thought to the issues under discussion. Such meetings become a pooling of ignorance.

3. *The leader does not control the meeting.* Even with clear objectives and specific agendas, meetings can go astray. Some leaders do not follow the prepared agenda or fail to keep the group on target. Once they go off on tangents or other agenda items are introduced, the session becomes disorganized and chaotic. Participants are talking about different things and very little can be accomplished.

4. *The meeting is long and tedious.* Some meetings start out organized but deteriorate into long, boring ordeals. The meeting is scheduled for too long of a period of time, or the leader does not keep the pace moving. Participants lose concentration and energy in meetings that last longer than one hour. Effective meetings are fast paced. If the group is not pushed through the agenda, it will become bogged down on each issue.

5. *Individuals are allowed to dominate.* Many a productive meeting has been ruined by one person who rambles, takes the discussion in a different direction, or blocks the group's productive work. Some people come to a meeting with the intention of sabotaging the session. Or the dominator is simply long-winded or lacking in group-interaction skills. Group effectiveness wanes and frustrations mount when one or two members hinder its progress.

There may be other reasons why meetings fail. These are merely the most common problems. If you and your colleagues find yourselves dreading or resenting business meetings, try to identify the pitfalls that plague meetings in your organization. That is the first step in creating more effective meetings in the workplace.

Reasons for Holding Meetings

Many advantages of group meetings cannot be realized when you work alone. Better decisions or solutions frequently emerge from well-run meetings. More heads are truly better than one. Members can challenge and stimulate each other in meetings. Information can be given to lots of people at once. Differences of opinion can be aired and settled. Participants can learn more about each other and develop support for each other through the process of group meetings. Managers who lead meetings will want to give specific thought to the particular reason they schedule a meeting. Such reasons include:

- *Obtaining information.* We often present information via reports (oral or written) in a meeting. If many people need the information, then a series of succinct reports in a group meeting can be an effective way to exchange information. Report givers must be skilled at presentation for this type of meeting to be effective. Listeners can ask questions or engage in discussion about the material presented. If there is no opportunity or need for follow-up discussion, then the meeting was unnecessary. If there is no need to hear or discuss the reports, then distributing the information in writing to individuals would be a better approach.

- *Solving a problem or making a decision.* Some decisions are best made by a group. We give more support to a decision that affects us if we have input into the decision initially. Many complex decisions need the deliberation of several individuals who bring in different perspectives. A problem-solving team working together through meetings can thoroughly analyze a problem and creatively discover solutions. Decision-making and problem-solving activities are prime examples of the adage that two heads are better than one. Though group problem solving and decision making is a slow process, better and more acceptable decisions and solutions emerge from group deliberations than from individual effort. Progressive organizations use the talents of all their members by encouraging decision-making and problem-solving meetings.

- *Motivating people.* Bringing individuals together for a meeting can be motivational. This is the basis of sales meetings and major conventions. A group energy develops when many people with the same goals assemble. The excitement and interaction provides a momentum that can be harnessed by the organization. Other features such as the meeting location and program can add to the excitement. Group meetings can be used for ceremonies and extravaganzas essential to building company pride and loyalty.

- *Developing new ideas.* Creative ideas can occur when a group of individuals bounce thoughts off of one another in a meeting. Members use their imaginations to discover innovative concepts or approaches. They replace evaluation and analysis with speculation and curiosity. While one creative person can develop new ideas working alone, a group meeting has the potential of producing many more ideas. Members build on each others' ideas. Participants stimulate each other. One idea sparks another. This is the purpose, for example, of a brainstorming session of advertising specialists to think of new advertising concepts.

- *Making announcements.* You can use meetings to announce and explain new policies, programs, systems, or products. A meeting can be an effective alternative to memos and reports. By getting everyone together, you can go into more detail, use visual demonstrations, answer questions, and clear up misunderstandings. An announcement can be more exciting or more visible when presented in a meeting. Top-level management can show its support for a new policy or program by calling a meeting to announce it. The need to communicate information internally to employees or externally to dealers, customers, the press, or the community is a common reason why we hold meetings.

Characteristics of a Good Group Meeting

Effective group meetings look and feel different from ineffective meetings. A good meeting could be characterized by the following six attributes:

1. *Participants have a strong sense of belonging or unity.* If the right people are attending the meeting, they know that they belong there. There is a sense of mission and cooperation. Members want to be a part of the group and see a common purpose. In essence, there is a strong commitment and loyalty to the group, which translates into good attendance at each session, prepared and informed members, and a willingness to work hard for the group or the company.

2. *Everybody participates.* In good meetings, everyone feels comfortable contributing. There is a shared interaction among members. Regardless of actual status or position, each person feels that all remarks will be considered by the rest of the group. No one dominates or monopolizes the discussion.

3. *Discussion follows a clear plan.* Effective meetings have clear purposes, published agendas, and prepared members who stick to the purpose and stay on course. Everyone knows why the meeting was called, what the group is trying to accomplish, and where it stands in relation to the task. Keeping discussion on the subject allows for efficient use of time. Meetings need structure and a sense of purpose if they are to accomplish anything.

4. *Conflicts are managed.* Whenever we meet in groups to give or get information, to make decisions, to generate ideas, or to solve prob-

lems, differences of opinion will occur. When meetings are operating properly, we will feel free to disagree. Organizations that stifle conflict restrict the good ideas collegial bickering or friction can produce. On the other hand, meetings must not deteriorate into aggressive free-for-alls. In effective meetings, people can disagree while maintaining respect for one another.

5. *Task and people issues are considered.* In effective meetings, the group does its work while maintaining good relationships between the people involved. Both the task and the morale of the group are important considerations. A group that is all work and no play will quickly burn out. Nor should a meeting be all fun and games and no work. The more people like coming to meetings, the more productive the meetings can be. Meeting effectiveness is a combination of productivity and enjoyment.

6. *The group is aware of its process.* Effective groups have ways to examine themselves and their progress. At times, they step back from their job and look at their procedures, membership, and internal communication. Members can suggest alternative meeting times, propose new ways of operating, and comment on group problems. This is the only way that a group can solve its functional problems. By monitoring the group process, members can make sure meetings are purposeful, organized, enjoyable, and productive.

The Leader's Role

The leader of a meeting has several tasks before, during, and after the meeting. In preparation, you must decide if a meeting is the best way to achieve a particular objective. In other words, is a meeting necessary? What is its purpose? Could the purpose be achieved more easily or effectively through another means? If you decide that a meeting is the best strategy, then plans are necessary. You must decide who should attend, what the agenda will be, when and where the meeting should occur, and what information, materials, or equipment will be needed.

Strategically selecting meeting participants is an important consideration for effective meetings. Some meetings automatically dictate the participants. For example, a staff meeting typically includes the full staff of a department or unit. Rather than having a standard composition of members for all meetings, however, consider the issue carefully. Is there a reason why all participants should be there? Should other individuals be present? Selecting the right mix of people for a meeting is a crucial factor in its success or failure.

You should carefully prepare and circulate an agenda ahead of time. It is important to be realistic about what can be accomplished in the allotted time period. Some leaders provide suggested time limits for each agenda item. Sometimes it is necessary to circulate a tentative agenda and ask participants to suggest additional agenda items. You then circulate a revised agenda to members before the meeting. If members are expected to bring information to the meeting or to present reports, they should receive advance notice. A carefully planned and communicated meeting agenda will more likely result in informed participants who efficiently use the meeting time.

The time and place of a meeting are other important considerations. Choose a time that accommodates members' schedules and energy levels. Monday mornings, Friday afternoons, and time slots immediately after lunch should be avoided. Likewise, people will not be at their peak concentration level the day before holidays or vacations. The location of a meeting can also affect its outcome. Rooms that are too crowded, too hot, or have poor acoustics lead to lifeless sessions. Chairs should be arranged to best serve the purpose of the meeting. Motivational meetings should be held in exciting, off-site locations. This adds a note of importance and visibility to the meeting and can make participants feel special.

You should also arrange for necessary materials and media equipment to be used at a meeting. Such fine points of preparation give the meeting an atmosphere of efficiency and enhance your credibility.

You must take an active role in running a meeting. The following are some suggestions for conducting an effective meeting:

1. *Create a member-centered meeting.* A dominant leader will stifle a meeting. Members resent meetings where the leader does all the talking and they cannot have input or ask questions. In this situation, they are not participants in a meeting but an audience to a speech. Even in meetings where the purpose is to make announcements or give information, you should not be the sole presenter. You can announce the information and then have key people explain it and answer questions. Some authorities suggest that the leader talk less than 20 percent of the time in a meeting. You should not give opinions or evaluations unless asked and should refrain from offering your opinions until everyone has had a chance to be heard. Good ideas are lost when subordinates are reluctant to contradict or disagree with a manager who has already stated a position.

2. *Stimulate discussion by asking questions.* An effective meeting is more than a series of monologues. It should be an exchange of information and ideas. To accomplish real interaction, you should be skilled at questioning. A good way to stimulate discussion is to

ask open-ended questions, which cannot be answered by yes/no responses or short reactions. Examples of open-ended questions are "What do you think?" "How should we proceed?" "Why?" "What should we do?"

3. *Avoid idea killers.* Make sure that everyone has a chance to be heard and that everyone's comments are taken seriously. Comments and behaviors that kill enthusiasm must be prohibited. Treating a participant as inferior, uninformed, inexperienced, or naive will suppress discussion. Sometimes the best comments come from organizational newcomers whose ideals are not dimmed by skepticism. You should monitor and disallow idea-killing remarks such as "It won't work," "You'll learn in time," and "You're kidding."

4. *Keep the group on the subject.* It is your role to move through the agenda and to keep the group from going off on tangents. Frequent summaries are a good device for keeping the group organized and for keeping the pace moving. If several members are interested in discussing another subject, make that a topic for a subsequent meeting. Make sure that no one dominates or sabotages the meeting. You must be skilled at maintaining control of the meeting without being dominant. A few well-placed, tactful remarks can keep the group on its agenda.

5. *Summarize the meeting and give assignments.* A good leader does not let meeting time run out. You should draw the session to a close by summarizing information, suggesting unresolved issues for future meetings, and giving participants tasks to work on before the next meeting. Thus, people leave the meeting with a sense of accomplishment and future direction.

There are still some tasks after the meeting has concluded. Prepare and distribute minutes, notes, or publicity of the meeting as soon as possible. You may want to begin planning the agenda of a subsequent meeting while ideas about this meeting are still fresh in mind. Finally, good leaders review and analyze the meeting process. Assess the meeting effectiveness and your own leadership style; then use that information to make the next meeting better.

Special Techniques

Some techniques are especially useful for achieving certain meeting purposes or facilitating the meeting process. Three techniques applicable to business meetings are the problem-solving method, brainstorming, and teleconferencing.

The Problem-Solving Method

The problem-solving method is a logical format for working through a problem to a solution. By following an established series of steps, the meeting progresses smoothly and logically. Everyone is working together on the same part of the problem. This eliminates the confusion that occurs when some people are focusing on possible solutions while others are still characterizing the problem. Groups engaged in problem-solving meetings should follow these five steps:

1. *Describe the problem.* What exactly is the problem at hand? Are there several interrelated problems? Are there problems underlying the obvious one?
2. *Discuss history, causes, and effects of the problem.* How long has the problem existed? Has anything been done to solve it before? What are its obvious and subtle causes? Who is affected by this problem? How serious are the effects?
3. *Suggest many possible solutions.* What are all the possible actions that could be taken to solve this problem? What are some immediate solutions, long-term solutions, and creative solutions?
4. *Identify the best solution.* Which solution is most practical, easiest to implement, most cost-effective, most acceptable, or most permanent? The best solution is one that fits whatever criteria the group thinks is important.
5. *Make recommendations for implementation.* Who will implement the solution? How? By what timetable? What resources will be required? Whose support is essential? By what means will the effectiveness of the solution be evaluated?

Brainstorming

Brainstorming is a method for stimulating the creative thinking of meeting participants. It encourages the free flow of ideas. It is especially useful to generate many ideas. The rules of brainstorming follow:

1. *Members present ideas rapidly as they come to mind.* Do not self-censor thoughts. Free-associate without worrying about the logic or quality of ideas.
2. *Members should briefly suggest ideas.* Speak just long enough to present an idea. Do not explain it or justify it.
3. *Members should not analyze or evaluate others' ideas.* The goal is a quantity of ideas. The quality of the ideas will be considered later. Members are not allowed to comment on, criticize, praise, or debate ideas that have already been presented.

4. *Members are encouraged to build on the ideas of others.* The advantage of group brainstorming is that one person's idea can trigger another person's thoughts. Piggybacking on previous comments is part of the creativity of this activity.

5. *Someone records each idea where everyone in the group can see it.* By putting ideas on newsprint or on a board visible to the entire group, members can see and build on previous comments.

Through this free-wheeling process, novel, creative, and even bizarre ideas emerge. Some seemingly absurd ideas that may be workable would never have been suggested if the group were evaluating them. The freedom from criticism protects egos and stretches minds. Once a long list of ideas emerges, the brainstorming process is complete and the group can move on to analyzing the ideas.

Teleconferencing

Teleconferencing is the use of telecommunication systems by groups of people at two or more locations for the purpose of meeting with each other. Participants can be geographically dispersed and meet via technology rather than through face-to-face contact. Teleconferences can range in size from three to thousands of participants at two or two hundred different locations. Advocates of teleconferencing use the technique for sales meetings, press conferences, shareholders' meetings, management meetings, fund-raising events, promotional programs with customers, and training programs.

Using teleconferencing for meetings has its advantages and drawbacks. Perhaps its greatest attraction is that it saves time because it reduces the need for travel. Additionally, it allows more people to have easy access to communication, provides a greater sense of participation in the organization as a whole, and creates an improved organizational image because of state-of-the-art technology.

The limitations of teleconferencing include the cost of the technology to provide full-motion, interactive video; the resistance of some participants to this technology; the impersonal nature of teleconferencing meetings; and technical or security concerns.

The following are suggestions for conducting effective meetings via teleconferencing technology:

• The individual scheduling a teleconference should determine its purpose, set an agenda with time estimates for each item, determine the list of participants, invite the participants in advance, disseminate the participant list and agenda ahead of time, gather all support material, and moderate the meeting by keeping the group on the agenda and time line.

- In a voice-only teleconference, it is advisable to send pictures of the participants along with the agenda. This is especially necessary if participants have not met each other before. This allows participants to visualize others in the meeting. Pictures of the various conference sites and working environments also help familiarize participants with each other.

- Those speaking in a teleconference other than for the purpose of a lecture should keep their remarks short and solicit frequent responses. Always give your name and location before making a remark, and solicit responses from specific individuals. Address other persons by name. Wait for a break in the discussion before contributing. Try to avoid off-microphone discussions in the background and extraneous movement. Never call on an individual or site without some warning.

- The teleconference room should look more like a meeting room and less like a radio or television studio. If the equipment and the technical production become the focus, people will become formal, rigid, and uncommunicative. It is important to preserve the spontaneity and informal exchange of a face-to-face meeting.

- For a video teleconference, there are some techniques to enhance individuals' visual images. Do not wear white or close-knit plaids. Look at the camera. Do not read from notes. Avoid nervous mannerisms. If image is very important, practice speaking before a camera or with a teleprompter before the actual teleconference.

- When using graphics, make sure all material can be seen or read. Opt for less rather than more information per graphic. Determine your worst-case viewing situation when judging the readability of material on slides or television still images.

For Additional Information

Elton, Martin C. J. *Teleconferencing: New Media for Business Meetings.* New York: AMA Membership Publications Division, 1982. A fifty-seven–page introductory guide to the types of teleconferences, research on teleconferencing as an alternative to travel, and some basic advice on selecting and implementing a teleconferencing system.

Fletcher, Winston. *Meetings, Meetings.* New York: William Morrow and Company, 1983. A witty look at the dos and don'ts of meetings.

The goal is to manipulate meetings to make them more fun. Topics include effective behavior in meetings, the leadership role, games played in meetings, brainstorming, and negotiation.

How to Run Better Business Meetings: A Reference Guide for Managers. New York: McGraw-Hill Book Company, 1987. Prepared by the 3M Meeting Management Team. A wealth of practical information for making meetings more effective. Topics include meeting dynamics, meeting rooms, leadership and participation skills, visual aids, and special meeting types such as technical, financial, multilingual, staff, and committee meetings.

Kirkpatrick, Donald L. *How to Plan and Conduct Productive Business Meetings.* New York: AMACOM, 1987. Ways to make meetings more productive. Content covers causes of unproductive meetings, guidelines for successful sales meetings, the use of teleconferencing equipment, the achievement of meeting objectives, the use of questions, and strategies for developing enthusiasm and maintaining control.

Lawson, John D. *When You Preside.* Danville, Ill.: The Interstate Printers and Publishers, 1980. Aimed at leaders of both volunteer organizations and work groups on the job. Three sections cover people issues, group-dynamics techniques, and special forms such as panel discussions, club meetings, and parliamentary procedure. Numerous lists, charts, and checklists make the information easy to grasp.

Sigband, Norman B. "Meetings with Success." *Personnel Journal*, Vol. 64 (1985), No. 5, pp. 48–55. A recommendation that companies have policies for effective meetings.

Mentoring

MENTORING involves the formation of relationships between senior and junior employees for the purpose of career development. The mentor (or sponsor) holds a higher position in the hierarchy and has demonstrated some degree of organizational success. Thus, the protégé can benefit from the mentor's information and advice. The mentor is interested in the career growth of capable younger colleagues and is willing to devote time and emotional energy to helping them. The mentor receives satisfaction and recognition from assisting the protégé. In some organizations, mentors receive tangible rewards for their involvement in mentoring relationships.

Benefits of Mentoring

Junior employees receive the most obvious benefits from mentoring. But mentors themselves and the organization as a whole reap advantages as well. Some advantages mentoring relationships provide to protégés are:

- *Assimilation into the organization.* Mentors can help newcomers learn about organizational norms, understand the unique culture of a particular organization, and deal with corporate politics. There is no way, other than through observation over time, to learn about the important aspects of a workplace without the help of a seasoned veteran of the organization.

- *Sharing of information.* A mentor can provide "inside" information that a protégé cannot obtain as easily or as quickly through other means. The mentor can be a direct conduit to supervisors' thoughts and reactions. The wise protégé listens carefully, honors the trust in the relationship, and is discreet with confidential information provided by the mentor.

- *Opportunities for career growth.* The many valuable functions performed by a mentor combine to offer career growth opportunities to a protégé. Mentors can help younger colleagues set goals, plan careers, and develop skills necessary for career advancement. They can nominate protégés for key projects, bring them visibility, speak favorably about them to others, and introduce them to key people in the organization.

- *Support and understanding.* Mentors are workplace friends. They can listen to problems, calm fears, and boost the confidence of protégés. Because mentors are more experienced and trusted colleagues, they can be an excellent sounding board for concerns and offer empathy and advice.

- *Provision of a role model.* Individuals who have achieved success in an organization can serve as valuable role models to newcomers. Astute protégés learn by observing the subtle behaviors and reactions of the mentor and incorporating such observations into their own repertoire of behavior.

Mentors can also realize benefits from their relationship with protégés. The fresh insights of younger talent can challenge and motivate older employees. Protégés can help senior employees stay abreast of new developments in a field or refine their outdated skills. Mentors can obtain information about subordinates from protégés that they could not obtain from other employees, who are often reluctant to share negative information with supervisors. Competent protégés make a mentor look good. A senior employee who has helped develop a young "star" shares in the visibility and prestige of the protégé's success. The protégé speaks favorably of the mentor and offers admiration and respect to the mentor, who in turn realizes great satisfaction by passing on information, insights, and wisdom and seeing these ideas continue through others. Some organizations formalize the mentoring process and offer rewards such as recognition dinners, travel perks, or funding for pet projects to those willing to serve as organizational mentors.

Organizations benefit whenever talent is nurtured. Mentored individuals learn faster, become socialized into the organization more easily, and enhance their chances for success. Through mentoring, the talents of younger employees are tapped and the motivation and skills of older employees are maintained. Thus, organizations can reduce turnover and realize a greater human resources potential.

Issues of Cross-Gender Mentoring

Many organizations use mentoring relationships to assist women and minority employees who may face unique career challenges in traditional organizations. The following are some dynamics of cross-gender mentor relationships that must be dealt with if such mentoring is to succeed in an organization.

Some women report difficulty in using male mentors as role models. What is considered appropriate behavior for a male in the workplace may not be considered appropriate for a female employee. At the very least, a female protégé must adapt behaviors modeled from a male mentor to fit her own style. The relationship of a male mentor to a female protégé may reinforce stereotypical roles of male power and female dependence. Issues of intimacy and sexuality surface in cross-gender mentoring relationships. Frequently, cross-gender mentor relationships receive more attention and resentment from co-workers than same-gender mentor relationships do. Workers may become suspicious of and impugn the motives of a male senior manager who takes a special interest in a younger female employee.

It is difficult to provide remedies to problems of sex-role stereotypes and sexual tensions that can affect cross-gender mentoring. At the very least, mentors, protégés, and organizations should be aware of such possible complications and should ensure that mentoring facilitates rather than impedes career growth.

Fostering Mentoring in Organizations

Mentoring is an aspect of human resources development. To encourage it, organizations must relate mentoring to its overall human resources development effort. If a company pays only lip service to the importance of employees, then mentoring will not work. An organizational culture to support mentoring must exist. A teamwork environment is more conducive to mentoring relationships than an environment of individual competitiveness.

Managers should be made aware of the mentoring process, functions, and advantages. Educational programs can highlight the topic of mentoring and teach support skills such as listening, coaching, counseling, motivating, and giving feedback.

The mentoring function can be built into goal-setting and performance-appraisal criteria for managers. If you are aware of the need to mentor junior employees and possess mentoring skills, you can allocate part of your time for this activity. Likewise, if mentoring becomes a management function in an organization, the performance-appraisal system can review and reward your success at mentoring others.

Organizations committed to mentoring can establish a formal mentoring program by disseminating a policy and setting up procedures for pairing senior- with junior-level employees. In such programs, however, participation should be voluntary. For a mentoring program to work, neither the mentor nor the protégé should feel coerced into the relationship. Once employees have expressed interest, a formal system can encourage the development of mentor relationships. There should be a mechanism for reassigning mismatched pairs and for evaluating the effectiveness of a formal mentoring program.

[See also Career Development]

For Additional Information

Collins, Nancy W. *Professional Women and Their Mentors.* Englewood Cliffs, N.J.: Prentice-Hall, 1983. Written for the professional and managerial woman who wants to seek and work effectively with a mentor. The man mentor of a woman protégé will also benefit from this book. Collins presents the results of surveys and interviews on mentoring and includes such areas as mentoring functions, selecting a mentor, multiple mentors, sex and mentors, and becoming a mentor.

Kram, Kathy E. *Mentoring at Work.* Glenview, Ill.: Scott, Foresman and Company, 1985. Information for employees as mentors and as protégés, for practicing managers who want to foster mentoring, and for human resources specialists and organizational researchers who want data on the topic. The author presents interview data to illustrate various types of developmental relationships in work settings and to explain benefits and limitations of mentoring. Ten pages of references are included.

Zey, Michael G. *The Mentor Connection.* Homewood, Ill.: Dow-Jones-Irwin, 1984. Based on interviews with managers in small and large corporations, a discussion of how mentors can be employed as a means of gaining upward mobility. The book covers such issues as the strategies for acquiring a mentor, the handling of relationships with peers and supervisors, and guidelines for avoiding pitfalls in mentor relationships. It provides examples of formal mentor programs in government and private industry.

Motivation

BECAUSE PRODUCTIVITY IS A GOAL IN ALL WORKPLACE ORGANIZATIONS, MANAGERS must deal with the concept of employee motivation. Part of your role is to encourage subordinates to behave in ways that stimulate organizational productivity. In order to be a skilled motivator of others, you must understand the concept of motivation and the complex array of factors that affect it, and be able to influence others toward greater productivity. You must also learn to deal with motivational problems.

The Concept of Motivation

The term *motivation* relates to the energy that initiates and directs behavior and concerns the choices that we make about our goal-directed behavior. Presumably, we have a wide range of choices about behavior. Motives prompt us to act in certain ways as opposed to other ways. Motives are the "why" of behavior. By understanding the inner urges that direct behavior, you can influence the way your employees behave toward work-related goals.

An understanding of the following five characteristics of motives will help you to motivate your employees more effectively:

1. *Motives are hierarchical.* The motives for our behavior vary in strength and importance. Some are more powerful than others. They exist in a type of rank order. When contradictory motives exist, the more powerful motive will guide our behavior. For example, an employee may be simultaneously motivated to earn more money and to have more leisure time. The employee will choose to work overtime only if financial motives are stronger than the desire for

leisure time. If the desire for free time is ranked higher than the desire for money in the motivational system, the employee will not opt to work overtime.

2. *Motives may be unconscious.* Frequently, we are unaware of the motives for our behavior. When asked why we are behaving a certain way, we may state a variety of reasons unrelated to our actual behavior. We may think these are our motives or wish they were our motives. Rarely are we fully aware of the inner needs and drives affecting our behavior.

3. *Motives must be inferred.* We can observe behavior, but we can only infer the motives underlying that behavior. Trying to understand our own and others' motivations is guesswork. At best, we can try to extrapolate motives from observed behavior coupled with stated beliefs, attitudes, and intentions. Even licensed psychologists cannot be certain about the motives for our actions.

4. *Motives are individualistic.* The motives of each of us differ. We each have a different motivational hierarchy comprised of different desires with different priorities attached to each one. Because motives are based on needs, rewards, and values, they obviously vary from person to person. One employee sees promotion as an incentive to perform; another behaves in ways to avoid the anxiety and responsibility associated with a promotion. Some of us find personal fulfillment through work; others derive no fulfillment at all.

5. *Motives change.* Motives are not stable. Because our motives fit together as a set, different ingredients of that set may change or vary in importance over time. What motivates us today may not motivate us tomorrow. Public recognition of success may have been a prime motivator in the past for a particular employee. But money may replace recognition as a motivator if that person incurs a major debt, for example. Even if we could ascertain all of the elements in a person's motivational system, the dynamic nature of motives would complicate our understanding.

Job and Organizational Factors Affecting Motivation

You must take many factors into account when trying to understand the process of motivation. So far, we have talked about motivation as an individual, internal phenomenon. But people do not behave in a vacuum. In addition to understanding inner needs and goals, you must identify factors of the job and the organization that influence behavior if you are to understand the motivational process.

Many characteristics of a job affect an employee's motivational level and either encourage or discourage the desire to perform well. Some types of jobs are more intrinsically satisfying than others, that is, in certain types of jobs, an employee is motivated by the work itself. Studies of motivation based on job content show that employees want to feel challenged in a job, they want feedback about their performance, they want to feel that the job is valued or important, and they want some degree of control or autonomy over setting work goals and determining the paths to reaching those goals. Keep in mind that because motives are individualistic, the extent to which employees are motivated by these job requirements will vary. But in general, employees find them intrinsically rewarding.

It is human nature to want to be challenged by work. We want to feel the sense of accomplishment that comes from testing our abilities. A job that requires little effort or thought is boring. We have difficulty sustaining the drive to perform it.

We all need some indication of how well we are performing in a job. Job performance feedback may come from others or be self-directed. Whether feedback is internal or external, employees will be more motivated on jobs that provide it. A job without feedback is discouraging.

Employees will be motivated if they perceive their jobs as valuable. The more they can see how their jobs fit into larger jobs or goals, the more value they can attach to their function. This means that it is best to work on whole projects or products. If there is just one small piece of a project, then employees must see how their part is meaningful to the whole.

Finally, jobs that allow some degree of autonomy are motivating. Obviously, we vary in the amount of autonomy versus direction we want in the workplace. Nevertheless, all employees want some control over setting and achieving their own goals.

Many features of the organizational environment also affect motivation. People and jobs do not exist in a vacuum, but within a larger organizational system. Employee motivation can be affected by the company's personnel selection and placement procedures, training and development system, performance-appraisal methods, supervisory styles and practices, and reward and compensation system. Indeed, just about everything in an organization can affect an employee's motivation to perform.

If the wrong people are hired for jobs, then motivation will suffer. An underqualified person will be discouraged by the inability to perform well and may be motivated to avoid work-related behavior because of a fear of failure. An overqualified person will be discouraged by the lack of a challenge. When job success requires little effort, there is little drive to perform well.

Employee training and development can be a valuable tool for developing motivation. Through training, employees can gain the skills necessary for success, can develop positive attitudes toward performance, and can develop challenging career goals. The opportunity for specialized training can reward performance and inspire improvements.

Performance feedback is an essential ingredient of intrinsically motivating jobs and a prerequisite to performance-based rewards. It is difficult to encourage employees to improve if you have no reliable way of assessing their current performance. Likewise, you cannot reward excellent performance without a means of judging excellence. A good performance-appraisal system should support your methods of motivating employees.

Effective supervision is closely tied to employee motivation. Subordinates will be motivated to perform well if they have a good relationship with their supervisor and feel that supervisory practices are fair. Indeed, supervisors are the key motivators of their staff. Effective supervisors motivate by giving regular and specific performance feedback, by coaching employees to improve their performance, by encouraging employee growth and development, and by rewarding good performance.

Motivation increases when employees receive desired rewards as a result of their performance. Rewards can take the form of raises, bonuses, promotions, recognition, prizes, or time off. The key points are that the employee must value the reward and the reward must be based on performance. Obviously, the importance of compensation and rewards as motivators will vary from person to person. But an organization with a fair compensation and reward system is likely to have an easier time motivating its members.

Types of Motivators

There are a variety of strategies you can use to motivate subordinates. Four types of workplace motivators are needs satisfiers, rewards, job design, and employee participation.

Needs and Motivation

Some outcomes are desired by employees and others are not. One reason for this involves the concept of human needs. If certain needs are important to individuals, then they will act in ways to satisfy those

needs. In other words, needs drive or motivate behavior. By understanding what pressing, unfulfilled needs people have, we can motivate
them. By showing how certain behavior leads to a desired outcome, we
can motivate others to perform certain kinds of behavior. The key
point, which can be difficult to achieve, becomes the accurate identification of a person's needs. Psychologists have theorized that any of the
following sets of needs may govern human behavior:

1. *Need for achievement.*   Employees motivated by a need for achievement want the satisfaction of accomplishing something challenging.
   They want to exercise their talents, to surpass others, to attain
   success. Such people are self-motivated, given a sufficiently challenging job to do. They set realistic goals and achieve them. To allow
   these employees opportunities for meeting their needs for achievement, you must provide new and challenging assignments. It is
   important to provide avenues by which they can stretch and test
   their abilities.

2. *Need for power.*   Employees with a high need for power derive
   satisfaction from influencing and controlling others. They like to
   lead, to persuade, and to have an impact on situations. Such people
   are motivated by positions of power, leadership, and authority. They
   become informal group leaders, hold leadership positions in community or civic groups, and strive for supervisory or management
   positions. These people should be given opportunities to influence
   others, to make decisions, and to direct projects.

3. *Need for affiliation.*   Employees motivated by an affiliation need
   derive satisfaction from interacting with others. They like to be with
   people, develop friendly relationships, and find the social aspects
   of the workplace rewarding. You can motivate such people by
   providing them with opportunities for interaction in the workplace:
   teamwork projects, group meetings, company athletic teams, or jobs
   involving communication with others. Obviously, they should not
   have jobs that isolate them from other people.

4. *Need for autonomy.*   Employees with the need for autonomy want
   freedom and independence. They want to direct their own efforts
   and will resist close supervision. You can motivate them by allowing
   them to make their own choices, set their own schedules, and work
   independently of others. Give them responsibility for their own
   work.

5. *Need for esteem.*   Employees with high esteem needs like to be
   recognized and praised. They want others to acknowledge and
   appreciate their work. Attention and respect from others motivates

their work. Give them ample feedback, public recognition, or tokens of appreciation for good work.

6. *Need for safety or security.* Employees motivated by this need derive satisfaction from job security, a steady income, health and life insurance, and a hazard-free work environment. They will seek jobs with tenure or protection. They may also want predictable work with little risk or uncertainty. Salary and fringe benefits are very important to them.

7. *Need for equity.* People driven by a need for equity want to be treated fairly. They have a strong sense of conscience or ethics. They may compare their work hours, job duties, salary, and privileges to those of other employees and become discouraged if they perceive inequities. They want to see that standards are being applied consistently and that dishonesty and favoritism are not being tolerated in the organization.

8. *Need for self-actualization.* This refers to the satisfaction gained from growth and self-development. It may mean creative expression on a job or learning just for the sake of learning. People motivated by this need may take on challenging work not for the sense of accomplishment or to gain recognition, but only for the sheer enjoyment of a new experience and self-discovery. Such people need jobs that help them reach their potential.

Rewards and Motivation

Extrinsic rewards are another type of motivator. Managers in work organizations typically give tangible rewards based on performance, such as raises, bonuses, status symbols, fringe benefits, prizes, and incentives. Employees who value such rewards put forth considerable effort to obtain one. But extrinsic awards can be quite costly to an organization. If you want to use extrinsic rewards to motivate employees, make sure that the following conditions are met, without which any reward system can actually hinder motivation and negatively affect performance.

1. *Employees must perceive the rewards as valuable.* Some companies offer trinkets as rewards and wonder why employees are not motivated to earn them. You should determine what rewards employees like. A banquet for the top-performing department may be appropriate for groups that value affiliation or recognition. Other employees might see a banquet as just another work obligation and would prefer a day off with pay. An employee who travels extensively on the job may not value a trip to an exotic location. A better

office or a training opportunity might effectively reward a career-minded individual.

2. *The reward must be tied clearly to performance.* Both the recipients of rewards and their colleagues who observe the process must see that the reward was earned through superior performance. If employees perceive that rewards are given on a capricious or arbitrary basis, then motivation will suffer. In fact, a subjective system of rewards will demoralize them.

3. *There must be objective criteria for evaluating performance.* People must know exactly what they have to do to obtain the reward. There should be no surprises. When employees disagree on who deserves rewards because assessment methods are vague or invalid, then morale and motivation will decrease. But rewards linked to clear and attainable standards of performance are effective motivators.

4. *Information about the allocation of rewards should be shared openly.* There should be no secrecy about who got what rewards and why. A performance-based reward system will serve as a motivator only in an atmosphere of trust and open communication.

Job Design and Motivation

Because certain job features are intrinsically satisfying, redesigning jobs can be a way to motivate employees. It is, after all, easier to change jobs in an organization than it is to change the people in an organization. Basically, there are three ways to redesign jobs:

1. *Job rotation*—moving employees through a variety of jobs, departments, or functions. It is especially useful for someone who has been on a job for a long time, who is no longer challenged by a job, or who has a strong need for activity or change. By giving an employee the opportunity to change jobs, you can prevent boredom and develop a more versatile worker.

2. *Job enlargement*—expanding an employee's duties. Once an employee has demonstrated the capacity to handle the current work load and has indicated a desire to expand into new areas, adding new responsibilities may be necessary to keep the employee motivated. Talented employees become especially frustrated and demotivated if a job is too simple or too limited.

3. *Job enrichment*—an attempt to make jobs more desirable or satisfying. Give employees more autonomy, input into decision making, more interesting projects, whole rather than fragmented tasks, or more information about company goals.

Participation and Motivation

Many organizations use systems of employee involvement to increase motivation, company loyalty, and quality performance. Evidence shows that employees are more motivated to implement decisions if they have had input into those decisions. There is little support for decisions that others impose on us. Employees who feel that they are an integral part of an organization will be motivated to do good work. Those who merely put in their time to earn a paycheck will care little about the quality of their work.

You can spark motivation by asking employees their opinions, encouraging employees to set their own goals and contribute to organizational objectives, and by developing organizational pride. Your subordinates have many good ideas and will want to contribute to organizational effectiveness if they feel that their contributions are valued.

Dealing With Motivational Problems

Employee motivation is an important part of your role. It does not just happen by itself. You and your organization must take an active role in hiring people capable of being motivated, training them appropriately, providing satisfying jobs in which they can meet your needs, and providing an environment and rewards to enhance motivation.

Even in situations where all those aspects exist, you will have to deal with motivational problems from time to time. Some managers opt for discipline as the only means of dealing with employee-motivation problems, but this alone is insufficient. Discipline can be effective with some specific and limited motivational problems such as tardiness or absenteeism. But you should take the following more comprehensive approach when trying to stimulate subordinates to set higher goals, to do more or better quality work, or to accept greater challenges.

1. *Try to understand an individual's motivational hierarchy.* What motives and needs are dominant? Talk to the employee about job goals, values, and needs. Observe behavior and listen to what the employee says about the job and the organization. This can provide clues to understanding an employee's motivational system.

2. *Analyze how needs can be satisfied through work.* Being a skilled motivator requires imagination and creativity. No one approach works for everyone. You must build a unique package of motivational strategies for each subordinate. Should rewards be given? What rewards? Should jobs be redesigned? How? Should this em-

ployee be praised, challenged, or reassured? Should opportunities
for leadership, freedom, or participation be provided?

3. *Work with employees in developing motivation plans.* Discuss
motivational problems with employees. Ask them what they need
from work. Rather than imposing rewards of little value or appealing
to unimportant needs, solicit employee input and commitments.

4. *Try to improve organizational features that support the motivational
system.* Work with personnel recruiters to hire the right people for
your jobs. Provide adequate training and development to your staff.
Work to improve relationships between supervisors and subordinates in your organization. Make sure your own management style
is fair and effective.

[*See also* Coaching Employees; Feedback; Quality Circles; Team Build-
ing]

For Additional Information

Losoncy, Lewis. *The Motivating Leader.* Englewood Cliffs, N.J.: Prentice-Hall, 1985. A practical guide to help leaders to motivate
others, to resolve conflicts, to increase productivity, to confront
others, to erase apathy, and to build team players.

Miner, John B. *People Problems.* New York: Random House, 1985,
chapter 4, pp. 83–114. The characteristics of motivation, and
advice to managers in dealing with motivational problems.

Nie, Oliver L. "Job Satisfaction: How to Motivate Today's Workers."
Supervisory Management, Vol. 31 (1986), No. 2, pp. 8–11. The
view that job satisfaction has replaced money as the primary work
motivator. Five aspects of job satisfaction are discussed.

Nash, Michael. *Making People Productive.* San Francisco: Jossey-Bass
Inc., 1985. An examination of productivity throughout the employment cycle that integrates the processes of selection, training, and
motivation. It translates research findings into concrete recommendations managers can use to make employees more productive.
Chapters cover such concepts as productivity, effective selection,
training, motivation, goal setting, performance appraisals, compensation strategies, turnover, and job satisfaction.

Quick, Thomas L. *The Manager's Motivation Desk Book.* New York:
John Wiley & Sons, 1985. A view of motivation as a system of such
elements as organizational culture, goal setting, delegation, confidence building, feedback, performance appraisals, coaching, coun-

seling, and training. Practical advice, checklists, and inventories are provided for each topic.

Sherwood, Andrew. "A Baker's Dozen of Ways to Motivate People." *Management Solutions*, Vol. 32 (1987), No. 5, pp. 14–16. Thirteen fundamental principles of motivation.

Stanton, Erwin S. *Reality-Centered People Management*. New York: AMACOM, 1982. Reasons for employee productivity problems, an evaluation of traditional management theories, and a management system based on a flexible approach to motivation and a comprehensive human resources program that supports the manager's motivational plan.

Negotiating

Whenever we exchange information with the aim of influencing or persuading others in order to meet our own needs, we are involved in the process of negotiation. Sellers and buyers negotiate the price and terms of large-scale purchases such as real estate. Husbands and wives negotiate to settle arguments. Teenagers negotiate with parents for privileges and freedoms. Unions and management negotiate labor contracts. And managers negotiate with countless numbers of people in the course of a week to make decisions, promote projects, or settle problems. The managerial role fits the very definition of negotiation. We share information for the purpose of achieving the needs of our departments and organizations.

The essential characteristics of negotiation, which distinguish it from other types of communication, are the notions of give-and-take, mutual fulfillment of needs, the use of strategies, and some amount of conflict that must be resolved. People usually enter negotiations with predetermined objectives that they expect to readjust along the way. Through the mutual exchange of information and concessions, they expect to be able to reach agreements. Needs fulfillment is the very purpose of negotiation. Each party is dependent on the other for something. Both parties want their needs to be met. Conflict occurs because the needs of each party are often mutually exclusive. The achievement of one person's needs may automatically frustrate the fulfillment of the other's needs. Finally, strategies come into play whenever negotiators plan methods or tactics to influence each other. Strategies of negotiation need not be devious schemes to manipulate or deceive. They are merely well-conceived plans and preparations developed prior to the face-to-face interaction of a negotiation.

Preparing to Negotiate

In many instances, effective negotiators spend more time preparing for a negotiation than they spend actually communicating in a negotiation session. The exact nature of the preparation depends on the type and importance of the negotiation, though all negotiations require that you set objectives, collect information, analyze the other parties' objectives, identify needs of both sides, and give some thought to the process of negotiating.

Setting Your Own Objectives

What do you want to accomplish by negotiating? You may have several objectives or goals, which may relate to long-term or short-term needs. It is wise to establish some priorities to your set of objectives: Which goals are least important and most important? Clearly, some points are major and others are minor. Make these distinctions ahead of time. Also, whenever possible, think of objectives not as fixed goals but in terms of flexible ranges.

For example, imagine a manager negotiating a temporary contract with an external consultant. The manager and consultant may not be able to reach an agreement if each begins negotiating with the following fixed goals: The manager wants to pay a $400 per day rate, wants the consultant to work exclusively for this company during the contract period, and wants to make all decisions about the project. The consultant, on the other hand, wants to earn $600 per day, wants no restrictions on simultaneously working for other clients, and wants to make all decisions about the project. With the discrepancies between those fixed objectives, it is unlikely that the manager and consultant will be able to negotiate an agreement. Imagine, though, if each party set the following range of objectives: The manager would be willing to pay between $300 and $500 per day, wants to restrict the consultant from simultaneously working for companies that are direct competitors, and wants significant input into project decisions. The consultant wants to earn between $500 and $700 per day, wants to be able to retain other steady clients and regular monthly income, and wants sufficient freedom in making project decisions. It is easy to see the points of agreement in these ranges. Both parties can meet their needs by agreeing to a fee of $500 per day, the right of the consultant to retain all clients except any company that is a direct competitor to this client organization, and a collaborative style of decision making during the project.

Collecting Information

The more informed you are as a negotiator, the more effective you will be. It is imperative that you collect all the facts related to a particular negotiation. What led up to this negotiation? What agreements were made between the parties in the past? What is the history of the situation? What solutions have other groups used in similar situations?

For example, imagine you are negotiating with supervisors for additional secretarial support for your department. Your supervisor's goal is to cut operating expenses. Your goal is to secure additional funds for secretarial assistance. Unless you have plenty of information and documentation to justify your need, you will not have much of a chance of obtaining your objective. Why is the current secretarial situation inadequate? Can you show that some clerical personnel were taken from your department in the past? Have more employees been added to your department recently, thereby increasing the ratio of managers to secretaries? Were any promises made about future secretarial increases? Do other departments of comparable size and complexity have a larger secretarial pool? Are there smaller departments with more office personnel than you have? Are there organizational precedents of sharing secretaries between departments, using temporary clerical personnel, or readjusting budgets for this purpose?

Analyzing the Other Party's Objectives

Besides knowing your own goals and being well informed about the negotiation issues, try to identify the objectives the other party will be attempting to achieve. With some knowledge of who you are negotiating with and why you are negotiating, you should be able to estimate some of your partner's goals and priorities. Imagine yourself in your partner's position. If you were on the other side of the negotiation, what would you be attempting to obtain? How would you go about obtaining your major goals?

Imagine that you are a manager negotiating the purchase of a computer system for your department. You may have established flexible objectives to meet your needs. You may have researched thoroughly the state of the art in available systems and the background of the company from which you are considering a purchase. You will have additional negotiation insights if you consider the vendor's objectives. Is their goal to obtain the best selling price? To obtain your business because of the reputation of your organization? To gain a foothold in your type of industry? To clear their inventory of a particular model of computer that will soon be replaced? To obtain testimonials of customer satisfaction from you for their marketing literature? To sell you a service contract? To receive cash from your purchase? To earn profit through the financing of your purchase? To minimize the training they provide to your employees in how to use the computer system? Obviously, your negotiating partner can have many objectives in mind. The more accurately you assess your partner's priorities, the more prepared you will be for the negotiating session.

Analyzing Both Parties' Needs

All negotiators are trying to meet human needs, which underlie all negotiation objectives. In fact, successful influence or persuasion usually appeals to basic human needs. By understanding how human needs relate to motivation and action, we can be more skilled negotiators.

The noted psychologist Abraham Maslow categorized human needs in a hierarchy from most basic to most advanced. He theorized that, at the lowest level, humans must have their physiological needs satisfied. These include food, shelter, and basic bodily needs. If these needs are met, then the next level of need fulfillment becomes safety/security. Next comes the category of needs called love/acceptance/a sense of belonging. People need to be accepted, to identify with others, and to give and receive love. Esteem needs are next on Maslow's hierarchy. People need self-respect and the esteem of others. They need to feel self-worth and competence. Finally, the highest need of human beings is for self-actualization, which means growing to one's full potential.

By understanding human needs, we can understand what motivates behavior. In negotiations, it is important to understand what needs motivate your own behavior. Are you negotiating, for example, for a sales manager position because of the financial stability and security it will provide? If so, then your negotiating priorities should be salary, benefits, and job-security items. Or does that sales manager position fulfill a need to lead the sales force and be a valuable member of the company? If your motive is group leadership and acceptance, then financial issues in the negotiation will probably be secondary to issues of power, recognition, and input. If obtaining a sales manager position fulfills an esteem need for you, then job title, office, and company car probably become important bargaining points.

In addition to identifying the needs that underlie your own negotiating goals, try to analyze the needs of your negotiation partner. Realize that a satisfied need is no longer a motivator of behavior. Emphasizing safety or security when the other person is craving self-respect will be fruitless. Highlighting the prestigious nature of a job does little to motivate someone who feels underpaid and financially insecure. By matching your strategies to the other person's needs, you will enhance your negotiating success.

Thinking About the Negotiation Process

The final step in preparing to negotiate involves learning about the negotiation process. It helps to be aware of specific skills involved in negotiating. Think of all the situations in which you practice negotiation. Analyze behaviors that help and hinder the achievement of desired outcomes. Give thought to the particular negotiating situation you are about to face. What is the time frame for negotiating? Will there be several interactions over a period of time before agreement is reached, or is there a one-shot chance for agreement? Will you continue to have a relationship with this person after the negotiation? Do you care about the nature of that relationship? Or is it unlikely that the negotiating parties will ever interact again? Are you negotiating as individuals or do you each represent constituencies? What is the distribution of power between you and the other negotiating party?

While there are not automatic strategies based on the answers to these questions, it is wise to consider such aspects of an upcoming negotiation. Just thinking about these and other issues helps you prepare for the negotiation interaction.

Developing the Right Attitude and Atmosphere

Somehow, the process of negotiating has earned a negative reputation. Negotiation conjures up images of stalwart opponents in poker-faced deliberations who fight for their positions by using misinformation and manipulation. In reality, negotiators can be more effective if they discuss principles rather than positions, promote trust, allow each other to save face, use a collaborative style of communication, and try creative problem solving. A key difference in the philosophies of collaborative versus competitive negotiation is the perception of each other as partners rather than opponents. To view the other as an opponent automatically creates an atmosphere of hostility and a goal of win-lose. Such a view promotes stalemates, calls for third-party interventions provided by mediators and arbitrators, and hinders the success of a negotiation. Viewing the other as a partner acknowledges that you depend on each other for the fulfillment of needs and that you want to be able to reach an agreement. It helps to create an atmosphere of collaboration and a goal of win-win or mutual problem solving. The following guidelines on personal attitudes and negotiation atmospheres will help you enhance the likelihood of a successful and fair negotiation outcome.

Negotiating Over Principles, Not Positions

Negotiators usually articulate positions that must be defended. To ensure that they obtain most of their goals, they exaggerate their position initially. Once they state a position, they feel compelled to defend it or they lose face. Egos become inextricably linked to each position. Any movement from a position is seen as a concession, a loss, or a weakness. It is easy to see where such an approach encourages threats, holdouts, and walkouts.

A better approach is to identify the principles or needs underlying a negotiation. State your objectives or needs rather than stating a position. There can be many options for satisfying an objective, but there is only one position. When each party has directly communicated its needs, some clear overlap will be revealed. Ironically, the principles underlying different positions in a negotiation can be quite compatible even when the positions are opposing. For those divergent interests, you can consider options that take both parties' interests into account. By revealing principles or needs, you are discussing a mutual problem. By stating positions, you are imposing predetermined solutions. It is much easier to find creative solutions once you both understand each other's needs than it is to compromise positions once opposing solutions have been put forth.

Consider, for example, the principles that a purchasing agent shares with a prospective vendor. Both want to establish a working relationship with each other. Each wants to stay in business and wants the other to stay in business. Both want to negotiate a fair deal and receive their part of the exchange as soon as possible. The purchasing agent wants to take possession of the purchased goods within a reasonable amount of time. The vendor wants to receive prompt payment. Already, they share many of the same needs. By acknowledging shared principles, they become partners in an exchange rather than opponents in a battle. As partners, they find it easier to deal with their divergent needs such as quality or price. They are likely to reach agreement on issues of price or quality by avoiding firm positions that must be defended. By examining their respective needs in relation to price or quality, they may find an option that satisfies both sets of needs. They become collaborators in mutual problem solving. That problem solving may not be easy, but at least the negotiators are in the proper mind set to find an acceptable solution. They are not in a combat where one wins and the other loses or both lose because of their inability to reach an agreement.

Promoting Trust

Collaborators trust each other. Competitors do not. Negotiators can develop trust by acknowledging common ground, by presenting accurate information, by listening to each other, and by aiming for an agreement that is fair to both parties. Realizing that you both share similar interests helps build trust. By discovering where principles overlap, you can identify with each other. You are not so different from each other. Trust involves an accurate prediction about the other person, and means knowing what behavior to expect, having faith in the accuracy of information, and seeing integrity in the other person's motives.

If we have experienced fairness and honesty from our previous dealings with a person, then we predict a similar behavior in the current negotiation. In effect, we trust the partner. Any behavior that contradicts our expectation destroys our trust in the other person. In other words, trust is built on past experience with a person or an organization. If the other negotiator has been competitive or manipulative in the past, then we enter the negotiation with suspicion and caution. Past experience tells us not to trust the other person. If we have no past experience with the partner, then we have a choice of expecting honesty and fairness or deception and competition. With no reason to distrust our fellow negotiator, why not expect fair treatment and a positive outcome? Such a positive prediction only increases the chance of a positive outcome.

As negotiators, we earn trust by considering the needs of both parties, by being honest and direct with information, and by genuinely trying to reach an agreement. That means avoiding bluffing, exaggerated claims, and other game playing. In effect, when both parties trust each other, they care about their ongoing relationship with each other rather than defeating each other and taking everything for themselves. Contrary to some views of negotiation, a trusting style does not put you into a weak position but increases your chances of a fair and successful outcome.

Encouraging Face-Saving

When there is a winner and a loser in a situation, the loser cannot help but feel dejected. It is impossible to save face in the event of a loss. If one person's position is accepted over another, the loser's ego is bruised. By avoiding win-lose styles of negotiating, no one has to save face. There is no winner or loser in collaborative problem solving. Together, two people arrive at a solution that fulfills as many of both parties' needs as possible. Both people can feel successful and satisfied.

Sometimes the need to save face leads to negotiation stalemates. Negotiators will hold out not because a position is unacceptable, but because agreement would be seen as giving in. And it is difficult to save face when you perceive yourself as conceding. To promote face-saving, it is important to create a negotiation atmosphere that avoids situations of backing down, giving in, or losing.

Promoting Collaboration

Collaborative negotiators perceive each other as partners, not opponents. They discuss principles, objectives, and needs rather than positions, demands, and sides. They want a win-win outcome where both parties benefit from the negotiation. A collaborative style of negotiating depends on mutual trust and a willingness to share information. Each negotiator begins with a range of objectives and is willing to be somewhat flexible. Each shares the goal of reaching an equitable agreement rather than cheating the other. Both are willing to take the time to listen to each other, to identify mutual and divergent needs, and to work at a mutually beneficial solution.

Thinking Creatively

Negotiators must be creative to find solutions that truly satisfy both parties. When negotiators have a history of being on opposite sides of the bargaining table, when they begin with different objectives, and when the fulfillment of one person's need seems to automatically negate the other's need, a mutually satisfying outcome is not readily apparent. But by using creative thinking in an atmosphere of trust and collaboration, a fair outcome can be reached.

When negotiators think creatively, they reject the obvious solution, even though it may be easy to obtain and requires little time or thought. But obvious solutions are seldom the best solutions. Creative negotiators strike out in new directions and consider original ideas. Rather than diluting the principles or needs of each party, as compromise solutions typically do, creative solutions represent entirely new options neither party has originally considered.

There are several ways to promote creative thinking in negotiations. One strategy is to use brainstorming. Once the partners understand each other's needs, they generate as many options for meeting those needs as they possibly can. The goal of brainstorming is to develop a large quantity of ideas. Avoid evaluating the ideas until an exhaustive list has been developed. Many of the options will be unfeasible or will be rejected by the negotiators. But in that long list may be one or two unconventional or unusual options that have merit and are acceptable to both negotiators. Without engaging in the freewheeling process of brainstorming, the negotiators would never have arrived at such a creative alternative.

Other suggestions for promoting creative thinking involve being open-minded, having a questioning attitude, drawing examples from seemingly unrelated situations, and persevering in problem solving.

Conducting a Negotiation

A negotiation is a type of communication and should follow principles that promote clarity and understanding. Ironically, though, negotiations have come to be associated with vague statements, distorted information, deceptions, bluffing, and threats. Some people think such strategies give the negotiator an advantage. More often than not, though, they lead to walkouts, stalemates, and the need for a third party to reestablish appropriate lines of communication.

If negotiators look at each other as partners trying to solve a problem together rather than as adversaries, they will be clear and direct in their communication. They will realize the value of stating specific needs, sharing information, listening, questioning, and building a good working relationship. What follows are not negotiating tricks but principles of effective communication in negotiations:

1. *State your principles directly.*   Early on, both parties should clearly indicate their needs, principles, or objectives. Remember, this is not a position, but a statement of problem parameters. Do not hold back in indicating your objectives. Do not exaggerate or distort your needs.

2. *Listen to each other.*   Pay attention to what is being said. Paraphrase to show your understanding. Check out assumptions. The sooner you understand the other's needs, the sooner you will find points of commonality and divergence. Once you clearly understand where the points of divergence are, you can begin to develop options to satisfy differing needs.

3. *Take your time.*   It takes time to find equitable solutions to problems. Creative options do not come easily but require much deliberation and contemplation. Partners must avoid defensiveness and be patient with the negotiation process.

4. *Use questions.*   Questions enable you to clarify your partner's point of view, separate facts from assumptions, and check out your perceptions. Straightforward questions allow negotiators to deal in specifics. Imagine the progress that a negotiation could take if each person honestly answered the question "What would you like to accomplish from this negotiation?" Effective questions in a negotiation are sincere attempts to elicit information or clarify understanding. They should not be devices to steer the conversation or lead to a particular answer. They should not come across as hostile or interrogating.

5. *Allow emotions.*   It is appropriate to have an explicit discussion of feelings in a negotiation. Feelings cannot help but underlie issues

and contribute to the atmosphere in a negotiation. To deny emotions is to fuel a heated eruption. When negotiators can release their feelings, they talk more rationally. The best way to deal with feelings in a negotiation is to state them and to discuss them rather than to make a dramatic display of them.

6. *Summarize agreements.* Negotiators frequently focus more on points of disagreement than they do on points of agreement. It is important during a negotiation, and especially at the closing of a negotiation, to summarize each element of an agreement. That way, each party knows exactly what has transpired and each defines outcomes similarly. A summary prevents people from selectively perceiving agreements in ways that favor them. If you hear an inaccurate statement during a negotiation, say, "No, that's not how I understood our decision. I thought. . . ." Then you can eliminate misunderstandings.

Special Forms of Negotiation

Not all negotiations involve just two parties in a face-to-face deliberation. There may be negotiating teams, mediators, or arbitrators involved in the process.

Some negotiations are so complex that they require the involvement of two groups of people. A labor-contract negotiation may involve various divisional heads and personnel specialists from management as well as several elected union representatives. Team negotiations provide the advantage of broader perspectives, informational expertise, and specialized roles. With more people present, more issues can be represented and more information provided. Each person brings a particular skill to the process, such as listening, questioning, creative thinking, summarizing, or trust building. The disadvantages of team negotiations include scheduling difficulties, human resources costs, and role coordination. If each negotiating team has four or five members, it may be difficult to find time for discussions in light of everyone's schedule. It is also more expensive to use several people rather than one person. Finally, team members may contradict each other, may disagree about desired outcomes, or may have difficulty working together as a team.

Mediators can be used when a negotiation reaches an impasse. If negotiators have taken sides and are rigidly defending positions, then progress is impossible without the help of a third party. The mediator intervenes between conflicting parties to promote understanding and agreement. The mediator does not make decisions or impose solutions, but helps establish cooperation between the negotiators. Mediators help negotiators clarify objectives, understand needs, and identify areas of agreement and disagreement.

Arbitration is used when the negotiation process breaks down and is beyond repair. While associated with negotiation, arbitration actually discourages negotiation. Arbitrators hear the issues of both sides and make a binding decision. Once a problem is in the hands of an arbitrator, the negotiators lose all power to make decisions. In effect, because they cannot agree, they allow someone else to determine a solution for them. The use of arbitration represents negotiation failure. Nevertheless, because not all negotiations can produce settlements, arbitration is a necessary and valuable option.

[See also Conflict Management; Dispute Resolution]

For Additional Information

Brooks, Earl, and George S. Odiorne. *Managing by Negotiations.* New York: Van Nostrand Reinhold Company, 1984. The various negotiations we perform internally as well as with clients, vendors, and suppliers. The authors talk about realizing sources of power, dealing with opposition, sticking to decisions, and persuading others.

Byrnes, Joseph R. "Ten Guidelines for Effective Negotiating." *Business Horizons,* Vol. 30 (1987), No. 3, pp. 7–12. Managers may spend up to 20 percent of their time negotiating, but they spend little time considering how to negotiate. Guidelines that you can use in both your professional and personal life.

Fells, R. E. "Managing the Process of Negotiation." *Employee Relations,* Vol. 8 (1986), No. 1, pp. 17–22. A model of the negotiating process and outlines of specific negotiating behaviors.

Fisher, Roger, and William Ury. *Getting to Yes: Negotiating Agreement Without Giving In.* Boston: Houghton Mifflin, 1981. The method of principled negotiation as an alternative between hard and soft negotiations. Readers will learn how and why to avoid positions; how to develop options and objective criteria; and how to deal with powerful, resistant, and manipulative negotiators.

Harris, Charles Edison. *Business Negotiating Power.* New York: Van Nostrand Reinhold Company, 1983. Negotiating principles and tactics, popular ploys used in sales negotiations, and ways to manipulate your physical and psychological negotiating environment. Chapters cover how to negotiate and administer specific contractual agreements. An executive's guidebook on basic contract law is included.

Nierenberg, Gerard I. *The Complete Negotiator*. New York: Nierenberg & Zief Publishers, 1986. Comprehensive information on the negotiation process, human behavior in negotiations, needs and motivation, reasoning, and effective communication. Nierenberg presents applications to purchasing, corporate negotiations, labor relations, real estate, and lawsuits.

Shea, Gordon F. *Creative Negotiating*. Boston: CBI Publishing Company, 1983. A set of techniques for developing win-win outcomes to negotiations. The author outlines a philosophy of cooperation, trust, supportiveness, and creativity that opposes traditional views of negotiating. Chapters cover such topics as bargaining drawbacks, conflict, problem solving, defensiveness, creativity, and third-party interventions.

Sparks, Donald B. *The Dynamics of Effective Negotiation*. Houston: Gulf Publishing Company, 1982. A pragmatic approach to negotiating in business and industrial settings that explains the characteristics of negotiations, the need for preparation, commonsense methods for conducting negotiations, and skills for dealing with style-oriented opponents. Sparks emphasizes issues rather than gimmicks for a win-win outcome.

Networking

SUCCESSFUL MANAGERS USUALLY develop methods for staying abreast of the latest developments in their fields; for meeting important people in their organizations, professions, or industries; for getting informal information useful to performing their jobs; and for cultivating a circle of allies or helpful colleagues. This process of establishing connections within and across organizations is called networking. While the label "networking" is relatively new, the activity of developing business contacts is not. Many women in the workplace have embraced the concept of networking as a way to penetrate the "old-boys network." Successful managers, be they male or female, understand the networking phenomenon and engage in it for career advancement.

Networking is somewhat difficult to define. It is an amorphous concept consisting of a variety of activities. Some people engage in networking without being consciously aware that they are doing so. For others, networking is an intentional and strategic activity. Suffice it to say that networking is the process of developing and using contacts for career support or advancement. Networking means building a system of interrelationships of people who can help each other's careers. By expanding the number of people you know and linking together the people you know with the people they know, a network of organizational contacts can be created. The number of connecting points in the network can grow exponentially. An examination of the types of possible networks, their purposes, and methods of developing networks will help define and illustrate the concept.

Network Types

Some examples of career networks include the following categories:

178

- *Occupational.* Anyone in a particular occupation can affiliate with others in the same occupation. The affiliation can be through informal contact or through formal organizations. Accountants meet with other accountants; journalists, architects, machinists, plumbers, or nurses meet with others in their occupation to learn from each other. The possibilities are endless.
- *Horizontal.* People at similar job levels, whatever the field, meet together. Presidents of various organizations in a city, for example, can have contact with each other. Groups form for professionals or executives from a variety of fields, with the assumption that people from similar career levels have common concerns.
- *Special-interest.* Individuals seek contact with others who are demographically or philosophically similar. Groups based on gender, race, age, ethnicity, or other demographic factors related to career progress are common network types. Likewise, employees can seek contact with others internal or external to organizations who share views about their treatment, benefits, or company policies. Professional groups of women, blacks, Latinos, environmentalists, older citizens, gays, political activists, or handicapped people are a few examples of special-interest networking.
- *Occupational/horizontal.* This type of network involves people at the same level in the same occupation. Examples include high school principals, hospital administrators, construction-company owners, general managers of automobile dealerships, or personnel administrators in the transportation industry.

Network Purposes

There are many reasons why people develop career networks. Most importantly, you can learn from organizational contacts. Talking to someone in the same profession or someone with the same job title can give you insights about how to perform your own job. You can share stories, examples, ideas, or advice. You can borrow techniques from each other. By interacting with someone else in your occupation, you may learn about new developments in your field. Clearly, more heads are better than one. Managers who do their job in isolation without seeking out professional colleagues will tend to become parochial and outdated in their ideas and methods.

Another reason to develop career connections is to acquire sounding boards. If it is risky to test new ideas within workplace organizations, an associate in a different organization who understands your job can provide valuable feedback about your new ideas, methods, or projects. Likewise, when your job is frustrating or a relationship with a supervisor is troublesome, complaining to an associate across town or across the country can be more productive than talking with internal colleagues or with family members. Your neighbor who is a manager in a different industry may be the best person with whom to discuss a work-related problem. A fellow black lawyer across town may have empathy with your job frustrations. The colleague you met at a conference a few months ago may be willing to give you feedback about your project proposal.

A well-developed network of business associates can provide referrals for a variety of needs. By talking with acquaintances in the world of work, networkers have found clients, customers, new jobs, consultants, partners, and friends, to name a few. Anytime you need to reach a large number of people or to expand the number of people you know, networking is an effective strategy. An independent consultant, for example, can find clients by cultivating a network of contacts. If each of five people recommend the consultant to several well-placed managers they know, the number of connections and possible clients increases rapidly.

Networking is especially useful for people who feel isolated in their work. The self-employed, employees of small organizations, people in remote geographic areas, salespeople in one-person branch offices, or the sole woman in an organization all must develop a network of people if they are to have work colleagues at all. Going to meetings or having lunch with others who can understand your job is imperative to work motivation and career growth in these instances.

Overall, people engage in networking to promote their careers. Knowing someone in a particular company can improve your chances of getting a job in that organization. Attending meetings or conferences with colleagues in your field keeps you current and enhances your promotability. Having lunch regularly with other women executives provides business contacts that enhance your organization's revenues. Knowing influential leaders in your city increases your visibility and prestige on the job.

Finally, networking can be fun. It gives you a chance to meet new people, to socialize with business associates, and to expand your horizons. For most managers, talking shop with people in similar or in different occupations is an enjoyable way to spend time. Discussing common business interests, empathizing with each other's workplace experiences, or discovering people you know in common is an exciting part of the organizational environment. Work would be boring without networking.

Networking Methods

There are as many ways to cultivate career networks as there are unique compositions of networks. Managers who are skilled at networking use all the available resources. You never know what the source of contacts, information, or opportunities will be. The secretary in your office may be related to your largest client. The parent of your child's best friend may be a potential benefactor to your nonprofit organization. A former college classmate may be the personnel specialist of the organization in which you would like to work.

Meeting lots of people and discovering the ways in which you can help each other's careers are the key points of networking. Possible sources for meeting people who could help your career include professional associations, volunteer organizations, classes and lectures, network directories, community groups, alumni associations, social events, and the people you already know.

Every job has some type of affiliated professional or trade association to which you may belong. Joining the groups related to your occupation or industry is an excellent way to make career contacts. But this method of networking is effective only if you are an active, outgoing member of the group. Merely paying membership dues or attending an occasional meeting is not enough. Joining committees and working on behalf of the organization will have greater career payoffs than passive membership.

The business and professional leaders of a community often volunteer their time and talents to nonprofit organizations in the community. Your willingness to participate in volunteer organizations could have long-term career benefits. By helping with artistic, educational, or civic endeavors, ambitious managers contribute to their own career contacts as well as to their communities.

Taking classes related to your line of work or attending business lectures in the community is another method of networking. Such educational activities attract a motivated group of individuals who have a common interest in the topic of the class or lecture. Both the leader and the participants represent fine sources of career information, contacts, and opportunities.

There are countless formal groups that exist to unite individuals with occupational, demographic, philosophical, or life-style similarities. The sheer variety of such groups makes it difficult for the average person to be aware of all the possibilities. Checking directories of network groups would be a wise way to locate sources of organizational contacts.

Having attended the same school often creates a psychological bond between people. Strangers who are graduates of the same school have been known to help each other. Typically, the alumni of any school will include many individuals with prestigious positions. Being active in alumni associations and contacting fellow graduates who may be valuable business associates is another networking strategy.

Many astute managers have stumbled on valuable business contacts at social events. Merely mingling and introducing yourself to a variety of people in social situations can expand a career network. Follow up on the casual meeting with a lunch invitation or with some business correspondence to develop the business relationship.

Finally, using your existing network of familiar people is an easy and effective way to make career contacts. Think of everyone with whom you have a relationship—relatives, friends, co-workers, neighbors. Talk to them about the people they know. Ask for an introduction or ask permission to use their name when contacting other people. Make contact with potential business associates. Discuss ways in which developing an association may be mutually beneficial. Remember, there are people who want to network with you because of the ways you can help them. They will be delighted that you took the initiative to contact them first.

Dos and Don'ts of Networking

In some circles, networking has come to have a negative connotation because of a seemingly callous purpose or because of inappropriate methods. Some people are overzealous in making career connections. Others try to use networking as a substitute for professional competence. By following some guidelines for networking, you can retain it as a valuable tool for professional growth and career advancement.

1. *Make sure networking benefits both parties.* Just like mentoring, networking should benefit both people in the relationship. Some managers make the mistake of developing contacts only as a way to benefit their own careers. They forget that networking is a two-way street. Successful networking means that you give as much as you get from the relationship. It is presumptuous to expect people to help you in your career if you cannot help them in return.

    Aspiring managers who join professional organizations only for job-hunting purposes, for example, do an injustice to the concept of networking. Such a self-centered purpose becomes quite transparent to network contacts as well. Even the neophyte person in a profession can help the careers of prestigious contacts by sharing an interesting article or by volunteering for undesirable tasks such as correspondence or clean-up at professional meetings. The more you can help your network contacts, the more they will want to help you.

2. *Always observe businesslike conduct.* Treat a networking relationship as you would treat any important business relationship. It is important that you not impose yourself on the contact person. You must make appointments and adhere to schedules. Realize that people are busy and workplace demands must always take precedence over networking activities. Networking relationships should be characterized by respect and professional integrity rather than pushiness and self-interest.

3. *Don't expect miracles.* Effectively developing career contacts should be an ongoing process throughout your working life. It is not something that you do intensively for a short period of time and then reap startling rewards. The positive outcomes of networking are not immediately apparent. The benefits often are subtle. A network contact may affect your career without your even knowing it. A business colleague may speak on your behalf behind the scenes. Networking is a slow, steady process of building workplace alliances. It may be years before you realize the benefits of a networking connection. You may never be able to state explicitly the mutual rewards of a long-standing professional relationship.

4. *Make time for networking.* Because the results of networking are intangible and work deadlines constantly threaten, some managers claim that networking is not worth the time. Attending meetings, actively participating in professional associations, and cultivating business relationships can be time-consuming activities. But if done effectively, networking is time well spent. It is important to schedule a certain amount of time into your work routine just for networking purposes. Make sure you touch base with business acquaintances often enough to maintain the relationship. Do not fall into the trap of becoming isolated in your own workplace tasks.

5. *Remember, networking presumes competence.* Competent individuals make successful networkers. Nobody wants to invest in relationships with incompetent associates. Successful, capable managers want to surround themselves with competent associates. Networking is a tool to advance your career, but the foundation of the career rests on competence in your profession. It is a myth that who you know will substitute for what you know. Perhaps a well-placed contact can get you an opportunity initially, but what you

make of the opportunity will depend on your technical and managerial competence rather than luck of association.

[See also Career Development]

For Additional Information

Harris, Philip R. *Management in Transition.* San Francisco: Jossey-Bass, 1985, chapter 9. A discussion of both personal networking and electronic networking as strategies for performance improvement. Harris explains the purposes and advantages of networking; describes behaviors necessary for effective networking; and discusses the use of communication technology for networking by electronic mail, teleconferencing, or videotext exchanges.

Welch, Mary Scott. *Networking.* New York: Harcourt Brace Jovanovich, 1980. Focused on women's networks, but nevertheless a thorough examination of the networking process useful to all managers. Welch defines networking, discusses its advantages, provides case studies, presents the mechanics of networking, and gives advice on how to start a network group.

Nonverbal Communication

MOST MANAGERS realize the need to be effective writers and speakers. Many recognize the importance of interpersonal competence, including being skilled at listening, giving feedback, dealing with conflict, and having a conversation. Fewer managers realize the pervasiveness and importance of nonverbal communication in the workplace. Nonverbal communication accompanies all interactions. It is present whenever people talk to each other. In many instances, it is the more important or dominant form of communication. Your appearance and demeanor in a job interview are often as crucial as your job competence. The firmness and confidence of your voice in a business negotiation can be as powerful as your actual words. The location and decoration of your office will convey powerful impressions to visitors.

Nonverbal communication is referred to popularly as body language. This aspect of communication is complex and includes all the sights and sounds that accompany our messages. Think of nonverbal communication as any messages a person receives about you through means other than your words themselves: your facial expressions, postures, gestures, clothing and appearance, as well as your use of space, territory, touch, and voice.

There are many reasons why you should be aware of nonverbal communication. Because nonverbal communication is present in all dealings with other people, it cannot be ignored. The sheer amount of nonverbal communication that occurs in organizations should compel you to pay attention and develop your skills in this area. Competent nonverbal communication can reduce misunderstandings in the workplace. By paying attention to both explicit information and the subtle nonverbal cues that accompany it, you can more fully understand messages. When you become aware of your own nonverbal communication, you can realize all the unintentional messages you convey.

Likewise, you can strategically control your nonverbal behavior to make your messages more powerful and to shape your image. You can improve your nonverbal communication skills by understanding the functions of the various categories of nonverbal communication and by following some simple guidelines in using it.

Categories of Nonverbal Communication

To improve nonverbal communication skills, we must realize the impact of facial expressions, posture, gestures, clothing and appearance, space and territory, touch, and voice.

Facial Expressions

We pay attention to the messages we receive from the faces of others. Subordinates judge the seriousness of your reprimand by the look on your face when you're talking to them. We may determine whether someone is telling the truth or lying by whether they can look us directly in the eye as they speak. While facial expressions can convey a multitude of messages, there are some standard types of information revealed by the face. Facial expressions tend to communicate emotions, show interest level, and regulate conversations.

Even when we try to hide emotions, they can leak through. We may say that we are happy for a promoted colleague, but show signs of disappointment or jealousy through our facial expressions. Certain expressions such as a blush of embarrassment or a nervous eye twitch are often involuntary reflexes.

Interest level and responsiveness reveal themselves primarily through the face. Eye contact, blank stares, and yawns all say something about the listener's interest level. We can regulate a conversation, perhaps without conscious realization, by smiling, frowning, nodding, raising an eyebrow, or winking. Recall the situation of being "called on" in a meeting by your supervisor looking directly at you and giving you a silent nod. Has anyone ever signaled you with a serious stare to be quiet?

Posture

Body movements associated with walking, sitting, or standing are aspects of nonverbal communication that people do not routinely notice. Unless they are distinctive, a walk or a posture can fade into the background. Nevertheless, postural cues frequently indicate degrees of liking, status, and tension. Business associates who like each other show relaxed postures, lean toward each other, and open or spread their arms and shoulders. Of course, other nonverbal information such as smiles, touch, and laughter can accompany the postural cues of liking.

How you stand, sit, or walk gives impressions about your status or power. Standing with arms folded across the chest, especially when others are seated or are in rigid formation, is an authoritative posture reminiscent of school principals or military sergeants. Imagine a subordinate leaning back in a chair with feet on table while meeting with you in your office. That could indicate an equal-power relationship between the two of you or could be seen as a disrespectful challenge of your status. Walking tall with long, confident strides gives the impression of status, while walking with stooped shoulders and a hesitant gait conveys inferiority.

The openness of your posture reveals your degree of relaxation. The person who takes up a lot of space by sprawling out when sitting will seem comfortable and relaxed. Arms across the back of a chair or a backward lean with hands across the back of the neck are not signs of a tense person. Picture, on the other hand, the tension exhibited by someone sitting on the edge of a chair with ankles crossed and hands clenched tightly in the lap.

Gestures

Gestures usually accompany words to illustrate or to emphasize the words. Throwing your hands up in frustration, when attached to words and facial expressions of frustration, helps to make the point. Some gestures, though, can stand alone to replace words. Pointing, the hitchhiker's thumb, waves, and the gesture for OK, among others, stand alone and convey rather automatic meaning.

What kinds of impressions do gestures convey? Your colleagues make judgments about your energy and confidence levels based on your gestures. One gesture that has acquired much symbolic meaning in business organizations is the handshake. Firm, strong handshakes are associated with confidence and credibility. Think of all the nervous mannerisms that reflect on your confidence level. People interpret a host of body-focused gestures such as scratching, nail biting, tugging at clothing, and hand wringing as signs of nervousness. Managers who unconsciously use these gestures may not realize the poor image of themselves they are revealing. Using your hands while talking conveys energy, enthusiasm, and dynamism. Such animated gestures help keep listeners' attention. If used excessively, however, they become distracting and may stereotype you as an emotional person.

Clothing and Appearance

It is a rare manager who does not realize how appearance affects credibility in the workplace. Indeed, in some organizations there is a conformity of dress that approaches an unofficial uniform. Dressing inappropriately in some industries or organizations can negatively affect your career. While it seems trivial to make business decisions on the basis of appearance, that can be the reality in many organizations. Business deals can be lost because of unshined shoes, stained ties, or excessive jewelry. Some professions require actual uniforms to enhance the recognition, credibility, and authority of the wearer.

Appearance factors such as general body build and physical attractiveness also carry powerful messages in our society. Think of the stereotypical characteristics associated with people who are fat and round-faced or tall and thin. We form definite impressions about the power and authority of tall individuals versus short individuals and will never know how many careers are advanced or stalled because of perceptions of physical attractiveness, which can be an unspoken prerequisite for success in public relations, receptionist, or broadcast-journalism positions, among others.

Space and Territory

The ways in which physical space is used in organizations says a great deal about individual and organizational power and image. The size, location, and privacy of your workspace is a powerful symbol in organizations. The higher you are in the organizational structure, the more likely it is that you will have a large, private office with windows. Low-ranking employees, on the other hand, probably work in crowded, open, noisy spaces. Astute visitors can read the power structure through the use of physical space and territory in an organization.

Another way that space and territory reveal power on the job is through the invasion of space. A manager can walk through the secretarial pool or onto the shop floor, but subordinates must be invited into the manager's office. Seating arrangements in business meetings will likely give clues to the leadership and influence of participants. For example, the person running a meeting often sits at the head of the table or at the front of the room surrounded by other key managers.

Experienced negotiators know the power of territory. They can hold negotiations on neutral territory to eliminate advantages to either side meeting on its home turf and can make business deals at restaurants, on the golf course, or over drinks rather than at the office of either party.

The type of furniture and artwork in lobbies and offices, the color schemes and neatness of the business environment, and the personal momentos placed on desks and shelves say something about an organization and its people. The physical image of a company directly affects its public image. The layout and the look of a department store or a restaurant will dictate its clientele. We judge people by the image of their workspace. We may not have confidence in an accountant or a lawyer whose office is cluttered with stacks of paper. Placing family photos, fresh flowers, or sports trophies in your office shapes the image that others form of you.

Touch

This category of nonverbal communication is not as prevalent in most organizations as other aspects of nonverbal behavior. Nevertheless, when touching does occur on the job, it carries a message. In some professions, like medicine, dentistry, athletics, dance, and hair design, touching is a legitimate job function. For most managers, though, touching does not go beyond a ritualized business handshake. You should be cautious when using touch in the workplace, for intentions behind touch are easily misunderstood. A friendly pat on the back or a tug on the arm to get someone's attention, intended as innocuous gestures, may offend the recipient. Any touch, unless it is invited, is an invasion of personal space. A unexpected touch can be intimidating. If you touch a subordinate, you may come across as aggressive. Finally, even the most well-intended touch of an opposite-sex business associate may be mistaken for intimacy or harassment.

Voice

What you say is verbal communication, but how you say it involves nonverbal communication. How you sound helps shape your image and the tone of messages helps you to interpret them. Vocal features include volume, rate, pitch, expressiveness, accent, diction, and fluency.

In some instances, the way you say something contradicts what you said. Imagine a financial officer using a hesitant, soft voice with little expression to assure managers that the company is in sound financial shape. Few listeners would be convinced. Likewise, a supervisor who solicits subordinates' reactions in a loud, forceful, low-pitched voice may stifle input. How you say things is as important as what you say. When words and tone contradict each other, people interpret the tone as the more reliable indicator of the real message.

Voice reflects image and affects persuasiveness. What image do you have of someone who mumbles? Speaks in a monotone? Has a squeaky voice? Has a deep, resonant voice? Sounds nasal? Shouts? Voice is such an important determinant of image that some managers opt for voice coaching to train their voices to sound more authoritative, personable, assertive, or confident. If you do much speaking in your career, develop careful diction and vocal expression while eliminating vocal clutter words like "you know," "um," "ah," and "OK."

Since so much of the management role involves trying to influence and convince others, you should also be aware of the relationship between vocal features and persuasion. Research shows that low-pitched, moderately loud, moderately fast, and expressive voices with clear diction, no accent, and no disfluencies are the most persuasive of all voices. By paying attention to vocal tone as well as developing convincing arguments, you can increase your persuasiveness.

Improving Nonverbal Communication Skills

There is a great deal to be aware of in the broad and complex area of human behavior known as nonverbal communication. Being aware of the communicative potential of facial expressions, posture, gestures, clothing and appearance, space and territory, touch, and voice can create more enlightened managers. But what are you to do with all this information? How can it improve your nonverbal communication skills? The following guidelines can help you become more competent at both displaying your own nonverbal behavior and more accurately interpreting the nonverbal cues of others.

1. *Do not take nonverbal communication out of context.* A little knowledge of nonverbal communication can be a dangerous thing. We have a tendency to look at isolated bits of behavior and draw incorrect assumptions from it. Remember that nonverbal cues are just that—cues to help you understand someone's message. You can best understand that message by looking at all the verbal and nonverbal features in context. The meaning of a certain facial expression will depend on a person's posture, gestures, and tone of voice as well. How you interpret that facial expression will also depend on who the person is, where the person is, and what was said. By taking any piece of nonverbal communication out of context, you decrease the accuracy of your interpretation.

2. *Avoid automatic interpretations of nonverbal behavior.* It is important to be flexible in your interpretations of nonverbal cues. Consider that a gesture, a facial expression, or a touch can mean many different things. People differ in their use of nonverbal communication. It is impossible to have dictionary definitions. You should not automatically interpret a smile, for example, as a sign of happiness. People smile when they are being polite, when they are nervous, when they are insecure, and when they want the approval of others.

   The interpretation of nonverbal behavior is not an exact science. It is simplistic to try to read someone like a book. This does not mean that you should completely give up trying to understand other people's nonverbal behavior. Astute managers will become skilled in observing people. But you also need to realize that the meaning of nonverbal behavior varies from person to person, from situation to situation, and from culture to culture.

3. *Practice perception checking.* Because interpretations of nonverbal communication are often wrong and because there can be many explanations for a given behavior, you should develop the habit of perception checking, a communication skill used to clarify the meaning of others' nonverbal messages. It is a way of making sure that you don't draw the wrong conclusions about the meaning of someone's behavior. Rather than interpreting a colleague's frown or loud voice as anger directed toward you, ask the colleague if something is wrong. Say something like "You look and sound angry. Is there something wrong?" It is wise to check out your perceptions of others' feelings, moods, and attitudes with them.

4. *Use nonverbal behavior to convey the messages you desire.* By being aware of the field of nonverbal communication, you can use nonverbal behavior to your advantage. You can strategically select nonverbal behavior to create the image you want, to emphasize messages, or to increase your effectiveness with people. Why let nonverbal cues convey unintentional messages about you when you can use this powerful form of communication to make it say what you want it to?

Being a more competent nonverbal communicator means becoming acutely aware of how you use your body, voice, clothing, and territory. It means not leaving nonverbal behavior to chance. Whenever you interact with others, make sure that your nonverbal behavior as well as your words help you achieve your objective.

For Additional Information

Caudill, Donald W. "The Image Management Puzzle." *Supervisory Management*, Vol. 30 (1985), No. 6, pp. 22–26. Body communication, dress communication, and social communication as ways of enhancing management success.

Druckman, Daniel, Richard M. Rozelle, and James C. Baxter. *Nonverbal Communication*. Beverly Hills, Calif.: Sage Publications, 1982. Research findings on nonverbal aspects of impressions, deception, and cross-cultural interaction as well as an overview of nonverbal aspects of voice, face, and body language.

Heslin, Richard, and Miles L. Patterson. *Nonverbal Behavior and Social Psychology.* New York: Plenum Press, 1982. Nonverbal behavior as it relates to social psychology themes such as attraction, influence, regulation, emotions, gender, culture, and personality.

Malandro, Loretta A., and Larry L. Barker. *Nonverbal Communication.* Reading, Mass.: Addison-Wesley Publishing Company, 1983. An introduction to various aspects of nonverbal communication including appearance, body movements, gestures, facial expressions, eye behavior, physical environment, territory, touch, voice, taste, smell, culture, and time. Each chapter includes a summary and references.

Patterson, Miles L. *Nonverbal Behavior.* New York: Springer-Verlag, 1983. The goals or purposes served by nonverbal behavior. Topics include nonverbal behavior as information giving, as a regulator of conversation, as an expression of intimacy, as a means of social control, and as a characteristic of certain professional or service relationships.

Older Workers

It IS CERTAIN THAT IN THE NEXT TWO DECADES THERE will be more older employees in the work force. The prediction is based on several factors. Demographers project a decline in the number of twenty- to twenty-four-year-olds from the mid-1980s to the year 2000. Thus, there will be fewer younger workers to fill the number of available jobs. At the same time, because of longer life spans and better health care, there will be a larger pool of older individuals from which to draw employees. By all accounts, the population of the United States is getting older. Recent legislation that has eliminated mandatory retirement in most professions and increased age-discrimination protection measures will lead to a larger proportion of older individuals in the work force. As a result, managers must learn to deal with older workers, to adjust their attitudes toward them, to develop appropriate personnel policies, and to assist older employees with the complex issues surrounding retirement decisions.

How Organizations Deal With Older Workers

Overall, our society regards older workers negatively. We consider older employees to be less productive, less flexible, less likely to keep up with new developments in their fields, more difficult to supervise and to train, and more likely to miss work for health-related reasons. The stereotype is of washed-up individuals who are biding their time until retirement and costing companies money in high salaries and health insurance costs while taking jobs away from competent, younger workers. Age has helped determine whether someone remains in the work force and influenced the value employers place on that worker. Stereotyped notions have led to personnel and pension policies that discourage older employees from remaining in the labor force and provide incentives for early retirement. The following are some of the ways in which society and workplace organizations have traditionally discouraged the retention of older employees:

- *Social Security Administration eligibility limits of 65 for full coverage and 62 for partial coverage of retirement benefits.* For all workers participating in the Social Security system, this provides a powerful message about appropriate ages for withdrawing from the labor force.

- *Private pension plans that require an employee to terminate in order to receive pension income.* Typically, employees cannot receive even partial payment from a pension plan until they completely sever ties with their current employer. This forces workers who may want to work a reduced schedule to retire completely or to semiretire and seek work from a new employer.

- *Benefit plans geared to the needs of younger employees.* Older employees who are eligible for Medicare will not need major medical and hospitalization coverage. Likewise, dental and obstetric benefits are geared to young families and will have little appeal for older workers. Short-sighted benefits packages not only have financial implications for older employees, but give subtle messages that the workplace is not geared to accommodate them.

- *The attitude that career-development and training opportunities for older workers is a poor investment for organizations.* While this assumption obviously will not be stated explicitly in organizations, younger workers are nonetheless favored for promotions, new responsibilities, and training programs. Companies consider it a waste to provide development opportunities for a 62-year-old worker who will be encouraged to retire at 65, for example.

- *Expectations that employees retire sometime in their sixties.* Progressive federal and state statutes regarding mandatory retirement ages will be useless if the majority of people believe that older workers are a burden and a barrier to others in a workplace. Taking status, responsibility, and opportunities away from older employees in the workplace clearly discourages older people from remaining on the job.

Innovative Personnel Policies

To retain older workers, organizations can adopt the following policies and practices:

1. *Company policy statements that older employees are valued* and will receive the same opportunities for meaningful work and career development as their younger counterparts.

2. *Flexible working arrangements.* Increasingly, varied job designs and schedules are becoming effective ways to retain various classes of employees including working mothers, those pursuing education on a full-time basis, and older workers. Some specific types of organizations, such as retail or service firms, have developed flexible working arrangements as a way to ensure large pools of qualified workers for 24-hour operations or peak-time needs. Flexible working arrangements can take many forms, including:

   - *Job sharing*—two people doing the same job on a part-time basis during different hours
   - *Flextime*—employees selecting their own arrival and departure times within limits set by management
   - *Part-time work*—allowing a full-time employee to change to part-time work within the same job level and function within the organization, and prorating benefits according to the hours worked
   - *Retiring*—allowing former employees to work as independent contractors or consultants

   Clearly, some types of organizations lend themselves to these alternative work arrangements more easily than others do. The full-time 40-hour work week is just one option for a work schedule. The more flexible you can be in providing varied work arrangements, the more likely you are to retain valuable employees. Flexible work options can save money by reducing benefits, turnover, and replacement and retraining costs.

3. *Job reassignments.* Older workers considering retirement may want to volunteer for jobs in their firms with less responsibility or stress than their previous positions. Such demotions or lateral moves may be preferable to retirement from the perspectives of both the employee and the employer. Older workers may also be interested in transfers, especially if such moves are to geographic areas with warmer climates. By relocating, they can fill a company's need and also find a better climate for eventual retirement. The organizational longevity of older workers may make them particularly suitable for special projects such as employee-involvement programs, problem-solving teams, and employee-performance-assessment projects. Reassigning older employees to special projects will simultaneously allow the company to utilize valuable experience and enhance motivation and productivity at a critical point in an older worker's employment history.

4. *Phased retirement.*   Employers can provide older workers gradual transitions to retirement by allowing them to reduce their hours of work as they approach retirement. There may be creative ways to provide partial pay and partial pension benefits.

5. *Flexible benefits packages.*   Some companies are opting for a cafeteria approach to fringe benefits, whereby individual employees select the particular benefits they need. This arrangement saves the employer money by eliminating unnecessary benefits for older workers. At the same time, it encourages older employees to stay on by providing benefits that are attractive and necessary to them.

6. *Education and training to prevent obsolescence.*   It is ironic that older workers are often denied training when they may be the segment of the work force most in need of it. Training to preserve older workers' competence in current jobs, to equip them with technological changes, and to prepare them for continued career advancement promotes their productivity and morale. Such efforts are worthwhile for organizations that want to retain older workers and get a decade or more of productive work as a return on the investment.

A recent decision by the Equal Employment Opportunity Commission (EEOC) regarding pension plan accruals should provide further incentives to retain older workers. Previously, employers could freeze pensions to the level reached at age 65 for employees who postponed retirement beyond age 65. The EEOC action in March 1987 mandates the continuation of pension accruals for older workers.

Preretirement Counseling

Increasingly, organizations are adding preretirement counseling to the benefits and programs they offer to employees. Some companies feel that they have a responsibility to provide such counseling because the issues surrounding retirement are so complex that older workers have difficulty making informed decisions. Also, because people tend to make several career or job changes in a lifetime, they may have accumulated a variety of retirement annuities. Preretirement counseling, especially regarding the financial aspects of retirement, is therefore becoming common in the workplace.

Company-sponsored preretirement counseling can take many forms, ranging from a mere cursory explanation of the company's pension plan to comprehensive sessions covering financial, medical, psychological, and social issues of retirement. In the financial area, preretirement counselors discuss retirement income options, tax options, housing decisions, and estate planning. Programs with components on medical information discuss nutrition, fitness, supplementary medical insurance options, and health care. Older workers may need counseling on the psychological effects of retirement even more than they need financial information. Coping with attitudes toward aging, retirement, and self-image are important ingredients in a preretirement program. Finally, some counselors explore with older workers questions of leisure time, hobbies, volunteer activities, and social support systems. Social counseling may be essential for retiring workers who are widowed or whose families are geographically separated.

Organizations considering preretirement counseling programs should focus on such aspects as the program's purpose, workers' rights to privacy, the competence of counselors, and the legal ramifications of such programs for the employer. Good preretirement counseling programs benefit both the company and the older employee and should not provide advice that solely benefits the company. Organizations that use preretirement counseling programs as a device to get rid of costly, unpopular, or outdated employees are clearly unethical.

Some older employees are reluctant to disclose private information such as finances, health status, and personal feelings to a representative of the company. Yet, to be successful in providing advice tailored to the needs of individual workers, preretirement counselors need such sensitive information. Overcoming workers' initial skepticism or fear can be the first step in establishing a viable preretirement counseling program.

The success of a preretirement counseling program also depends, in large part, on the competence and credibility of the counselors. They must possess up-to-date information in many areas related to retirement. They must be qualified counselors who can earn the trust of clients and, at the same time, have business expertise for organizational success. Organizations can hire psychologists specializing in gerontological issues or can purchase prepackaged preretirement counseling programs.

Because counselors can be held legally liable for the advice they give, some companies refrain from giving investment or legal advice to preretirees. Their preretirement programs offer only general and, consequently, less effective information to employees. Effective preretirement counseling programs must have counselors who are licensed and competent, must provide information that is complete, up-to-date, and accurate, and should have the advice of legal counsel.

For Additional Information

Copperman, Lois F., and Frederick D. Keast. *Adjusting to an Older Work Force.* New York: Van Nostrand Reinhold, 1983. A comprehensive treatment of management policies regarding older workers in organizations. Data on demographic shifts, personnel policies to retain older workers, and recommendations for public policymakers and employers are included.

Humple, Carol, and Morgan Lyons. *Management and the Aging Workforce.* New York: AMACOM, 1983. A management brief that dispels myths of older workers, presents demographic factors affecting the work force, and presents a vision of the progressive workplace. Chapters deal with organizational policies as well as training and development decisions affecting older workers.

Keiffer, Jarold A. *Gaining the Dividends of Longer Life: New Roles for Older Workers.* Boulder, Colo.: Westview Press, 1983. Social and economic reasons as well as strategies for retraining older people in the work force. Keiffer discusses the origins and inadequacies of present retirement strategy and presents guidelines for encouraging longer work lives. The roles of public agencies, businesses, educational institutions, and private and voluntary organizations are presented.

Montana, Patrick J. *Retirement Programs.* Englewood Cliffs, N.J.: Prentice-Hall, 1985. A guide for the human resources practitioner to developing and implementing a preretirement planning program. Chapters cover the need for preretirement programs, needs analysis, and program development and marketing. The appendix includes a checklist for preparing for retirement, an annotated list of retirement-preparation programs and materials, a sample preretirement program, and a list of sources on finances, aging, estate planning, and the social-emotional aspects of retirement.

Ragan, Pauline K., ed. *Work and Retirement: Policy Issues.* Los Angeles: University of Southern California Press, 1980. A series of articles on public- and private-sector policy relevant to older workers. Information on personnel policies, performance assessment, the effects of aging on productivity, and preretirement counseling is included.

Rhine, Shirley H. *Managing Older Workers: Company Policies and Attitudes.* New York: The Conference Board, 1984. Findings of a survey of 363 companies regarding policies affecting older workers, perceptions of older employees, pension programs, and workforce composition.

Rosow, Jerome M., and Robert Zager. *The Future of Older Workers: New Options for an Extended Working Life.* Scarsdale, N.Y.: Work in America Institute, 1980. Data regarding demographic, employment, and retirement trends as well as forty-five policy recommendations related to hiring and separation; pay and benefits; assessment and counseling; and employer, government, and union options for extending working life.

Watts, Patti. "Preretirement Planning—Making the Golden Years Rosy." *Personnel*, Vol. 64 (1987), No. 3, pp. 32ff. The need for organizations to assist with preretirement planning and the impact this has on younger employees.

Organizational Culture

THE CONCEPT OF ORGANIZATIONAL CULTURE refers to a set of assumptions or beliefs that are shared by members of an organization. A system of shared values in the workplace can be considered a culture. Culture encompasses the assumptions, habits, customs, stories, practices, and traditions of a group. Typically, we think of culture based on nationality, religious affiliation, or ethnic origin. People from countries such as Australia, Egypt, or Brazil, for example, have different values and customs based on the unique cultures in their nations. Likewise, Jews, Hindus, Koreans, and Italians will be steeped in different traditions.

Just as nations, religious, and ethnic groups inculcate their members with beliefs and practices, so do organizations. Corporate cultures specify how employees communicate, dress, think, behave, work, and make decisions and are pervasive aspects of a workplace that people just recently have begun to acknowledge, analyze, and manage. While the idea has been intuitively understood for some time, the explicit discussion of corporate culture is a relatively new phenomenon in management literature.

Why Care About Organizational Culture?

Culture has a powerful influence throughout an organization. It guides behavior, affects morale, and creates an organization's identity. Something so pervasive and potent deserves attention. In addition to focusing on organizational culture merely because it exists in all companies, you should understand the culture of your organization for many pragmatic reasons:

1. *Fitting in.* Being in a new culture creates uncertainty and tension. You do not know what is expected of you in a new organization,

function, company site, or department. Assessing the culture helps you to respond appropriately. You can get cues about how to act and what to value. Do managers address executives by their first names? Do co-workers disagree with one another in meetings? Do some departments have larger budgets or better offices than others, thereby indicating their relative importance in the organization? Such expectations and values are not spelled out for newcomers. The only way to understand subtle organizational norms is to observe them through behavioral manifestations of the culture. Individuals who fail to analyze corporate culture will invariably violate its standards of behavior and have trouble fitting in.

2. *Understanding others' behavior.* Effective managers have insights into people and their behavior. Since an organization's culture shapes its people's assumptions, values, and behavior, you must work to understand cultural forces in the workplace. Perhaps a culture of competition is preventing people from working effectively as a team. Or maybe employee input is stifled because supervisors ask to be alerted to problems but reward workers who keep quiet. An awareness of culture helps you to understand people's motivations, standards of performance, and seemingly contradictory behavior.

3. *Managing intraorganizational conflicts.* Sometimes subgroups in an organization do not get along because they represent two very different cultures. Research and development specialists may be accustomed to a data-gathering, deliberate, slow, analytical type of environment and may not be able to work effectively with the action-oriented, fast-paced, flamboyant marketing people in the same company. An understanding of these different subcultures in your organization will lead to more realistic expectations of cross-functional teams and prepare you to handle intergroup conflicts.

4. *Coping with marketplace diversity and international business.* In a heterogeneous society, organizations employ and serve a diversity of people who differ according to racial, gender, ethnic, religious, age, geographic, and life-style factors. Organizations that understand how culture affects people can provide more enlightened and nondiscriminatory places to work. You can use cultural information to market products and services more effectively and to meet the needs of a diverse clientele or customer base. For multinational corporations or executives who travel to different parts of the world to do business, an understanding of culture as it affects the workplace is essential. Cultural insights prevent social blunders and give a company a business advantage in foreign markets.

5. *Shaping or redirecting organizational cultures.* A corporate culture is developed through the leaders of the organization. This may
be a conscious or an unintentional process. If you want to take a
proactive stance in shaping your company's image, values, and
standards of behavior for employees, you must understand cultural
forces in the workplace. Indeed, you shape organizational cultures
by most everything you do: the behaviors you show as a role model;
your hiring, promotion, and termination decisions; what you pay
attention to and reward; organizational creeds you create and stories
you tell; organizational structures and policies you develop; and the
physical space you occupy and allocate. Consciously affecting or
changing an organization's culture is a very slow and costly en-
deavor, though not an impossible one. Finally, by understanding
the workplace culture, you can realize the constraints that a culture
places on planned change. Strategic planning or organizational
development goals, for example, must be developed in light of the
organizational culture.

Elements of Organizational Culture

Because an organization's culture derives from all its structural,
procedural, and personnel aspects, the concept of culture is broad and
elusive. There are identifiable elements, however. Managers interested
in examining the culture of their organizations should focus on these
elements:

Values

Strong business leaders clearly indicate what they consider to be
important. By communicating values, the underlying assumptions
upon which organizations are based, you establish common goals and
standards of behavior and help shape your organization's identity. In
some cultures, creativity is valued and consequently rewarded. Other
workplace cultures value obedience, teamwork, seniority, or conflict.
By identifying the values of your corporate culture, you discover
preferences for how the organization should be run and guidelines for
individual behavior in the organization. Values are prescriptive in that
they specify what we ought to do.

Values as clues to organizational culture can be discovered in a
number of ways. Sometimes they are explicitly stated in company
philosophies, creeds, or policy statements. A company's slogans and
mottos usually reveal the essence of its mission. In addition, you can
analyze the physical environment created by an organization. An

organization occupying sleek corporate towers downtown gives a message different from that of the company operating in dilapidated warehouses by the railroad tracks. Vast differences in the offices given to various departments can reveal the value or status a company accords. You can discern organizational values by observing which behaviors are rewarded and which punished.

Communication

Every workplace culture will include assumptions about the correct way for people to relate to each other. Indeed, the styles of interaction and rules governing relationships in an organization reveal much about its culture. Some cultures promote informal interaction, reward dissent, and encourage social relationships between employees. Other organizations allow communication only through a strict chain of command or discourage disagreement.

To discover communication aspects of an organization's culture, pay attention to who communicates about what to whom. Culture dictates the topics worthy of communication in the workplace. An organization holding meetings, preparing reports, and developing plans related to productivity would reveal a culture different from the organization focusing on risk, innovation, and entrepreneurial activity. Do first-line supervisors have easy access to organizational decision makers? Does communication travel only downward from top levels to others in the workplace, or can lower-level employees give information, advice, and suggestions to their supervisors? Are meetings informational or problem-solving activities? Is gossip and rumor rampant? Are opportunities for social relationships provided through company dining rooms, softball teams, or annual picnics? Clearly, an organization's culture can be characterized by the content, amount, and direction of its communication as well as by the nature of workplace relationships.

History

Corporate founders are frequently colorful characters whose visions shape the organizations they develop. Founding figures and leaders throughout an organization's history have a powerful influence on its culture. Major developments or crises chart its course and image. An organization's culture is the sum of the major leaders and events of its past.

Thus, to understand your organization's culture, you must learn about its history. Who were the company founders? What were their visions, goals, and idiosyncracies? Who are the company's legendary heroes and what did they do to achieve such fame? What were the major turning points in the organization's development? The answers may entail the development of new products or services, expansion into new locations or markets, incidents of major restructuring, technological advancements, or responses to societal forces, among other things.

Just as a nation of people can appreciate their culture by learning about their history, so organizational members can understand workplace culture through significant people, events, and crises that affected the organization. Reading corporate histories, talking to veterans of the company, and listening to stories and legends can provide insights into present-day culture.

Symbols and Ceremonies

Organizations create objects and emblems to represent themselves. These contribute to an organizational identity. Employees can look to them as a source of pride, loyalty, and personal identity. Outsiders recognize companies by their symbols. Likewise, organizations stage many events for both insiders and outsiders that reveal their cultures. Company literature, advertisements, press releases, meetings, recognition ceremonies, and social events say something about the organizational culture.

To discover workplace culture through symbols, you can analyze company logos, mottos, and slogans. What image do they portray and what values do they embody? Decorations, artwork, or interior designs in company facilities may be symbolic of organizational philosophies or attitudes. Mahogany furniture in law offices and chrome or vinyl furniture in retail firms are strategic reflections of the different cultures in these professions. Documents such as annual reports, recruiting brochures, and employee handbooks serve symbolic as well as informative functions. Routine events such as departmental meetings or extravagant occurrences such as trade shows or stockholders meetings shed light on organizational culture. How often are ceremonies held? What is their purpose? Who is invited? Where are they held? How is achievement recognized? Answers to these questions can provide evidence of the culture of an organization.

Managing Organizational Culture

Astute managers are aware of the concept of culture and understand their roles in shaping or redirecting the cultures of their organizations. In essence, effectively managing a corporate culture means understanding it, consciously shaping it, and changing it, if necessary.

Understanding culture means recognizing the values, communication rules, history, symbols, and ceremonies of a particular organization and how they both affect and reflect everyday decisions and actions of people on the job. Paying attention to the more subtle aspects of the workplace, including both human and structural factors, provides a larger perspective on the organization. Enlightened managers do not underestimate the role of culture. They can articulate their organization's culture, point to its elements, and understand how culture influences their own and others' behavior.

Effective leaders of organizations realize that they can actively shape the culture of their companies. In many ways, business leadership is synonymous with the creation of organizational culture. Strong leaders have a vision of the type of organization they want to develop and they take steps to bring that vision to action. Through your own behavior, you provide role models of the values and practices you want others to embody. You reinforce your cultural vision every time you make decisions, delegate projects, reward performance, or preside over organizational events. Rather than haphazardly affecting workplace culture through random actions and messages, wise managers build and shape the culture of their organizations through clear and consistent actions. The ability to shape organizational culture rather than being constrained by it can distinguish legendary from average leaders.

When organizational leaders set out to change aspects of their organization's culture, their motivation may stem from changing marketplace dynamics, organizational restructuring, or the need for more effective management styles. They can affect cultural change through such intervention strategies as organizational development, team building, or training. Leaders who seek to change the culture of an organization must realize the enormous commitment their goal requires and must follow certain basic tactics to succeed.

Because culture is so pervasive and deep-rooted, it is not easy to change. Change projects may take years to accomplish, cost considerable sums of money, and try the patience of leaders and employees alike. External consultants are often necessary to help organizations embark on change and to cope with the resulting upheaval, confusion, and anxiety. Upper-level management must demonstrate visible commitment to change and must help others through the painful transition of organizational assumptions and values. A strong, visible person to spearhead a change project is necessary as a symbol and consensus builder. To accomplish change in an organization's culture, committed leaders must embrace the change process, equip the organization with skills for managing change, and have patience to let cultural change evolve over time.

New Organizational Cultures

Contemporary scholars of corporate culture point to evidence of a transformation in the American workplace. Some predict that traditional, hierarchical organizations with power centralized in the hands of a few will give way to decentralized, smaller, entrepreneurial organizations. Visions of this emerging work culture include information-oriented businesses with increased levels of productivity through the utilization of new technologies; more participation and involvement of employees especially through the use of telecommunication; smaller, highly motivated work units; egalitarian and flexible workplace structures; work environments that emphasize creativity, reward risk, and enhance the quality of life; and increased employee autonomy and control.

Some analysts of culture say we are already moving toward such a work macroculture. We must examine the cultural elements of specific companies to determine whether organizational culture is evolving.

[See also Intrapreneuring]

For Additional Information

Deal, Terrence E., and Allen A. Kennedy. Corporate Cultures: The Rites and Rituals of Corporate Life. Reading, Mass.: Addison-Wesley Publishing Company, 1982. A primer on cultural management for business leaders. The book explains such elements of culture as values, heroes, rites and rituals, and communication. In addition, it provides methods for identifying, managing, and reshaping cultures. Examples of cultural-management practices from actual companies are included.

Graves, Desmond. Corporate Culture—Diagnosis and Change. New York: St. Martin's Press, 1986. A research-oriented book that covers types of organizational cultures, the differences between cultures and climates, the ways companies reinforce culture through senior management training, generalizations about comparative culture, and ways to change culture.

Harris, Philip R. Management in Transition. San Francisco: Jossey-Bass Publishers, 1985. Written for both current managers who find themselves in the midst of role transition and future managers who will face new challenges. The book describes new work cultures, suggests new management and leadership strategies, and provides instruments for assessing managerial and organizational performance. There are chapters on dealing with innovation, technology, teamwork, employee wellness, and transitions.

Howard, Robert. *Brave New Workplace*. New York: Viking Penguin, Inc., 1985. An alternative vision of workplace culture characterized by a balance between equity and efficiency, meaningful work and high technology, worker satisfaction and profit, and social renewal and economic prosperity. Howard describes the elements of a "brave new workplace" and discusses the implications of organizational change on workers and on society as a whole.

Kilmann, Ralph H., Mary J. Saxton, and Roy Serpa. *Gaining Control of the Corporate Culture*. San Francisco: Jossey-Bass Publishers, 1985. A handbook of twenty articles by academics and practitioners on understanding, managing, and changing organizational cultures. Through numerous case illustrations, the following topics are discussed: methods of identifying cultural norms, ways leaders influence organizational cultures, the effects of culture on organizational performance and strategies, and guidelines for promoting cultural change.

Reynierse, James H., and John B. Harker. "Measuring and Managing Organizational Culture." *Human Resource Planning*, Vol. 9 (1986), No. 1, pp. 1–8. Describes a survey and analysis technique used to examine, measure, and manage organizational culture. The technique and its application are discussed.

Schein, Edgar H. *Organizational Culture and Leadership*. San Francisco: Jossey-Bass Publishers, 1985. Ways to understand organizational culture from either a theoretical or practical point of view. Schein covers the meanings and functions of cultures, their formation and development, and cultural change. He presents a thorough explanation of culture and leadership as complex and interdependent processes.

Orienting New Employees

SOME COMPANIES go to great lengths to recruit and select the right employees for jobs and then destroy all that careful planning by failing to provide adequate job orientation. For many new employees, the orientation to their job consists of nothing more than a few introductions, a brief tour of the facility, and the suggestion that fellow employees can answer further questions later. Consequently, the first few days on the job are filled with tension, uncertainty, embarrassment, self-doubt, resentment, and pessimism about future success in the position. This bad start may spill over to affect long-term perceptions about the job and the company.

Instead, an effective orientation program should ease the employee into the organization, celebrate the new employer-employee relationship, and provide information vital to functioning productively in the organization. Orientation sessions may seem like a waste of time because the employee is not working, but the commitment to new-employee orientation will pay for itself in less turnover and in more motivated, productive, and loyal employees.

New employees should receive two kinds of orientation training: orientation to the organization and orientation to the work unit and job. Each complements the other and contributes to a comprehensive new-employee orientation program. A discussion of the purposes and components of each follows.

Orientation to the Organization

The purpose of this information is to acquaint new hires with the nature of the organization—its structure, mission, philosophy, and goals. Also, new employees should learn their responsibilities to the organization and the organization's responsibilities to them. This aspect of orientation gives them a sense of organizational identity. The specific topics of an organizational orientation should include:

1. *Company history.* Explain the founding of your company, its progress, accomplishments, key figures, and the path it took to its present status. This helps new employees see the larger picture and feel proud to be affiliated with the company.

2. *Nature of the industry or profession.* Explain how the organization fits into the overall picture of the particular industry or profession. What have been major developments in the industry? What are some current trends in the field affecting your company? This acquaints employees with the forces and constraints affecting the organization and can provide background information about why the company functions as it does.

3. *Organizational philosophy, mission, and structure.* The new employee should learn about the guiding principles of the organization. What are its values? What does it stand for? Next, why does the organization exist? What is its overriding purpose? A sense of the organizational structure should be provided. What are the various divisions or units in the company? Understanding the organization chart will help new hires see how they fit into its structure.

   You need not provide too much detail here. It is important not to overwhelm new employees. On the other hand, they should not feel that they are working in a vacuum. An introduction to the organization's philosophy, mission, and structure provides a sense of identity, helps shape work values, and creates pride in and loyalty to the organization.

4. *Employment benefits.* New employees should be made aware of the various benefits provided by the organization, such as medical insurance, life insurance, sick leave, vacations, holidays, retirement plans, education and training, and child care. It is not necessary to explain all the features of these benefits, lest information overload set in. But new hires should be aware of their benefits options and should schedule an individual appointment with a benefits counselor to make decisions and to process paperwork.

5. *Organizational policies and procedures.* These are general rules about how the company functions. For example, statements should be made about affirmative action and equal employment opportunity (EEO) policies, performance standards and evaluation processes, safety and security practices, and any standards regarding salary increases and promotions. Remember that the orientation

session is only an introduction. All rules and regulations cannot be explained at this point. But new hires should acquire a sense of what is considered acceptable behavior in the workplace.

6. *Facility tour and introduction to key people.*   It is essential for new employees to see how the organization operates, learn their way around the physical facility, and be able to associate names with faces of key people. They should be escorted to all departments and receive a brief statement about the function of each department and the interrelationships of departments. The tour should point out the location of employee lounges, lunch rooms, vending machines, and other pertinent areas such as exercise rooms, lockers, or medical or child-care facilities. The leaders of various departments should make a point of greeting and welcoming new employees.

Aspects of the organizational orientation will vary in length according to the size and complexity of the organization. In a small company, the information can be covered in a few hours. In large corporations, the orientation to the organization may take a full week. Such information should be supplemented with written materials wherever possible. Employee handbooks typically include information about company history, philosophy, mission, structure, policies, procedures, and benefits. The personnel department should provide brochures about various benefits and distribute policy manuals, facility maps, and organizational directories.

Remember, new employees may be overwhelmed with the amount of information provided in orientation sessions. Written materials to read at home or to consult as a later reference can ease the feeling of information overload. All aspects of organizational information are not pertinent to new employees on the first day of work. They are more concerned with their daily job duties. However, general information about the organization provides a framework for doing a job and will interest the new employee more after a few days in the organization. Thus, it is important that the employee have written materials to consult and avenues for asking questions both during and after the formal orientation program.

Orientation to the Department and the Job

Once the new employee has been introduced to the organization, it is time to provide an orientation to the particular work unit and job duties. This session should take place in the work unit and be conducted by a member of that department. The topics to be covered in the departmental orientation include:

1. *Department mission and relationship to the organization.* What are the responsibilities of the department? What is its role and how does that role relate to the overall organizational mission? The new employee should learn what the work unit does in the short term and long term and how work flows into and out of this work unit. It is important to explain how work in this unit affects and is affected by work done in other units.

2. *Departmental structure.* Who is in charge of what in the department? Who supervises whom? New employees should be aware of their reporting relationship and, in the case of supervisory positions, should know what employees they supervise.

3. *Work supplies.* The person doing the departmental orientation must show new employees their work station or office and explain where to get supplies, tools, or equipment necessary for carrying out the job; the phone system; and policies regarding the use of office equipment or clerical staff.

4. *Job description and standards of performance.* Employees should know exactly what they are responsible and accountable for. What tasks are they expected to perform in the new job? How are they to do their job duties? What are acceptable standards of performance? By what criteria will their job performance be measured? During the departmental orientation, they should be guided through the actual work performance. Perhaps they can watch others perform the job and then do it themselves with follow-up coaching. Information about work priorities should be provided. Trainees should be encouraged to ask questions and be given ample feedback by supervisors.

    One method of orienting new employees to the job is to provide a work buddy or coach, who provides on-the-job training for a limited period of time. This role must be taken seriously and far surpasses the question-answering role that colleagues often perform for new hires. Of course, the buddy must show excellent work performance and be skilled as a teacher or coach.

5. *Work schedule.* Departmental orientation sessions should acquaint new employees with expectations about work hours: starting and stopping time, lunch and coffee breaks, overtime, and scheduling sick days and vacations.

6. *Departmental policies.* New employees will need to know work-unit rules about dress codes, smoking, personal calls, visitors, and disciplinary and grievance procedures. They should be apprised

about norms of acceptable and unacceptable behavior in the work unit.

The departmental orientation is not as much of a distinct informational session as the organizational orientation is. The first few days in the work unit may be spent in orientation to the department and to the job, or the process may intermittently span several weeks. It is not clear where the orientation process ends and ongoing job-performance coaching begins.

Interspersed with all the orientation information, there should be attempts at hospitality and rapport building. Small talk about non-work-related topics can ease the stress of those first few days on the job. New employees should be invited to lunch during the orientation period. In short, they should feel special and welcome during the first few days on the job. The more co-workers take new employees under their wing, the more successful the formal orientation program will be.

Dos and Don'ts of New-Employee Orientation

1. *Don't neglect new-employee orientation.* Beware of letting new employees sink or swim on their own. You may not realize all the areas of uncertainty for a new employee. Avoid a haphazard or rushed orientation. Take the time to provide a comprehensive introduction to the company and to the job, which will reduce misinformation and job errors and create a more satisfied and productive worker.

2. *Provide follow-up to orientation training.* Don't think that a new employee is acclimated after a few days or weeks. Provide detailed information, at a later time, about policies and procedures and company benefits. Schedule several feedback sessions about job performance. Give new employees plenty of opportunity to ask questions even months into the job tenure.

3. *Make orientation exciting.* Since this is the introduction to the firm and to the job, the first impression should be positive. Orientation should not entail an endless stream of factual information. Group orientation sessions for all new hires throughout the company can lend an air of excitement to the process. Social events mixed with various formats for presenting information can add a memorable and beneficial impact. Make sure speakers are dynamic, discussions are lively, tours are productive, and orientation leaders are helpful and friendly. Orientation should make new hires happy

about their decision to join the organization and make them look forward to beginning their actual work.

4. *Don't sour new employees.* All organizations have problems, drawbacks, and troublesome people. Orientation is not the time to alert new hires to problems or to make disparaging remarks about the company or any of its people. Reality will hit soon enough. The new employee will have enough information to digest without having to hear company gossip.

5. *Hold separate orientation sessions for exempt and nonexempt employees.* While information about company history, philosophy, and mission will be applicable to all levels of employees, much of the information and tone of orientation sessions will vary according to employee status. Supervisors and managers may be more interested in organizational structure, training opportunities, and career-advancement issues than nonexempt employees would be. Information on policies, rules, and disciplinary procedures may vary across employee groups. Benefits likely will differ. Rather than trying to orient diverse employees together, tailor separate sessions to meet specific needs.

6. *Solicit feedback about orientation effectiveness.* New hires should provide feedback to orientation leaders about the effectiveness of both organizational and departmental information sessions. Participants should indicate to what extent their needs were met and their questions answered during the orientation period. The input should be used to revise subsequent orientation training.

[*See also* Training]

For Additional Information

Addams, H. Lon. "Up To Speed in 90 Days—An Orientation Plan." *Personnel Journal*, Vol. 64 (1985), No. 12, pp. 34–40. Explains that the first few weeks on the job are the best opportunity management has to set the tone for a worker's entire period of employment and offers a complete ninety-day orientation program.

Arthur, Diane. *Recruiting, Interviewing, Selecting, and Orienting New Employees.* New York: AMACOM, 1986. Includes one chapter on orientation and covers such issues as acclimating the employee to the first day of work, conducting organizational orientations, and performing departmental orientation. Sample orientation programs of topics, schedules, and formats are included.

Desatnick, Robert L. *Managing to Keep the Customer.* San Francisco: Jossey-Bass Publishers, 1987. A book on customer service that includes a section on the importance of orienting new customer service employees. It includes a list of characteristics of successful orientation programs and a sample program from a large corporation.

Klubnik, Joan P. "Orienting New Employees." *Training and Development Journal,* Vol. 41 (1987), No. 4, pp. 46–49. An example of one company's program of making new hires part of the team right from the start.

Performance Appraisals

PERFORMANCE APPRAISAL is the observation and evaluation of an employee's work behavior and accomplishments for the purpose of making decisions about the employee. Decisions may include wage, salary, and benefits determinations; promotion, demotion, transfer, or termination actions; and counseling, training, or career-development options. Systematic methods of identifying and measuring performance can assist human resources planning and improve an employee's future performance.

Many benefits result from an effective performance-appraisal system. Organizations can control marginal performance, reduce losses from ineffective performance, and make more efficient use of personnel. Individuals can realize rewards for effective performance, eliminate uncertainty about others' perceptions of their performance, and have a clear understanding of their career pathing.

While performance appraisal is an essential part of most managers' jobs and a vital aspect of the human resources function in organizations, problems and dissatisfactions surround the appraisal systems in many companies. To improve performance appraisals, you must be aware of the psychological-measurement principles, legal implications, and communication elements affecting the process of performance evaluation and review.

Who Should Evaluate Performance?

There are various options for determining who will perform the assessment task. Possibilities include immediate supervisors, self-appraisal, peer review, subordinates, evaluation committees, personnel department staff, training department staff, and external sources. An organization can use one or any combination of these sources to conduct performance appraisals.

Probably the most common evaluator of performance is the employee's immediate supervisor. Often, the supervisor is in the best position to observe a subordinate's behavior in relation to job objectives. Employees regard supervisors as legitimate performance evaluators who are qualified to make career development-decisions affecting them.

Self-appraisals contribute to employees' satisfaction with the evaluation process. When employees participate in setting performance goals, determining evaluation criteria, rating themselves, and discussing their performance with supervisors, they tend to be less defensive about appraisals and show greater improvement in performance. Some drawbacks to self-appraisal include the time needed to involve employees, the problem of discrepancies between self- and others' ratings, and the loss of control some supervisors feel in inviting employee participation.

Peers often have firsthand knowledge of one another's performance. Research has shown peer appraisals to be reliable and valid predictors of job performance. The average of several peer ratings is probably more reliable than a single rating. Potential problems include the unwillingness of peers to evaluate each other, friendship biases, and competition within the work group.

Subordinate evaluations allow for multiple ratings and encourage subordinates to view workplace demands through the eyes of their supervisors. Subordinates are in an excellent position to comment on their supervisor's leadership ability. The method promotes an environment of participation and provides valuable feedback to supervisors. On the other hand, some supervisors are threatened by subordinate evaluations and apply negative sanctions to the work group for poor reviews. Subordinates may inflate ratings because they fear reprisals. Also, subordinates may not fully understand a supervisor's job requirements or may emphasize criteria relevant to their own relationship with the supervisor.

A committee of evaluators can increase accuracy due to the number of independent raters but may be time-consuming for the organization and threatening to the employee being rated. Problems of confidentiality of information and lack of direct observation of job behavior can result. Members of personnel or training departments may be the most qualified in appraisal techniques, but often do not have the time to participate in performance appraisals. Also, they are so removed from the employee's actual job that evaluation accuracy suffers. External evaluators such as consultants or assessment-center raters can also conduct performance appraisals. While they often employ stan-

dardized techniques that are statistically accurate and legally protected, external evaluators are costly and typically evaluate behavior in
hypothetical rather than actual situations.

Performance-Appraisal Techniques

Just as there are many options for deciding who should rate
performance, there are numerous techniques of structuring and guiding
a performance appraisal. Evaluation procedures vary according to (1)
the extent to which they assess personal versus performance criteria,
and (2) the extent to which they use objective versus subjective judgments. Organizational sentiment and practice in performance appraisal
is shifting away from subjective ratings of personal factors (traits) to
objective evaluations of performance factors (behavior). While it is
more difficult to obtain valid and reliable ratings of actual job-related
behavior, organizations find these techniques to be more effective and
legally defensible than subjective judgments of character traits. Explanations, advantages, and disadvantages will be presented for the following commonly-used performance-appraisal methods, such as trait-
based measures, narrative essays, the critical-incident technique,
checklists, graphic rating scales, behaviorally anchored rating scales,
cost-related outcomes, and Management by Objectives.

Trait-Based Measures

In some organizations, performance appraisals are based on personal qualities or traits. Common traits included in performance evaluation forms are dependability, honesty, creativity, resourcefulness,
integrity, decisiveness, judgment, tact, initiative, leadership, cooperation, enthusiasm, personality, and loyalty. The assumption underlying
this approach is that such traits manifest themselves on the job and
affect work performance. Raters indicate their perceptions of the employee on these factors through a checklist, yes/no scale, or graphic
rating scale indicating a relative quantity of the trait.

As might be expected, there is ample room for error when you
use trait-based measures. Raters may vary considerably in their perception or understanding of these traits, be forced into the role of judge,
and have difficulty defending their decisions. By what criteria does a
rater award a numerical value of 3 versus 4 for creativity on a 5-point
scale, for example? Judgments on trait-based measures are subjective
and prone to litigation. Research shows that high ratings on trait-based
measures do not necessarily correlate with good job performance.

Despite these serious problems, trait-based measures continue to be used for many reasons. Raters often prefer such personal criteria because trait measures are easy to develop and simple to use. Because the same list of traits can universally relate to a variety of people across job lines, the organization may be able to get by with just one performance-appraisal form. In some cases, certain traits do indeed distinguish between satisfactory and unsatisfactory performance of a job. These arguments notwithstanding, organizations would be wise to use trait-based items sparingly in conjunction with other techniques or to avoid them altogether in performance evaluations.

Narrative Essays

This involves a written description of an employee's qualities, attitudes, and behavior. The appraiser, who is familiar with the employee's performance, produces an unstructured, candid statement about the employee's strengths, weaknesses, and areas needing improvement. The method provides specific performance feedback to employees and can be a springboard for open communication between a supervisor and a subordinate, as well as a catalyst for goal setting and individual development. Of course, the essay method is subjective, legally questionable, and dependent on the appraiser's writing skills. Also, because the appraiser chooses the criteria to discuss, comparisons across employees are difficult.

Critical-Incident Technique

With this method, the supervisor makes periodic notations of important performance actions, both positive and negative, of subordinates. In essence, the supervisor develops a file of effective and ineffective actions or performance by an employee. The file can serve as a jog to the memory while a performance review is being conducted, can give employees meaningful feedback about specific work-related behavior, can serve as the basis for completing other performance-appraisal instruments, and can provide written documentation for personnel decisions in the event of appeals or litigation.

This is a time-consuming technique when performed conscientiously for all employees. Also, supervisors may be biased in what they choose to record. They may record more negative incidents for a disliked subordinate or fail to document poor performance of a well-liked employee, for example.

Checklists

Checklists can range from lists of traits to descriptive statements of job-related behavior. The rater indicates with a checkmark traits the employee manifests or job-related behaviors the employee performs. Because a checklist ensures that all employees are assessed on the same items, comparisons are easier. The more specific and descriptive the items are on the checklist, the more objective the method is likely to be. Checking a form to indicate whether an employee has "initiative," for example, requires much interpretation on the part of the evaluator. Checking an option on a continuum of "initiative" indicators, however, depends more on the observation of an employee's behavior than on subjective judgment. Such categories on a checklist might include (a) needs substantial encouragement and direction in beginning projects, (b) starts some projects with minor prodding, and (c) launches new projects through individual motivation.

Graphic Rating Scales

Graphic ratings scales contain a number of job-performance qualities and characteristics worded into statements. The rater typically responds in one of two ways: (1) how frequently the employee demonstrates the behavior or quality (always, often, sometimes, rarely, never) or (2) the extent of agreement with a descriptive statement about the employee (strongly agree, agree, undecided, disagree, strongly disagree). Examples of statements include "The manager takes corrective action to solve poor performance problems of subordinates," "The manager motivates subordinates to perform their jobs well," or "The manager meets reporting deadlines."

The items on graphic rating scales typically involve job behaviors rather than generalized traits. In that respect, they are more objective than some other evaluation techniques. Graphic rating scales do vary, however, in the extent to which they define or provide examples of performance dimensions for the rater. For instance, there is still ambiguity in the statement "The manager takes corrective action to solve poor performance problems of subordinates." Examples of "corrective actions" can be provided such as "gives employees oral feedback about poor performance," "sets goals with employees to improve performance," or "coaches employees to improve work performance." By providing specific examples of job-related behavior, you can avoid discrepant definitions of terms. Of course, a rater's perception of whether the employee "sometimes" versus "rarely" performs the behavior can still be subjective.

Graphic rating scales do not provide as much depth as essays or critical incidents do, but they are more objective, less time-consuming, and allow comparisons among employees. They lend themselves to an easy comparison between self-appraisal and supervisor evaluation. If they are constructed carefully and used with reliability and validity data, graphic rating scales can provide an efficient, standardized, and legally sound means of structuring performance evaluations.

Behaviorally Anchored Rating Scales

The behaviorally anchored rating scales (BARS) is a type of graphic rating scale with specific behavioral descriptions for each point along the scale. The descriptions are anchors to aid the rater in defining outstanding, good, average, or poor performance.

Ideally, both evaluators and employees to be rated contribute to the development of the scale, which is a complex process essentially involving the collection of incidents describing competent, average, and poor performance of a particular job; categorization of those incidents into overall performance dimensions (technical ability, communication skills, leadership, and so on); and rating the incidents to assign numerical values that translate into anchors along a continuum.

The following is an example of an item from a BARS for a training manager:

Dimension: Organizational skills

3 *Excellent:* Follows a training outline; presents material in logical units; ties one idea into the next; summarizes information often.

2 *Average:* Prepares a training outline but only follows it occasionally; presents material in no particular order; ties some ideas to others; summarizes information at times.

1 *Poor:* Neither provides nor follows a training outline; presents material in a random order; ideas seem unrelated to each other; rambles.

There are both advantages and disadvantages to the BARS method. The scales tend to be precise and objective because there are behavioral anchors for each decision option. But there is little inference about what constitutes excellent, average, or poor behavior on a certain dimension of a particular job. The anchor descriptions, because they are created by people familiar with the job, tend to be accurate illustrations of the range of job performance. The descriptions use actual job terminology. Sometimes, however, the specific examples of behavior used as anchors on the scale do not correspond to the employee's actions. In that case, the appraiser's decisions revert to general estimates of competence on a dimension. BARS are time-consuming to develop for every job in an organization. Also, to be legally defensible, ratings must be backed by documentation of specific instances in which the employee performed or failed to perform a certain action.

Cost-Related Outcomes

This technique uses quantitative measures of performance outcomes or results. Criteria might include sales volume, claims processed, reports written, units produced, turnover rate, absences, and accidents, which can serve as absolute indicators of an individual's, a department's, or an organization's effectiveness. Measurement is very precise and objective.

The problem is that not all jobs or all aspects of jobs lend themselves to quantitative measures. How does one quantify problem solving, interpersonal sensitivity, or employee-development activities, for example? Nor do cost-related outcomes indicate how well something was done; they just tell how often something was done. A variety of factors beyond an employee's control can affect such quantitative criteria. For jobs that lend themselves to cost-outcome criteria, this method of performance appraisal may be effective when combined with other measures.

Management by Objectives

Management by Objectives (MBO) is a technique whereby supervisors and subordinates mutually agree on measurable performance goals for a certain time period. They develop plans of action and specify resources for achieving the goals. Then they monitor progress and evaluate goal achievement in a performance-review session.

Thus, employees have maximum input into the criteria by which their performance will be evaluated. The performance evaluation focuses exclusively on job behavior and accomplishments rather than on personal qualities, traits, or work attitudes. There is less uncertainty and defensiveness about the appraisal process because objectives are jointly defined from the start. The method enhances cooperation and communication in the workplace.

Problems with MBO can occur if supervisors and subordinates disagree on performance goals for a given time period. Whose goals become the evaluation criteria? Also, MBO focuses on a number of small, specific accomplishments to the exclusion of broader, less measurable, long-range objectives. Finally, resources must be provided for the attainment of goals. Otherwise, an employee's failure to meet objectives may be due to external forces and performance appraisals become unfair.

Problems With Performance Appraisals

Organizations must be conscientious about using an appraisal technique that is fair, objective, and related to the job requirements of the individual being evaluated. Nevertheless, because performance appraisals are based on human judgment, they are prone to subjectivity and error. In order to make the appraisal process as effective as possible, you will want to be aware of these common problems:

- *Rater's desire to be accepted.* Some people have a great need to be liked and accepted by others, which interferes with a rater's objectivity. In evaluating another employee's job performance, raters with this need inflate ratings in order to be liked by the employee being appraised.
- *Friendship between rater and ratee.* Raters who like the employee being appraised may be favorably biased when observing and evaluating that employee's job performance.
- *Concern with self-protection.* Some raters are reluctant to make negative evaluations of an employee's performance for fear of violent reactions, reprisal, or making their own departments look bad.
- *Fallible memories.* Performance appraisals are often inaccurate because the rater cannot recall important job-related behaviors and has no documentation to jog the memory.
- *Lack of rater motivation.* Some raters dislike conducting performance appraisals and have little motivation to do a competent job. They simply go through the motions or try to complete the process as quickly as possible.
- *Lack of rater skill.* Some appraisers do not have the skills to make an accurate observation and fair judgment; others are unfamiliar with the form of evaluation being used.
- *Little opportunity to observe employees' behavior.* Raters cannot make an accurate appraisal unless they have had ample opportunity to observe emloyees' performance and understand the requirements and constraints of the ratee's job.
- *Discrimination.* Errors occur because of unintentional bias or overt discrimination based on the sex, race, age, religion, or political ideology of the ratee.

Common Rater Errors

There are many documented human errors in the use of evaluation instruments. *The halo effect* occurs when a strong perception of the employee's performance in one area distorts the rater's judgment in other areas. For instance, perceiving an employee as motivated may lead to the erroneous judgment that the employee is competent. *The spillover effect* occurs when conclusions from a past performance appraisal interfere with judgments on the current appraisal. *The status effect* is documentable when people in higher-status jobs automatically receive better ratings than people in lower-status jobs. *The central-tendency effect* refers to raters' judging all employees at the middle or average point on all performance dimensions on a rating scale. Sometimes raters also err by being overly harsh or overly lenient in the evaluation of employees.

While the potential problems with performance appraisals are numerous and discouraging, the desire to develop an effective appraisal system is not futile. Research shows that raters who receive training in how to conduct performance appraisals do a better job than untrained raters do. Organizations committed to the performance-appraisal process should equip appraisers with the knowledge and skills to be effective evaluators.

The Need for Documentation

There are many reasons why performance appraisals should be supported with thorough written documentation. Documentation consisting of notes and files of specific actions during a review period serves as a reminder at the time of a formal appraisal and guides the rater to an accurate judgment. Also, the rater can provide specific examples to clarify points and help employees understand the ratings. Thus, employees know not only how they were rated, but why they received those ratings. When personnel decisions are based on performance reviews, the supervisor with documentation is more likely to receive quick approval for actions. Finally, and perhaps most importantly, proper documentation is imperative when you have to defend job evaluations and decisions legally.

The following guidelines should be followed to achieve proper and thorough documentation:

1. *Be fair.* Do not try to create a slanted case. Document all major job behaviors, not just positive or negative ones. Trying to build a case against an employee or showing favoritism toward an employee will be seen as prejudice. Logically, any employee file should include instances of good and bad behavior.
2. *State facts, not opinions.* The file should include examples of observable behavior, not inferences of attitudes or motives.
3. *Document actions when they occur.* It is important to record actions immediately. Trying to recall actions even after a few weeks will result in inaccurate information.
4. *Keep documentation on all subordinates.* Keeping perfor-

mance records just for poor performers or for certain categories of employees (women, minorities) could be viewed as harassment. It is important to keep thorough and balanced documentation on all employees.

5. *Make documentation consistent with oral comments and actions.* What you write about employees' performance must be consistent with what you tell them and what actions you take. Some supervisors will write negative evaluations but tell employees that they are doing well. Others write a glowing evaluation but fail to recommend a raise or a promotion (which other employees with less satisfactory evaluations may receive).

Legal Considerations

Federal and state employee statutes, as well as court decisions, point to the following nine prescriptions for performance-appraisal practices:

1. The appraisal process should be formalized, standardized, and as objective as possible. Subjective supervisory ratings do not comprise an adequate performance-appraisal process.

2. The criteria in a performance-appraisal method should be as job-related as possible, based on a formal job analysis for all employment positions. Ratings should not be based on attributes of the employee.

3. Appraisal ratings should be uncontaminated (not affected by factors outside of the employee's control) and nondeficient (important aspects of job behavior are not omitted).

4. Employees must be aware of the performance standards to which they will be held accountable.

5. Evaluators should have substantial opportunities to observe job-related behaviors of the employees they appraise.

6. The validity of ratings should be determined. Various types of validity issues affect the adequacy of rating instruments and raters. Organizations whose performance-appraisal systems are questioned must show that ratings are valid reflections of past behavior and valid predictions of future behavior. It is wise to have specialists in psychometric testing document the adequacy of your performance-appraisal system.

7. When possible, more than one rater should be used.

8. Documentation to support ratings should be kept.

9. Employees should have the recourse of a formal appeal process. Because errors can be made, all performance appraisals should be subject to an impartial review. Assure employees that using the appeals process will not result in punitive actions.

The Performance Interview: Feedback to Employees

The performance interview provides an opportunity to review job-related behaviors and performance expectations with the subordinate. The supervisor and subordinate should engage in an honest, two-way discussion about the latter's performance and set performance goals for the future. The interview process can be divided into three phases: preparation, communication, and follow-up.

Preparation

The appraiser should set a time, place, and agenda for the appraisal interview and notify the subordinate of those details. Both parties should have sufficient time to prepare for the appraisal interview. If self-review is part of the process, the employee will need time to complete a self-rating scale or set performance goals, in the case of an MBO approach. The rater must gather necessary data and complete appraisal forms. Find a private and comfortable location, preferably a neutral site, for the session. Allow enough time for both parties to discuss all the points they want to without feeling rushed. The rater should consider how to deliver feedback, how to handle employee reactions, and how to effectively coach for improved work performance.

Communication

Communication during the performance review should follow the guidelines for conducting effective interviews. The supervisor should try to put the employee at ease, discuss the purpose and agenda for the meeting, and then get to the information about job performance. Comments about job performance should be specific and illustrated with examples. Basically, the appraiser evaluates the employees's job performance against objectives and standards that have already been agreed to by the employee. If self-review has occurred, the supervisor and subordinate should examine and try to clarify areas of discrepancy in ratings. Together, in a problem-solving format, the two parties should discern causes for variations in ratings or causes for below-standard results.

The appraiser must be skilled in giving constructive criticism, showing empathy, listening, probing, managing conflict, and avoiding defensiveness. An appraiser skilled in interpersonal communication will be nonthreatening, sensitive, objective, firm, composed, and helpful in the interview.

After communicating ratings on the various dimensions, move on to plans for development. Areas needing improvement should be discussed, one at a time. The supervisor and subordinate should agree on work objectives for the next period and determine how each of them will contribute to the goals. Joint commitment and action for improved performance are a critical part of the appraisal and development process. To conclude the interview, summarize what was discussed, what was agreed to, and what will happen next.

Follow-Up

The rater should record all pertinent information as soon as possible after the interview. This includes an objective account of the information exchanged as well as personal reactions and impressions of the interview climate and tone. Both parties should keep written agreement of the understandings reached, actions planned, and commitments made.

Informal Appraisals

Although the formal performance-appraisal process is a crucial aspect of all organizations, it should exist within a larger appraisal system. It is not enough to give performance feedback only at periodic intervals such as once or twice a year. Informal discussions of job goals and performance results, initiated by either the supervisor or the subordinate, should be a routine part of the supervisor-subordinate relationship. Open communication can make formal appraisals less threatening and focus on performance excellence as an ongoing organizational goal.

[See also Assessment Centers; Coaching Employees; Feedback; Interviewing]

For Additional Information

Bernardin, H. John, and Richard W. Beatty. *Performance Appraisal: Assessing Human Behavior at Work.* Boston: Kent Publishing Company, 1984. A review of research, methodologies, and uses of performance appraisal, as well as an extensive list of references. The emphasis is on developing and validating an appraisal system.

Caroll, Stephen J., and Craig E. Schneier. *Performance Appraisal and Review Systems.* Glenview, Ill.: Scott, Foresman and Company, 1982. Explores the performance-appraisal and -review process in relation to organizational research and theory. The authors discuss performance appraisal as a human resources management activity; performance appraisal criteria, methods, and raters; performance review as feedback; and the administration of a performance-appraisal system.

Clement, Ronald W., and George E. Stevens. "The Performance Appraisal Interview: What, When, and How?" *Review of Public Personnel Administration,* Vol. 6 (1986), No. 2, pp. 43–58. How often to conduct a performance review, what performance criteria to focus on, and what style of interview to use.

Eichel, Evelyn, and Henry E. Bender. *Performance Appraisal: A Study of Current Techniques.* New York: American Management Association, 1984. The results of a survey of management personnel on performance-appraisal practices. Sixty-four pages cover such topics as techniques of appraisal, who participates, problem areas, and the feedback interview.

Henderson, Richard I. *Practical Guide to Performance Appraisal.* Reston, Va.: Reston Publishing Company, 1984. A comprehensive and practical guide for designing and using a performance-appraisal system. Issues of measurement, training, government regulations, and communicating appraisal information are included. The book includes an annotated bibliography of sources, as well as media and training programs on the topic.

Morrisey, George L. *Performance Appraisals in Business and Industry.* Reading, Mass.: Addison-Wesley Publishing Company, 1983. Useful as a text for an organizational training program on performance appraisal or as an individual study guide for managers. Topics cover appraisal models and issues, appraising managers and supervisors, setting performance standards, documentation, and the development interview.

Politics in Organizations

ANYONE WHO IS PART OF A WORKPLACE ORGANIZA-TION is aware of the concept of organizational politics. Intuitively, managers realize the need to have political savvy for surviving and thriving in an organization. But just what is organizational politics? And how does a politically astute manager behave? Being competent at organizational politics means understanding the concept of workplace politics, recognizing the ways that politics function in organizations, and adopting appropriate behaviors to avoid political blunders in your organization.

The concept of being political in a workplace can have various meanings. Managers who are skilled in promoting themselves up the organizational ladder and gaining power can be considered politically shrewd. Being political can mean getting your view, actions, or contributions recognized and accepted. Politically astute employees tend to be well-liked and possess much credibility. They see to it that their ideas are implemented and they have many loyal followers. They have much influence on the organization, regardless of whether or not they hold key leadership positions.

Because of the ways in which organizational politics operate, the concept is somewhat amorphous. Politics is like a persistent but elusive undercurrent in the workplace. It operates with subtlety, below the surface. It is not explicit, and therefore not easy to describe or to grasp. Subtlety is one of the characteristics that makes political behavior successful. Someone who is blatantly trying to influence others or to gain power will meet with resistance. Attempting the same behavior inconspicuously will be more successful. For example, we are aware of the persuasive goal when a colleague is making a presentation in support of a pet project. We assume a critical posture and expect to question the validity of the proposal. The speaker, by being obvious in the influence attempt, will meet with resistance. But subtle attempts at influence, such as repeatedly portraying the project in a good light through brief comments exchanged in the hall or at lunch, may be powerful. Because you see these remarks as informational rather than persuasive, you will be less resistant and gradually become a proponent of the project.

Another characteristic of organizational politics is its pervasiveness. Political undercurrents exist in all organizations, though organizations vary in the extent to which political behavior is explicit and observable. But to deny the existence of politics in a workplace is to be naive. If you think that a political atmosphere does not exist in your organization, then probably you have been overlooking or misinterpreting some signs. Because influence, power, and hierarchical structures characterize organizational life, political behavior is inevitable. Anytime you talk informally in the workplace, you have the opportunity to promote yourself and your projects. Such influence occurs naturally, casually, and almost imperceptibly during interpersonal conversations. If politics entails affecting others' perceptions of us and our work in order to gain credibility and power, then everything we do is political. Managers who understand the nature of politics in their organizations can see its pervasiveness.

In addition to being subtle and pervasive, organizational politics can be positive. Many of us think of workplace politics as devious and manipulative. Some managers leave certain organizations because they find the politics to be too stressful or destructive. But political behavior is not necessarily devious, back-biting actions, which are merely one form of organizational politics. For some reason, workplace politics has come to be equated with self-serving actions that necessarily hurt others or the organization. It is important to realize that organizational politics can be positive. Presenting accurate information behind the scenes to advance yourself or your project is both ethical and appropriate. Perhaps organizational politics become negative when false information is presented, when others are slandered, or when too much political activity interferes with work.

Many would argue that political savvy is necessary for managerial success. Technical competence alone does not ensure career advancement. Competent work, combined with the ability to influence others while not offending them, is the hallmark of successful managers. You must be able to sell yourself and your ideas both publicly and behind the scenes in organizations. Without an understanding of the political dynamics of your organizations, you violate unwritten rules, undermine your own projects, and hinder your credibility and career opportunities.

By realizing the subtle, pervasive, necessary, and often positive nature of organizational politics, you will be well on your way to developing political awareness. Each organization has its own political rules of conduct. By being patient, cautious, and observant, you can learn to recognize and employ behavior that is politically correct for your particular workplace. In addition, there are some general guidelines for practicing organizational politics in most any workplace:

1. *Pay your dues.* You should not expect to receive any favors or support until you have contributed in significant ways to your department or organization. This is especially important advice for organizational newcomers. You earn credibility, support, and the right to influence others by working hard and demonstrating your trustworthiness. By accepting unpleasant tasks, assisting others, and working extra hours initially, you build up a reserve of credit for advancing yourself and your goals later on.

2. *Listen and observe.* Because the political atmosphere is implicit and subtle in most organizations, skills of listening and observing are important. By listening, you can notice who advances what ideas, who supports whom, what subtle suggestions are made, and what topics are awkward. Keen observation can reveal what projects receive high priority, where informal lines of communication occur, and the nature of alliances and animosities. The real power in organizations does not always lie with the visible power holders. By noticing the geographic placement of offices, seating arrangements in meetings, alternate meanings to statements, and the pattern of workplace friendships, you can begin to identify informal power, norms, and expectations.

3. *Understand the people in your organization.* In order to get along with and to influence others, you must pay attention to the personality traits and organizational interests of the political players. Being a good judge of character is an ingredient of political savvy that helps you determine allies and methods of influence. Who are the fence sitters? Who are the opinion leaders? Which colleagues make decisions based on tradition, evidence, cost-effectiveness, or majority sentiment? Some people need to be coaxed, praised, or reassured. Others welcome directness and debate. Some people are risk takers and others are cautious. Still others block every attempt to change. Remember that employees in an organization want to protect their self-interest. By identifying those interests and styles of behavior, you will become skilled at dealing with people.

4. *Identify power sources.* Because organizational politics is so closely tied to power, it is important to appraise the relative power positions of individuals and organizational units. Who makes what

decisions? Who controls what resources? Who has influence with supervisors? Learn to recognize both formal and informal power. For example, those in legitimate positions with the ability to reward or punish others are obviously powerful. But so are those who possess valuable information, indispensable skills, or charismatic personalities. Sometimes the least obvious person wields the most power.

5. *Build partnerships.* Most people operate according to the principle of reciprocal favors. If someone helps, supports, or acts kindly toward you, you are likely to feel obligated to return the favor. Maxims such as "One good turn deserves another" or "Scratch my back and I'll scratch yours" illustrate the reciprocity ethic. Politically wise managers build alliances based on this principle. By supporting each other, two colleagues have more strength as a team than they would individually.

    Two points about the judicious use of this strategy are worth mentioning. First, it is rarely necessary to remind people that they owe you a favor. To make such an explicit statement is to bring the political process to an awkwardly obvious level. It also insults others to imply that they aren't holding up their end of the bargain. Indeed, the best alliances are implicitly understood rather than fully expressed in the first place. The second caution concerns the overuse of predictable alliances. If the work group realizes that two people always side with each other regardless of the issue, the group will discount the partnership.

6. *Never overuse power.* Being blatant with power is a sure way to lose it. Power can be regarded as your ability to influence others minus the others' ability to resist. It is a transaction between people, not an entity one person possesses. A manager who is tyrannical with power will create much resistance. A better approach is to avoid obvious displays of power. Managers, for example, who arbitrarily mandate new procedures for reports often get complaints, refusals, and sabotage from their staff members. By gradually and subtly influencing staff members to see the value of the new procedure instead, you will find compliance and support. Indeed, even in the absence of supervision, the staff will continue to do the reports in the new way because they have internalized your perspective on the issue.

7. *Learn to negotiate.* Politically savvy managers are good negotiators who know when to make concessions and when to hold out. By compromising several smaller points, they can often win on big issues. Effective negotiation involves careful listening, a sensitivity

to nonverbal cues, the strategic use of questions, a knowledge of options, a sense of timing, and a confident style of communication. Negotiation is involved in many aspects of the managerial role. You may find yourself negotiating with supervisors, subordinates, colleagues, potential employees, unions, customers, or vendors. It is inherently a political process because it involves subtle attempts to influence others to gain power or achieve a goal.

8. *Never alienate supervisors.* It is political suicide to alienate supervisors. You do not have to agree completely with everything a supervisor does or says, because such obvious attempts to gain favor would hurt your credibility. But there are various aspects of maintaining a good relationship with supervisors. Never disagree publicly with them, nor create problems that make them look bad to their bosses. Get a supervisor's approval for unusual actions. Always follow the chain of command. Be a team player, not a pest or a constant complainer. Credit the contributions of your boss to your own successes, and thank the supervisor for assisting, supporting, or developing you. Find ways to make your boss look good. Say yes to most requests your boss makes of you.

9. *Develop loyal and competent subordinates.* Being politically astute involves not only interactions with supervisors and colleagues, but also relates to how you treat subordinates. Competent subordinates make you look good. Treating subordinates with respect and fairness will result in a group of loyal supporters. Managers who have good relationships with subordinates can also receive essential information and perceptions from this level.

10. *Be patient.* Developing political awareness takes time. It can't be rushed. Asking someone to acquaint you with the political dynamics of your organization is self-defeating, because the process cannot be articulated clearly; it must be sensed. Also, one person's perspective gives a limited and distorted picture of the political reality. Being patient also means taking time to build a reputation gradually, to influence slowly and subtly, and to acquire power incrementally. Being patient does not mean waiting idly for things to happen. Listen quietly, observe, and unobtrusively build good relationships and alliances, while cultivating competence, trust, and power.

[*See also* Negotiating]

For Additional Information

Beeman, Don R., and Thomas W. Sharkey. "The Use and Abuse of Corporate Politics." *Business Horizons*, Vol. 30 (1987), No. 2, pp.

26–30. Explains the foundations of political behavior, identifies highly political situations, and provides the new manager with tools to deal with negotiating political behaviors.

Block, Peter. *The Empowered Manager: Positive Political Skills at Work.* San Francisco: Jossey-Bass Publishers, 1987. The philosophy and practicality behind the notion of positive politics. Block sees politics as a way of replacing organizational bureaucracy with entrepreneurial spirit and helplessness with empowerment so that we can control organizations rather than be controlled by them. The book presents ways to encourage responsibility and self-expression in subordinates, to implement future visions in organizations, to deal with difficult people, to negotiate successfully, and to deal with organizational realities.

Culbert, Samuel A., and John J. McDonough. *Radical Management: Power Politics and the Pursuit of Trust.* New York: The Free Press, 1985. Ways to monitor the political dimension inherent to all workplace participation. Through numerous work-life vignettes, the authors cover such topics as why people engage in politics, situations promoting politics, management trust, power transactions, team building, leadership, and motivation.

Cummings, Paul W. *Open Management.* New York: AMACOM, 1980, chapter 10, "Power and Politics," pp. 173–184. The ramifications of power and politics and ways to acquire power and to use political techniques effectively.

Macher, Ken. "The Politics of Organizations." *Personnel Journal*, Vol. 65 (1986), No. 2, pp. 81–84. Contends that most people do not enter the work world with the skills necessary for human relations mastery. Organizations must do what they can to promote these attributes. The author discusses four organizational manageable factors that encourage productive human relations.

Payne, Stephen L., and Bernard F. Petting. "Coping with Organizational Politics." *Supervisory Management*, Vol. 31 (1986), No. 4, pp. 28–31. A brief review of what supervisors should know about basic organizational politics in order to survive in a heavily politicized firm.

Yates, Douglas, Jr. *The Politics of Management.* San Francisco: Jossey-Bass Publishers, 1985. Examines organizational politics from the perspective of managing conflict and bureaucracy. Yates discusses public and private organizations, the manager as political detective, political resources, conflict management, and policy-making.

Presentations

PERIODICALLY, MANAGERS must make presentations to internal or external audiences. Internally, you may find yourself speaking to a group of supervisors, subordinates, or colleagues. External audiences include customers, stockholders, the community, or the press. Through presentations, you try to inform, educate, persuade, build consensus, affect decisions, or stimulate action. Whether it is an informal talk to a small group of colleagues or a speech to an audience of hundreds of unfamiliar faces, you need essentially the same skills to make successful presentations.

Overcoming Anxiety and Building Confidence

Most of us, even the most experienced and effective of speakers, feel some amount of anxiety before making a presentation. It is normal to feel some emotional tension when faced with a situation where performance is important and the outcome is uncertain. Minor stage fright can be advantageous. Such normal anxiety creates physiological reactions that you can convert into presentational advantages. For example, fear causes the heart to beat faster and causes more adrenalin to flow through the body. This mental and physical alertness can produce energy for a dynamic and enthusiastic delivery. The secret is not to let speaking anxiety run rampant, but to control and channel it effectively.

The first step in building speaking confidence is to identify the specific causes of anxiety. Inadequate information, audience evaluation, hostile listeners, a weak delivery style, the attention of the spotlight, or question-and-answer sessions can all produce anxiety in a manager who must make a presentation. Some speakers fear that they will bore the audience, make themselves look foolish, appear overly nervous, or forget what they were going to say. By identifying the specific anxiety producers, you are in a better position to cope with anxiety.

Developing an appropriate attitude and relying on some anxiety-prevention strategies can help you build presentational confidence. The following are some general techniques. You can develop other devices for your own unique needs.

1. *Think positively.* Expecting failure will help to produce failure. By focusing on strengths and positive expectations, you will enhance your likelihood of success. Convince yourself that you will give the best presentation you can.

2. *Prepare thoroughly.* Once you have collected your information, organized your thoughts, and rehearsed your talk, anxiety about the presentation subsides. Never take a speaking situation for granted. Careful preparation builds confidence and success.

3. *Analyze the audience.* The more you know about the audience and can predict outcomes, the less nervous you will be. Analyzing the audience means knowing how many people will be present, who they are (gender, age, race, position), how much they know about the topic, why they are attending, and their attitude about you and your information.

4. *Learn to relax.* Techniques such as slow, rhythmic breathing, exercise, self-hypnosis, yoga, or meditation can help you relax. Some speakers take a few minutes before the presentation to think of something pleasant, to go for a walk, to talk to a friend, to sit quietly alone, or to engage in small talk with the audience. Discover whatever relaxation techniques work best for you.

5. *Acquire experience.* As in any hobby or sport, the more you do it, the better you become. Actual speaking experience is the best way to control anxiety and to develop skills. Taking communication courses or volunteering to speak in professional or civic organizations can provide nonthreatening opportunities to practice presentational skills. Analyze your performance and seek improvement after each presentation you make.

Organizing the Message

An organized message is crucial if an audience is to pay attention to, understand, accept, or remember your information. It also enhances your image and credibility. No matter how dynamic your style is, the presentation falls short if the substance of your message is not easy to understand and to follow.

The first step in organizing a presentation is to determine the objective of the message. Every presentation needs a single purpose or central idea. Managers who cannot translate their purpose into a central idea of the presentation tend to ramble and confuse listeners. A central idea is a way to narrow the focus of the presentation topic. For example, a branch bank manager plans a presentation to inform customers about individual retirement accounts. At this point, the topic is determined, but the purpose or central idea is vague. A more specific purpose would be "to convince customers to purchase an individual retirement account by explaining its value and showing them how to open an account."

Once you have determined the purpose, select a few main points to cover in order to achieve it. In the preceding example, the manager may want to include three points regarding the value of individual retirement accounts: current tax savings, favorable interest rates, and the building of retirement income. After determining main points, select facts, examples, statistics, quotes, or stories to explain each point. This is the substantive information of the speech.

Next, outline the main points and supporting information to see that it flows logically. Points may have to be rearranged, or material added or deleted as appropriate. Some people use this outline as notes from which to deliver the presentation. By seeing the arrangement of points, you can plan smooth transitions between ideas. Finally, the presentation needs an introduction and conclusion, important elements that capture attention and provide lasting impressions of you.

By preparing a purpose, main points, supporting information, transitions, outline, introduction, and conclusion, you will present an organized, coherent message. Of all the skills of making presentations, organizing information is probably most crucial to speaking effectiveness.

Delivering the Presentation

Delivery is the packaging of a message. While it is essential to organize a message, the skillful presentation of information is another important ingredient of presentation success. Dynamic delivery keeps an audience's attention and makes listeners more receptive to your ideas. Excessive delivery problems can undermine your credibility and information.

One way to improve presentation style is to realize common

pitfalls managers encounter when making presentations. Examine this list of presentation errors to identify your own potential problems.

- Monotone voice
- Filled pauses
- Speaking too softly
- Speaking too quickly
- Distracting gestures
- Stiff, tense posture
- Lack of eye contact with listeners
- Mispronounced words
- Dependence on notes
- Nervous habits
- Ignoring audience cues
- Losing train of thought
- Pacing

With practice, speakers tend to get better at delivering messages. There are a few strategies for achieving the dynamic delivery of ideas:

1. *Be dynamic.* A lively, energetic speaker is much easier to listen to than a slow, deliberate one. As a speaker, you should try to be outgoing and enthusiastic. This means speaking loudly, using vocal variety, and keeping the pace moving. A confident, prepared speaker can be more dynamic than a nervous, tentative one. Making presentations, at any level to any audience, involves a degree of showmanship. Listeners will pay attention to presentations that are interesting and enjoyable.

2. *Be conversational.* The best speaking style mimics ordinary conversation. Formal or pompous styles of talking strain listener concentration. Listeners will be captivated if they feel that the speaker is addressing them individually. To be conversational, voice tones should be informal, relaxed, and familiar. Avoid sounding as if you are lecturing or reciting information.

3. *Use appropriate physical movement.* Making an effective presentation involves nonverbal techniques as well as vocal ones. Natural gestures can illustrate or emphasize a point. Awkward or repetitive gestures can be distracting. Physical movement can parallel the movement through ideas in a presentation. Casually walking through the audience can capture attention and create an atmosphere of friendliness and informality. Remaining behind a podium or stiffly clinging to notes can undermine speaking effectiveness.

4. *Be fluent.* Speaking effortlessly and with grace captivates an audience and enhances your image. Successful presenters do not stum-

ble over words, lose their train of thought, or clutter their talk with meaningless vocalizations. For many speakers, being fluent means eliminating words like "um," "ah," "OK," and "you know" from their delivery. By being aware of such pet, distracting words and by being comfortable with silent pauses, you can develop a fluent speaking style.

5. *Give eye contact throughout the audience.*   Plan to have eye contact with every listener. Even in large audiences, you can scan all sections of the audience rather than looking just in the center. Eye contact during a presentation serves many purposes. It shows a speaker's confidence, credibility, and sincerity. It lets listeners feel that you are speaking directly to each and every one of them. It allows you to get feedback from the audience. By looking directly at all listeners, you can see signs of boredom, confusion, or disagreement. The effective speaker then adjusts to accommodate the audience mood.

6. *Use notes effectively.*   Good speakers usually speak from limited, unobtrusive notes. Notes should serve only as a guide to the arrangement of ideas. Occasionally, they may include information, such as a statistic or quotation, which the presenter wants to deliver verbatim. Managers who use extensive notes or complete manuscripts often fall into the trap of reading from the notes. Reading information is not the same as presenting a message. Too much dependence on notes is a sure way of putting an audience to sleep.

7. *Do not call attention to your delivery.*   The best presentation delivery is unnoticed. A speaking style that calls attention to itself defeats its purpose. Delivery is merely the mechanism for getting ideas across. The audience should be concentrating on the ideas, not the delivery style. If listeners are paying attention to the delivery, then you are probably using a distracting habit.

Choosing the Appropriate Language

To be effective, use words that are clear, specific, inoffensive, and vivid. In written communication, the reader can check the meaning of an unfamiliar word or reread a passage until it makes sense, but it is your responsibility to make sure that listeners understand the language in a presentation. That means avoiding specialized terms or jargon unless the audience understands it. If you must use jargon, take the time to define the technical or unfamiliar term. Simple, concise ways to make points are needed in oral presentations. Avoid long, complex sentences and eloquent displays of vocabulary.

Other devices for achieving clarity include sequencing words, transition words, and frequent summaries. Words such as "first," "second," "next," and "finally" help the listener follow your movement through a sequence of ideas. Such sequencing words reveal the pattern of organization of ideas. Transition words show the relationship of ideas. Words such as "however," "on the other hand," and "similarly" help orient the listener to your points. Presentations need enough restatement to emphasize points and to assist listeners' recall. A few well-placed internal summaries as well as a final summary can help the audience to grasp and remember your information.

In addition to using clear language, you should also use specific language whenever possible in a presentation. Instead of saying, "We will know our budget allocations soon," say "We expect to know our budget allocation by July 1." Besides spelling out the meaning of ambiguous terms, being specific also means giving examples to illustrate a point. Instead of saying, "This company cares about employees," say "This company has established flexible benefits, a complaint procedure, and a new lunchroom because it cares about employees."

Choose your words carefully to avoid offending listeners. This means avoiding sexist language, racial slurs, ethnic aspersions, or remarks that would provoke defensiveness. Also, certain subtly offensive words hinder your purpose. For example, asking a group "Would anyone be willing to serve on a committee to plan the spring meeting?" discourages response. However, asking "Would anyone like the opportunity to help plan the spring meeting?" will invite more volunteers.

Vivid language is descriptive and captivating. It paints a picture for the listener. It uses active rather than passive words. Note the difference between these two sentences: "The report was done by us." "We did the report." Perhaps a more exciting verb, such as "prepared" or "completed," would make the sentence even more vivid. "Profits soared" is more exciting than "profits rose." "Diversified and increased attendance occurred this year" sounds boring and vague. "Hundreds of new people attended this year" is a more descriptive and vivid alternative.

Give careful thought to your word choice in presentations. Clear, specific, inoffensive, and vivid language will capture attention, emphasize points, and spur listeners to action.

Using Visual Aids

Most business presentations call for the use of visual aids. Frequently, you place crucial information on flip charts, transparencies, or slides to include in a presentation. Some information, especially numerical data, is difficult to grasp except in visual form. Talking about accident rates over a ten-year period will overwhelm listeners, but showing those rates in a graph presented on a transparency, for example, will allow you to highlight points and the audience to study the information. A chart to show redesigns in the organizational structure or sales growth will have more impact than words alone. Slides or a video showing a foreign manufacturing location go far beyond a mere verbal description.

As a speaker, you should determine whether visual aids will enhance a presentation, the best form of a visual aid, and the effective use of visual material. Visuals will enhance a talk if they allow you to accomplish something you could not achieve through words alone. To visually present a few key words from a presentation will probably detract from rather than enhance a talk. Unless the words represent technical jargon, there is no reason to display them. When considering visuals, determine their purpose. If you cannot identify a specific purpose, then they are probably unnecessary. Another method for determining whether you should use visual aids is to assess their potential benefit in relation to the cost of preparation. For example, slides that are expensive and time-consuming to prepare are not worth the effort unless they make a significant impact on the presentation. Putting some figures on a flip chart may be worth the minimal effort involved, even if their impact is not great. Remember that visuals should aid a presentation. If they add nothing but time to the talk, then they are a hindrance.

Once you decide that visuals will aid your presentation, it is important to select the appropriate form of visual material. The type you use will depend on your speaking purpose, the nature of the information you are presenting visually, the size of your audience, and your visual resources. An informative presentation to a few colleagues will not require an elaborate use of visuals. A slide presentation in this situation is inappropriate. On the other hand, convincing potential investors to support a new project suggests the use of professionally prepared visual material as opposed to a few figures scrawled on a flip chart.

Certain information lends itself to particular forms of visual presentation. Illustrating a distribution system may require a map; a film may be needed to show how a piece of equipment operates; and a chart may be the best way to show operating costs. Give careful consideration to the most effective means of presenting information. In many ways, choosing the right method of visual presentation is a matter of common sense. The information itself suggests the best visual medium.

Suppose that you have decided to use a graph to present some financial information. Should you provide that graph on a flip chart, a transparency, or a slide? The audience size will dictate a method. An audience of more than twenty will not be able to see a flip chart. An audience of about 100 will be able to see carefully prepared transparencies displayed on a large screen. With groups larger than 100, slides should be used.

Finally, in terms of selecting visual aids, consider your available resources. Do you have the time, the money, or the professional assistance for producing slides? Is it possible to have a videotape produced professionally? Perhaps someone with excellent printing skills could draw flip charts by hand. It is better to use less sophisticated methods such as flip charts or transparencies than to create sloppy or amateur slide or video presentations. Remember that visuals must not be distracting nor call attention to themselves in any way.

You must be skilled in the use of visual aids. While it is important that visuals be selected and prepared carefully, they must be presented effectively as well. Even professionally prepared visual material will fail if you do not know how to use the material. The following are some guidelines for the use of any type of visual aid in a presentation:

1. *Check legibility.* Visual material should be large, bold, and simple. Excessive amounts of information, small printing, or delicate drawings cannot be seen even from a short distance. Light color markers on flip charts or transparencies do not show up well. After preparing a visual, test its legibility by positioning yourself at the back of the presentation room. If you cannot easily see the visual from there, then an audience member in that position will not be able to see it either.

2. *Have all materials with you at the time of presentation.* Many a presentation has been ruined by a missing chart, by the lack of an extension cord to run the slide projector, or by a marker that has run out of ink. Never search for materials during a presentation or leave the podium to retrieve anything. A practice session using the visuals aids will alert you to any malfunctioning equipment or missing material. Some speakers have backup equipment or materials just in case.

3. *Don't block the view of visual aids.* You must be able to refer to visual material without standing in front of it or looking at it rather than at the audience. Practice standing to the side of a flip chart and using a pointer. Become proficient at using overlays or pointers with overhead transparencies. Credibility plummets and distractions

abound when a speaker is not smooth and natural in the use of
visual material.

4. *Plan time appropriately.*   Visuals add time to a presentation. It is
   essential to determine how much time you will need for showing
   visual material. Give the group enough time to see, and in some
   cases to study, the visual material. You can quickly pace a slide
   presentation, where the impact comes from the total show rather
   than from any one slide. You need to display financial charts or
   graphs, on the other hand, for a long enough time for the audience
   to examine them.

5. *Make the visual aid secondary to the presentation.*   Visuals assist,
   but do not replace, a speaker. Some speakers fall into the trap of
   becoming narrators. Their entire presentation is nothing more than
   a series of visuals, with them announcing or reading from one. Do
   not plan to use visuals for more than half of a presentation. Orient
   listeners to a visual presentation and summarize after showing the
   visual material. Remember that the visual material is not the presentation, but merely an aid.

Handling Questions

It is a rare business presentation where the speaker is not called
on to answer questions. For most managerial presentations, the question-and-answer session is more important than the prepared talk.
Listeners will ask for more information, seek clarification, or challenge
the validity of information. In presentations that seek to persuade or to
stimulate action, questioners challenge assumptions, offer opposing
views, expose errors, or undermine speaker credibility.

Handling questions is the more difficult part of a presentation.
You can never be as thoroughly prepared for this aspect of speaking as
you can be for the planned remarks. There is always some element of
the unexpected in question-and-answer sessions. Inevitably, you lose
some of the control to the audience. On the positive side, if you can
handle listeners' questions effectively, you have passed a major hurdle
to the success of your presentation. Nothing builds your credibility
more than confidently and professionally handling a difficult question-
and-answer session. Follow these guidelines for becoming skilled at
fielding audience questions:

1. *Anticipate questions.*   Most questions are typical and can be expected to emerge from a certain topic or from a particular audience.
   Put yourself in the place of your audience. What questions would

you be likely to ask? By analyzing the common fears, assumptions, needs, or problems that listeners experience, you can identify likely questions. Anticipating probable questions is largely a matter of audience analysis. By thinking about the perspectives, values, and personalities of your listeners, you can anticipate issues and questions.

2. *Always repeat the question.* This will allow the entire group to hear the question. It is annoying for the audience to listen to a speaker give an answer to a question they did not hear. Repeating the question allows you to see if you understood the question correctly. Finally, it provides you some time to frame a response.

3. *Keep answers short and simple.* Remember that what is important to one person may be boring to the rest of the group. If the questioner wants detailed information and you can see signs of disinterest from the rest of the group, plan to discuss the question privately after the session or to send additional information to the questioner later. Providing short and simple answers keeps the pace moving. Question-and-answer sessions should not be tedious dialogues or debates but should provide a means for any listener to get quick clarification or a bit of additional information.

4. *Discourage monopolizers.* Never allow one person to ask several questions if there are others who have not had a chance to ask a question. It may be necessary to interrupt the monopolizer diplomatically. Say something like "You're raising some interesting points, but in the interest of time, let's move on to some other questions."

5. *Realize that some questions cannot be answered.* You cannot be expected to have answers to all questions that could possibly be asked. It is appropriate to say that you do not have that particular information. You might suggest an alternative information source to the questioner or promise to provide information as soon as possible. Never fake an answer. It is always more credible to admit a lack of information than to bluff or to provide misinformation. In some cases, you do not want to answer a question because it is sensitive or embarrassing. Gracefully sidestepping a question requires skill, but there are some techniques for the beginner. You can talk generally about the topic of the question without directly addressing the specific question. You can answer a slightly different question. You can indicate that because of a certain circumstance you are not at liberty to discuss the question right now.

6. *Maintain your composure.* Some people will ask irrelevant or hostile questions. Others will use the session as a forum to state

their own views. Some will attempt to sabotage your plan or your credibility. It is imperative that you remain friendly, calm, and composed in these situations. Do not argue, blame, threaten, preach, or ridicule. Do not become defensive, hostile, or attacking. You must remain confident, professional, and in charge of your emotions during a hostile question-and-answer session.

[See also Nonverbal Communication]

For Additional Information

Elsea, Janet G. "Strategies for Effective Presentations," *Personnel Journal*, Vol. 64, No. 9 (1985), pp. 31–34. Strategies to help managers prepare themselves and their remarks for a variety of audiences and situations.

Holcombe, Marya W., and Judith K. Stein. *Presentations for Decision Makers.* Belmont, Calif.: Lifetime Learning Publications, 1983. Designed to help managers develop and deliver effective oral presentations. Chapters cover audience analysis, organizing information, rehearsing and delivering presentations, using visuals, managing logistics, and speaking in contexts such as meetings, negotiations, panels, and videoconferences. Many checklists and worksheets are included.

Martel, Myles. *Before You Say a Word: The Executive Guide to Effective Communication.* Englewood Cliffs, N.J.: Prentice-Hall, 1984. Covers the basics of image, language, speech organization and delivery, visual aids, audience questions, and speech anxiety. Martel also provides information on speaking to the media and speaking in specialized contexts. The section on media covers press relations, news conferences, and crisis communications. Specialized contexts include meetings, teleconferences, executive testimony, debates, and panels.

Shea, Gordon. *Managing a Difficult or Hostile Audience.* Englewood Cliffs, N.J.: Prentice-Hall, 1984. Techniques for dealing with audiences and groups that are hostile, fearful, apathetic, bored, or negative. Chapters cover such topics as reading the audience, handling emotions, diffusing tension, listening, resolving conflict, maintaining the right attitude, and dealing with indifference.

Vanoosting, James. *The Business Speech: Speaker, Audience, and Text.* Englewood Cliffs, N.J.: Prentice-Hall, 1985. Examines the composition, delivery, and image of business speeches; the communication principles that govern public speaking in a business setting; and the practical aspects of persuading, convention planning, ghostwriting, introducing others, accepting awards, entertaining, selling, demonstrating, explaining, motivating, and oral reporting. Sample speeches, exercises, and critique forms are included.

Public Relations

PUBLIC RELATIONS (PR) involves the communication of accurate information about an organization in order to enhance the image, growth, and survival of that organization. Public relations involves the sending and receiving of information with individuals and groups who affect and are affected by the organization: employees, unions, customers, distributors, the community, stockholders, the media, and the government.

The image of the PR field and its functions have changed in recent years in light of far-reaching transformations in the social, political, economic, and business environments.

Public relations is a complex and vital function for any organization, large or small. To a large extent, the public relations manager or department coordinates the organization's responses to the social, political, economic, and business communities. Managers at all levels need to be aware of public relations objectives and must realize that they too carry the organization's image to the public. Progressive organizations orient their managers to the new business environment while encouraging them to make decisions and to demonstrate behavior consistent with the company's image. Managers are the organization's ambassadors; they, not just the PR department or the chief executive officer (CEO), must be responsible for promoting the company's image and reputation.

The following general orientation to the field of PR and its various aspects provides information that can help an organization develop or enhance its PR function, help acquaint management with its role in PR, and help public relations specialists better understand their job responsibilities. Seven aspects of PR will be discussed: media relations, community relations, customer relations, employee and labor relations, financial relations, government relations, and crisis management.

Media Relations

This aspect of PR involves communicating to the press, handling press inquiries, preparing others in the organization to interact with the media, and working with the advertising department on ads that fulfill a public relations role. The PR manager may write and disseminate news releases or feature articles on corporate social-responsibility programs, technical or environmental achievements, positions on legislative action, employee accomplishments, or human interest items. It is important to develop an extensive and up-to-date network of media contacts. The PR manager becomes the clearinghouse for information about the organization, prepares that information for media consumption, and knows the people to whom the information should be forwarded.

The PR manager often acts as the organization's spokesperson in print and broadcast media inquiries. PR specialists appear on televised news programs, entertainment or magazine shows, or talk shows to communicate with the public about almost any aspect of their organization. They also grant studio or taped interviews, make prepared statements for the news, or participate in call-in shows on the radio. PR specialists grant interviews to print journalists and represent the organization's interests in newspaper and magazine articles. Likewise, if the company has some information of interest to all the media, the PR manager will coordinate a news conference.

Sometimes the media want access to top-level executives in the company. In that case, the PR manager may work with CEOs or other top management to prepare them for radio or television appearances. Such executive coaching is especially important when the media or public is critical of the company. The PR manager may hire an outside consultant specializing in preparing executives for media appearances.

Finally, in terms of media relations, the PR manager may be called on to coordinate institutional or issues advertising with the organization's advertising department or agency. While advertising is not a function of public relations, some types of ads fulfill a PR role. Institutional ads promote a company's image by highlighting its history, achievements, or civic contributions. Issues advertising is a type of advocacy in which the organization states its position on some controversial topic. Because these advertising vehicles involve public relations goals, the PR manager should have input into them.

Community Relations

This aspect of PR involves the cultivation of a good business-community relationship. Because organizations need the physical and human resources of the communities in which they are located, they must be concerned with the health and prosperity of the communities. It is not only a sound ethical practice but a good business practice to be a responsible member of the community. The PR manager plays a vital role in community relations by coordinating and publicizing such organizational activities as corporate philanthropy and sponsorship, leadership in community-improvement projects, employee participation in social and civic groups, and cooperation with local government and educational institutions. In large organizations, a separate community relations specialist may coordinate these projects. The public relations manager must work closely with this person; however, the PR specialist would likely be responsible for publicizing, if not spearheading, community activities.

The business world realizes its responsibility to contribute to charitable organizations and encourage employees' charitable donations as well. Likewise, small companies and large corporations alike typically sponsor cultural, athletic, and recreational activities of the community and frequently provide funds and personnel to such community projects as neighborhood rehabilitation, child care, youth training or employment projects, and recreational programs. Many organizations encourage employees to join social and civic groups and to participate in local government. Wise organizations also make their facilities and personnel available to educational groups through company tours and speakers' bureaus. It is the job of the PR manager to apprise management of these obligations, help carry them out, and coordinate the company's information regarding all aspects of community affairs.

Customer Relations

An organization's products or services provide the direct link between the organization and the public. What a customer says about a company is probably the biggest influence on the company's image. Customer satisfaction, then, is the foundation of effective public relations. While the PR manager is not directly responsible for customer relations, a concern for customers must be part of a PR objective. People who purchase directly from a company are not the only "customers" whom organizations must court; consumer affairs groups, dealers, distributors, retailers, contractors, and suppliers also interact with a company and shape its reputation.

While most organizations will have separate customer relations or consumer affairs departments, the PR manager often must act as a liaison to and help with the publicity activities of those departments.

Thus, it is important that the PR specialist have an understanding of customer and consumer relations.

Many organizations take an active role in educating customers about product information, health and safety concerns, and consumer rights options. This may be done through owners' manuals, pamphlets, audio/videotapes, speakers, or training seminars. Likewise, progressive companies solicit customer feedback through surveys, hot lines, comments cards, and panel discussions. Two-way communication and the satisfactory handling of complaints strengthens the buyer-seller relationship, which makes the company look good and increases its profits. An effective public relations manager helps others in the organization see the relationship between customer relations and public relations.

Dealers, distributors, retailers, contractors, and suppliers are a customer segment that must be informed, supported, and listened to. Frequently, organizations will provide liaison personnel, brochures, sales literature, newsletters, and audio/videotapes to these groups to enhance relationships and promote the company's image.

The PR manager may be directly responsible for preparing customer-oriented news stories about new products or services; representing the company position to consumer activists; presenting statements about pending consumer-rights legislation; or communicating with the media in the event of a product recall, boycott, or liability suit. The PR specialist helps the company coordinate actions affecting consumers with overall public relations objectives.

Employee and Labor Relations

Organizations are developing a heightened sense of employees as a "public." Indeed, employees are a conduit through which organizational information reaches the larger community. The field of employee and labor relations uses knowledge of human behavior to improve the employer-employee relationship. Public relations departments can help promote the exchange of accurate information between employees, labor leaders, and management. By helping to build good employee communication, the public relations manager influences the positive image employees carry to their families, friends, and neighbors—all of whom are potential customers.

The public relations manager may be responsible for internal communication or may cooperate with the employee and labor relations specialist in promoting communication with employees. In either case, organizations use a variety of means to promote the exchange of internal information, including employee newsletters, magazines, handbooks, manuals, internal television programming, personal letters, meetings, and hot lines. Where many of these sources used to focus exclusively on social information such as promotions, retirements, marriages, births, and company recreational events, they now include information about substantive issues affecting the organization. Internal public relations means keeping employees informed about company plans for growth, new products or discoveries, economic news relating to the company, government regulations, employee training opportunities and benefits, key personnel changes, and company involvement in community affairs. Likewise, an employee feedback program is necessary for employee trust and satisfaction. Attitude surveys, quality circles, suggestion boxes, hot lines, and face-to-face communication give employees the chance for input. The effective exchange of information with employees provides a building block to a comprehensive public relations program.

There is another area of employee and labor relations that directly pertains to public relations: the dissemination of information during layoffs, contract negotiations, and strikes. The public relations manager may be called to issue statements to employees, the community, and the press during personnel cutbacks. The public relations manager typically presents information about progress in labor negotiations, being careful not to jeopardize those discussions or violate legal guidelines. Finally, the public relations manager usually acts as a company spokesperson during labor strikes. So in many ways, employee and labor relations impinge on the public relations function in modern organizations.

Financial Relations

Most organizations release some information about their financial condition. Public institutions have greater responsibilities in this area than do private organizations. They must communicate with stockholders and meet legal requirements for financial disclosure set forth by the Securities and Exchange Commission. A corporation's annual meeting and annual report serve not only a financial function, but a public relations function as well. While company financial officers, legal counsel, and investor relations departments handle these functions, the wise public relations manager realizes their potential as vehicles for developing positive attitudes in the financial community. The public relations specialist may also issue statements or write press releases concerning company acquisitions and mergers.

Government Relations

All businesses must be concerned with government decisions. Legislation regulates business and affects its bottom line. As a result, organizations have a role in informing legislators of their position on issues, and they communicate with government as one of their "publics" in many ways. Organizations work with industry councils or professional organizations for legislative counseling or lobbying. Lobbyists carry business information to government officials in the attempt to influence legislation. They also transmit information from government officials back to corporate executives. In essence, they act as ambassadors of goodwill, communicating an organization's image to the government and to the public at large. Although lobbying is handled by public affairs departments in organizations, the public relations manager must be aware of its impact.

The public relations department may also have a role in explaining a company's need for involvement with political action committees (PACs) to employees via internal communication media. The PR department may cooperate with the employee relations and public affairs departments to educate and involve employees in government advocacy and political issues. The PR function can be instrumental in changing negative perceptions about the relationship of government and business to society. Finally, public relations specialists sometimes assist business leaders who are called on to testify at government hearings. While the public relations job does not encompass public affairs duties, it is important to realize the inter-relationship between PR and government.

Crisis Management

Another aspect of public relations involves the ability to deal with the communication problems that occur during emergency situations. Types of crises organizations face include industrial accidents, product tampering, product failures, damaging rumors, boycotts, or well-publicized litigation. Anytime a company receives negative publicity, the situation should be considered a crisis. A company's ability to handle a crisis and restore public confidence can affect its very survival.

The public relations department has a direct role in crisis management. Before a crisis develops, the public relations manager should develop a plan to follow in the event of an emergency. A company credo of management philosophy and social responsibility can provide a foundation. In a crisis, the public relations function may have to set up a 24-hour press office, staff hot lines to handle calls from the public, and coordinate communication with the public, the media, senior management, the legal department, security, employees, the union, federal agencies, and community leaders. A crisis calls for the widespread and immediate dissemination of accurate information by the public relations department in order to preserve an organization's good image.

The Public Relations Specialist

As the many diverse aspects of the field reveal, public relations specialists must have numerous skills to perform several vital functions in an organization. PR managers contribute to corporate policy-making, collect information to survey attitudes and reactions, communicate with various publics, coordinate communication among various groups, and prepare other organizational personnel to act as company spokespersons.

PR specialists must possess numerous skills including newswriting and editing, technical writing, broadcast media production, graphic design and layout, public speaking, persuasion, group dynamics, and interpersonal communication. They must understand all the aspects of business, be good managers, possess excellent communication skills, and get along well with people.

Some large organizations with broad PR needs hire public relations generalists who can use the services of consultant specialists in aspects of PR such as crisis management, financial relations, government relations, or special promotions. On the other hand, some small organizations take care of all their PR needs through external PR consultants or agencies. Whatever the method, it is imperative that organizations appreciate the complexity and importance of the PR function and that managers realize their role in promoting a positive image of their organization.

[See also Corporate Social Responsibility; Presentations]

For Additional Information

Gray, James G., Jr. *Managing the Corporate Image.* Westport, Conn.: Quorum Books, 1986. Guidelines for defining, setting up, administering, and evaluating a corporate image program. The book includes advice, case studies, and research on media, employee, community, consumer, and government relations, as well as crisis management.

Jefkins, Frank. *Public Relations for Management Success.* London: Croon Helm, 1984. The role of management in PR, the costs of PR, setting up a PR department, and assessing the results of PR. Jefkins covers special aspects of PR such as crisis management, employee relations, PR for the professions, financial and political PR, and PR consultants.

Moore, George Stanley. *Managing Corporate Relations*. Westmead, England: Gower Press, 1980. The PR function as it relates to modern management practices, with emphasis on measurable objectives. The book covers the various aspects of PR as well as PR resources, actions, and responsibilities.

Sperber, Nathaniel N., and Otto Lerbinger. *Manager's Public Relations Handbook*. Reading, Mass.: Addison-Wesley Publishing Company, 1982. A handbook of information and action checklists for both the general manager and the public relations professional. Topics include crisis communication, media relations, consumer affairs, community relations, financial relations, special events, social responsibility, executive media exposure, and running a PR office.

Quality

REALIZING THAT PRODUCING THE HIGHEST-QUALITY PRODUCTS AND SERVICES IS IMPERATIVE TO STAYING IN BUSINESS, ORGANIZATIONS OF ALL TYPES have developed a renewed emphasis on quality. That focus may have emerged because of the threat of foreign competition, because customers increasingly demand satisfaction, or because most successful businesses tout quality as the secret to their success.

Certainly everyone is an advocate of quality. It is difficult to imagine an executive, manager, or employee at any level who would claim to be against quality. But what does quality mean? In order to embrace quality as a business philosophy or as a managerial practice, we must understand the concept.

What Is Quality?

When we think of quality, we think of excellence. Quality means meeting the highest standards, conforming to requirements, performing as expected, and preventing problems or errors. An organization dedicated to quality produces perfect products or services on the first try. Quality does not mean correcting problems after they occur or allowing a certain margin of error in production or service.

In most organizations, a short-sighted and costly definition of quality has evolved. Quality has come to be synonymous with inspection to pinpoint defects or problems and a system of correction so that a small rate of error is tolerated, which, ironically, promotes the absence of quality. Look at how quality-control systems as the only means of ensuring quality tend to operate in organizations. Quality-control systems maintain a desired level of quality in a product or process by carefully planning, inspecting, and taking corrective action where required.

The Costs of Lack of Quality

An inspection or correction approach to quality is costly. Whenever work must be redone to be corrected, the organization has incurred double costs: the cost to do the job the first time and the cost to redo it. Errors in production or services can result in exorbitant costs associated with warranty replacements, product liability suits, product recalls, malpractice suits, consumer actions, or lost customers.

Then there is the cost of having a team of inspectors to check all work. It seems wasteful to have a group of employees whose sole job is to spot mistakes and bring them to the attention of the people who made the mistakes. A more cost-efficient approach would be to teach employees how to perform the job right in the first place and how to prevent mistakes. At the very least, employees could be taught how to spot their own mistakes early enough to make correction easier and less costly.

Inspection or correction approaches to quality can even undermine quality. If you knew that someone would carefully check your work and bring problems to your attention, would you not become a bit complacent and careless about quality standards? A proactive, preventive approach makes more sense than a reactive, corrective philosophy. It is always easier to prevent problems before they happen than to try to correct them once they happen.

Emphasizing quality not only saves money but can also be the key to making or breaking a business. Customers naturally gravitate to the product or service that best meets their needs. From a customer standpoint, quality means that the product or service does what it is supposed to do consistently and without exception. If the product or service does not provide 100 percent satisfaction to customers, they will turn to your competitor. In the long run, the cost of not providing quality means going out of business. Even organizations that traditionally have not had strong marketing orientations, such as hospitals, banks, and universities, now realize the relationship of quality to organizational survival.

Developing Quality

There are some steps organizations can follow to develop a culture of quality. Throughout an organization, in many cases, it means changing the entire culture of the organization. Creating a system-wide philosophy and implementation plan for quality takes time. Quality is not produced just because we espouse it or reward it. All of the following steps must be implemented over a long period of time so that quality becomes the norm rather than the exception in organizations.

1. *Develop a system-wide commitment to quality.* Employees at all levels must begin to think about the meaning and importance of quality. They must see it not as a luxury but as a necessity. Some organizations make the mistake of expecting quality from hourly employees or from the manufacturing function without realizing the importance of quality at higher levels and in all functions. Every employee in the organization must develop a sense of pride in absolute standards of excellence. No employee should tolerate the slightest deviance from standards. Although creating such a system-wide vision is no easy task, total quality cannot be achieved without total commitment.

2. *Set standards and requirements for quality.* It is impossible to reach quality standards unless we know precisely what they are. For every job, a standard of excellence must be defined in quantifiable terms, wherever possible. For example, a quality operation in a hotel might be defined in this way: All guest rooms must be cleaned by 3 P.M., guests must be helped by a reservation clerk within ten minutes of their arrival, room-service deliveries should be made within thirty minutes of placement of the order, and the hotel operator must answer the phone within the first three rings. Such standards should be developed for every aspect of every job.

3. *Collectively create and communicate standards.* Because they are in the best position to know what reasonable standards are, employees should participate in the development of standards for their jobs. This way, they will understand the requirements, be more committed to achieving them, and be better able to help co-workers in their units meet standards of quality. This is teamwork at its best.

   It is imperative that employees know the precise standards they are to achieve. It is unfair to hold employees accountable to standards that are vague or unknown. The training function, supervisors, managers, and experienced employees can be resources for communicating quality standards throughout the organization.

4. *Provide the necessary tools for achieving quality.* Cheerleading about quality and establishing requirements for it are just one part of the process. Stopping here will merely frustrate employees. It is futile to motivate employees about quality and to communicate standards of quality without providing the tools for achieving it.

There are various tools. Traditional systems of quality control, already in place in many organizations, are one tool for maintaining quality. But keep in mind that quality control is just a tool, not a complete system, for achieving excellence. Also, quality-control procedures are applied only to technical, and not to managerial, jobs in many organizations. To be effective, quality-control systems must apply to all functions in an organization.

Some companies have turned to statistical quality control as a means of preventing problems. Each variable in a process is identified and then tracked or measured throughout the process. When a variable starts to deviate from requirements or go out of control, adjustments are made to bring it back in line. In this way, problems are identified as they initially emerge and are corrected before the product or service is produced.

The tools for achieving quality in many cases involve creating an adequate size staff for each unit. Consider the hotel management example discussed earlier. What does it take to get rooms cleaned on time, guests served on time, and telephones answered on time? Besides the existing staff operating efficiently, a larger staff may be necessary to provide impeccable service. Management must be committed to providing adequate resources to make excellence attainable.

Another tool for achieving quality is education or training. Employees at all levels need to acquire information and to develop skills to produce excellence. In other words, they need training to do their jobs without error. Management needs to learn how to implement quality-improvement programs. Even senior-level executives need education about their role in promoting and achieving quality. By teaching everyone to do their jobs more accurately and more conscientiously, organizations can achieve quality.

Many companies have turned to quality-circles programs as a way to both create standards of quality and equip employees with the skills for producing it. Quality-circles programs build teamwork, improve communication, increase commitment to quality, and solve problems before they become unmanageable. They help spread the concept of quality throughout the entire organization.

There are many other tools for helping employees produce excellent products and services. Businesses must examine their own quality standards and existing resources to identify the tools they need to bring about quality. Quality-control procedures, additional human resources, training and education of the work force, and quality-circles programs are a few of the common means of promoting quality.

5. *Measure quality.*   In order to determine whether quality standards are being met, measurement or assessment must take place. Periodically, you should compare work produced to quality standards to see how it measures up. Every work procedure must have its own standards of measurement, which must be applied often. This is the only way to determine whether quality is being achieved. If such assessment is a regular and routine part of all jobs, it will not be threatening to employees. Keep thorough data on the rate of compliance to standards throughout the organization.

6. *Reward quality.*   When assessments show that standards are being met, recognize and reward the achievement. People or units meeting quality standards should be singled out for praise, visibility, and rewards of some type. Examples of excellence can serve as models for the entire organization. Once employees realize that their company recognizes and rewards excellence, they will be motivated to excel.

7. *Coach for improvement.*   Where assessments show that quality standards are not being met, you must direct efforts at coaching for improved performance. Your organization must never tolerate failure to meet standards, nor should it lower them to accommodate areas of weakness. Individuals whose work fails to meet quality requirements should receive coaching, training, or other types of assistance to improve the quality of their work. Management should examine whether there are constraints affecting employees' abilities to meet quality requirements. You may have to discharge employees whose work consistently fails to meet standards despite ample assistance.

8. *Keep the entire process operating throughout the system.*   Quality can never be taken for granted. The entire process for developing and implementing quality must be ongoing if quality is to be maintained. It is not enough to follow the seven preceding steps just once. The workplace organization is dynamic: new jobs emerge, the composition of employees changes, and new requirements develop. Organizations should continually cycle through the various steps so that the emphasis on quality becomes perpetual.

Pitfalls in Achieving Quality

Many organizations have failed to institute quality because they have taken the wrong paths. Halfhearted attempts at quality improvement that doom themselves to failure should not be seen as indictments of the entire concept of quality in workplace organizations. Organizations can achieve consistently high quality by implementing the complete process of quality improvement and by avoiding these six pitfalls:

1. *Concentrating on intentions only.* It is a myth that asking for quality or promising quality will produce it. We all have good intentions about the quality of our work, but intentions play a very small part in the creation of quality. Thus, defining quality and committing employees to quality is not enough. Developing standards, providing tools, measuring progress, rewarding or coaching, and continually following through are indispensable parts of the process.

2. *Starting at the bottom of the organization.* As with most any program in workplace organizations, change must start at the top. Employees must be sure that upper management is behind a program before they will embrace the program. Why should lower-level employees dedicate themselves to quality if they do not see their supervisors doing so?

3. *Focusing on inspection.* Quality-improvement programs that emphasize inspection after work has been completed are doomed to failure. The key to generating excellence is planning before the output, not inspecting the output after the fact.

4. *Assuming that quality is a technical, not a managerial, concern.* Quality has come to be identified with design, engineering, or operations activities rather than with the managerial role. Isolating the concern for quality with one department rather than spreading responsibility for quality throughout the entire organization means that excellence cannot be achieved.

5. *Being impatient about quality.* Some companies give up on quality because they do not see immediate results. Because quick turnarounds do not occur, some managers believe that quality is impossible to achieve. True conformity to standards in all aspects of all jobs takes time. Committed organizations must be prepared to spend years developing quality and should never abandon the focus on it.

6. *Tolerating some rate of error.* Some managers believe that complete conformity to requirements is impossible to achieve. They think that because people are human and error is inevitable, some small rate of nonconformity to quality requirements must be tolerated. The notion defeats the whole concept of quality. Once some error is allowed, the company has admitted that quality is an impossible goal, and gives itself permission to err. After all, mistakes are inevitable. Every employee will feel free to make a few

little mistakes, and the amount of error will increase exponentially. Soon larger and larger margins of error must be tolerated. Then the goal of quality has disappeared.

[*See also* Coaching Employees; Customer Service; Quality Circles; Training]

For Additional Information

Crosby, Philip B. *Quality Is Free*. New York: McGraw Hill Book Company, 1979. Proposes that it costs nothing to do things right the first time, but that doing things wrong costs money. Crosby shows how quality is the responsibility of all employees and not just a manufacturing concern. Through a case-history approach, he provides a plan for achieving quality in organizations.

————. *Quality Without Tears*. New York: McGraw-Hill Book Company, 1984. Management actions as they relate to quality improvement. Information is organized around four questions: What is quality? What system is needed to cause quality? What performance standard should be used? What measurement system is required? Crosby takes the position that creating quality means changing the organizational culture.

Guaspari, John. *I Know It When I See It*. New York: AMACOM, 1985. A short, entertaining fable about quality that delivers some poignant messages about the importance of quality, myths associated with quality, and ways to achieve quality in manufacturing and service organizations.

Verry, Leonard L., Valarie A. Ziethaml, and A. Parasuraman. "Quality Counts in Services Too." *Business Horizons*, Vol. 28 (1985), No. 3, pp. 44–52. The nature and determinants of service quality from both consumer and executive perspectives.

Quality Circles

A QUALITY CIRCLE is a small group of workers from the same department or area who voluntarily meet together regularly for about one hour per week in paid time to identify, analyze, and solve work-related problems. They present those solutions to management, and, in some cases, implement them themselves. The group typically ranges from three to twelve people and works under its own supervisor. Quality-circle members receive recognition and, in some cases, rewards for their participation.

Many organizations regard quality circles as a way to tap employees' knowledge, creativity, and motivation to improve attitudes, work quality, and overall productivity. Who is in a better position to recognize and solve work problems than the employees who directly confront and are affected by those problems? Involving workers in problem solving not only provides a wealth of human resources to aid productivity, but also gives workers the opportunity for input in day-to-day operations. The participative philosophy behind quality circles can create a more efficient and satisfied work force.

Implementing Quality Circles

An organization desiring to establish quality circles should do the following:

1. Determine objectives.
2. Form a steering committee.
3. Select a facilitator.
4. Select and train circle leaders.
5. Develop policy and publicize the program.
6. Train members.

7. Conduct circles.
8. Evaluate the program.

Determining Objectives

It is important to articulate objectives of a quality-circle program at its very inception. Well-defined objectives can help guide the subsequent formation, composition, and evaluation of the quality-circle program. Early on, objectives may be general or specific, short-range or long-range. But the organization must specify, as clearly as possible, what it expects to accomplish with quality circles. Common objectives include:

- Providing job involvement
- Building teamwork
- Reducing job errors
- Improving safety records
- Enhancing communication
- Reducing waste
- Reducing cost
- Improving morale
- Improving management-employee relations
- Creating problem-solving abilities

The list is not comprehensive. Organizations should develop objectives to suit their particular functions, cultures, or problems. Be sure to consider both task-oriented and people-oriented goals expected of a quality-circle program.

Forming a Steering Committee

A committee of people from various levels and functions should be formed to oversee the entire quality-circle program. For the concept to receive widespread support in the organization, the steering committee must represent all interests. There should be a member of top management to show commitment, to provide financial resources, and to aid in policy-making. A member from middle management can inform this level of its role in the operation of quality circles. Supervisors are likely to be circle leaders and therefore will play a vital role in steering-committee activities. A union representative should be on the steering committee to provide union views and support, not merely to "monitor" the process. In addition, nonexempt employees should participate in the planning process, since they will comprise the majority of the operating circles. Members of the steering committee should represent various functions as well as various organizational levels. It is important to include individuals from such functions as production, quality control, engineering, research and development, personnel, training, finance, and marketing. All participation should be voluntary.

Unless there is a member of the organization with expertise in implementing quality circles, the steering committee should engage the services of a consultant who will structure a program to meet your organization's objectives, sell the project throughout the organization, and train the project facilitator, circle leaders, and members. The consultant can also assist with program evaluation and expansion.

The steering committee coordinates every phase of the project. Careful planning by a diverse and motivated membership can promote the acceptance of participatory leadership throughout the organization and enhance the effectiveness of quality circles.

Selecting a Facilitator

The quality-circle facilitator is the one person in the organization who ultimately makes quality circles happen. While the steering committee coordinates the project, the facilitator actually trains leaders and members, publicizes the program in the company, attends initial circle meetings, monitors ongoing operations of circle meetings, maintains records, and collects information needed to evaluate the quality-circle program. The facilitator must be committed to the project, must have the respect of the organization as a whole, must have knowledge and experience in quality circles, and must have excellent leadership, communication, and instructional skills. The facilitator should be a member of professional associations related to quality circles and will be expected to interact with other facilitators locally and nationally.

Typically, the facilitator's job is a full-time one. Exceptions occur in small companies. The facilitator usually reports to the director of manufacturing, the director of quality control, or the director of industrial relations. In some cases, the quality-circle facilitator will report to a vice-president or to the chief executive officer. Because of the variety of tasks involved in coordinating a quality-circle program, the facilitator should not try to handle more than twenty operating circles. Each separate plant may want to have its own facilitator.

The facilitator can be the key to the success of quality circles. The tasks performed by a facilitator include championing the concept; answering objections; soliciting and using the advice of others at all levels; motivating, training, and coaching others; and acting as a liaison and innovator in the organization.

Selecting and Training Circle Leaders

There are two schools of thought on the selection of leaders for initial quality circles. Since the concept usually begins on a small scale and gradually expands throughout the organization, you may want to select leaders who already have the skills to make the concept work. That is, select supervisors and department heads who already practice participatory leadership. They will have positive attitudes toward quality circles and will get the first few circles off to a successful start. On the other hand, such individuals are the ones who need quality circles the least. The opposing view recommends starting with departments in need of improvement and people whose management styles need changing. Careful training of more autocratic supervisors to encourage and accept input from their staffs may provide more dramatic examples of quality-circle success.

The quality-circle leader should be the person immediately above the employees participating in the circle. Quality-circle leaders perform a variety of functions including:

- Creating enthusiasm for circle meetings
- Meeting with the circle once a week
- Scheduling meetings and giving assignments
- Enforcing a code of conduct in meetings
- Acting as a liaison between members and the facilitator
- Helping to train members
- Keeping circle records

Quality-circle leaders should receive training in participatory leadership, group dynamics, team building, group problem solving, interpersonal relations, conflict management, and creative thinking. Not only must they be well acquainted with the quality-circle concept and organizational goals for the program, they must also be able to encourage their groups to solve problems in a democratic fashion. This can be a difficult task for some supervisors who have previously been encouraged to direct, give orders, and control workers. Quality-circle members initially may be suspicious of this new emphasis on equal participation. It is important to realize that leading a quality circle is not the same as supervising a work team. During the one-hour circle meeting, the supervisor/leader is just another member of the circle, with some special responsibilities.

Developing Policy and Publicizing the Program

An organization should develop an overall corporate policy regarding quality circles. A written policy statement will show top-level support for the concept, provide answers to certain questions, and can be disseminated as one means of orienting employees about the project. The policy statement should include a statement of objectives for the program and emphasize that participation at any level is voluntary. It should delineate the scope of permissible projects for circle meetings and indicate that circles will not discuss such matters as salaries and benefits, hiring and firing policies, interpersonal conflicts, grievances, and labor-contract issues.

Typically, corporate policy statements regarding quality circles also indicate when circles meet, how long they meet, the size of circles, how leaders are selected, what training will be provided, and what rewards are available, if any, for participation. It is wise, also, to indicate that while management will attempt to implement most solutions emerging from circles, it may not be able to implement every recommendation suggested.

There should be a plan for explaining and promoting the quality-circle program. Because the process involves changes in leadership philosophy in an organization, there will be numerous questions and objections to address. Likewise, the facilitator and leaders must advocate the program if substantial numbers of enthusiastic participants are to be found. Companies have found the following methods to be successful in promoting quality circles: program-announcement letters to employees, articles in company newsletters, formal presentations with question and answer sessions, recruitment brochures, sections in the employee handbook, program explanation in new-employee orientation sessions, and information on bulletin boards. Some organizations have distributed press releases to local newspapers or have advertised their quality-circle program as part of their sales efforts.

Training Members

All employees who volunteer to join quality circles should be trained to understand the concept of quality circles and develop some basic skills necessary to function in circle meetings. Members must become familiar and comfortable with these steps of the problem-solving process: identifying problems, consensually selecting a problem to solve, gathering information, generating alternative solutions, selecting the best solution from alternatives, making recommendations or implementing the solution, evaluating results, and presenting outcomes. Additionally, members may benefit from training in group interaction, listening skills, and speaking before groups. An organization should never sacrifice member training in favor of training circle leaders. Both are crucial. Because the real essence of the program is the actual circle meetings, it makes sense to provide members with the problem-solving and group-communication skills necessary for making discussions meaningful and productive.

Conducting Circles

As soon as member training is completed, the circle leader should schedule the first quality circle within the next two weeks. At this point, members are motivated and their recall of training concepts is fresh. Members begin the problem-solving process by suggesting problems they perceive need solving. They can brainstorm to encourage creativity and to identify the less obvious problems facing their department. The circle leader should not evaluate members' ideas to direct them to a certain problem to solve; the leader's role is rather to move the group along the problem-solving scheme and to make sure everyone gets the chance to participate in the discussion. Each week, the circle works on the problem according to the problem-solving model until a solution is implemented and evaluated. If the quality circle cannot actually implement a solution itself, it meets with a manager to recommend an implementation plan. A manager who cannot accept a recommendation should provide logical reasons for the refusal. Frequent refusals will undermine the members' confidence and the program credibility. Quality-circle members who see their input translated into action in an organization are likely to become more loyal, more motivated, and more productive employees.

Evaluating the Program

The steering committee will have developed criteria for evaluating program outcomes against initial objectives. Both the financial aspects and the human elements of quality circles should be considered in determining the success of the program. An impartial team of evaluators should develop objective procedures for measuring outcomes. Criteria for evaluating quality circles include:

- Increase in output
- Reduction in the amount of rework
- Cost reduction or waste reduction
- Improved safety record
- Reduction in absenteeism, tardiness, turnover
- Fewer customer complaints
- Fewer grievances
- Decrease in interpersonal conflict
- Improved motivation or morale
- Frequency and quality of communication
- Requests for additional quality circles
- More quality awareness

Cost Considerations

The quality-circle steering committee will want to prepare a tentative budget for the project. Costs incurred directly as a result of the program will fall into these categories:

- Facilitator's salary and benefits
- Consulting fees (optional)
- Training materials
- Promotional materials
- Reward program (optional)

In addition, there will be indirect costs of the steering committee's time, the leaders' and members' time, clerical costs, and meeting-room costs. Some organizations compute a return on investment by comparing these costs to the economic impact of problems solved by their quality circles, and some report a considerable dollar savings from quality circles. On the other hand, their effects on individual development and the evolution of a participatory culture in an organization are immeasurable.

Rewarding Quality Circles

While most quality-circle programs do not give monetary awards to participants, all programs must have some means of recognizing and rewarding employees for their participation. Management can send appreciation letters to the home address of all circle members, with copies placed in employees' permanent files. Certificates of achievement placed in visible locations can give public recognition to circle members, and special luncheons, picnics, or banquets for circle participants can boost cohesiveness as well as provide recognition. Some companies give members small gifts such as T-shirts, coffee mugs, or gift certificates to stores or restaurants. The actual token of appreciation is not as important as the fact that management express recognition and gratitude to circle participants. These individuals should feel special.

Members of mature quality circles often feel psychologically rewarded as a result of the training received and the opportunity for input. They can express their ideas, interact creatively with co-workers, and have a real impact on the organization. The individual satisfaction, pride, and fulfillment from involvement in quality circles is an enormous intangible reward.

Organizational Conditions for Successful Quality Circles

While quality circles can represent a positive tool for organizations and individuals alike, the process will not work in all organizations. The following are some organizational conditions or characteristics that are prerequisite to a successful quality-circle program:

- A general attitude of support for the program exists from the top down.
- The organization values people.
- The organization values innovation.
- Employees are generally satisfied with compensation and job security.
- Adequate staffing and funding for the program is provided.
- The economic climate is favorable.
- Management-employee relations are good generally.
- The organization wants to develop participatory leadership.

Because quality circles spread decision-making power from a few to many in an organization, the concept can be threatening. For quality circles to work, enough people at all levels in the company must truly want widespread participation. Supervisors and management must believe that workers are responsible and intelligent and have valuable contributions to make to the company. Employees must trust management and be enthusiastic and optimistic about the program. If workers want to do as little as possible for their paychecks or if they view quality circles as a manipulative tool of management, then the program will not work. Management must be willing to listen to employees and to give them the power to implement their own ideas for improvement in the workplace. In short, quality circles are based on respect among people.

Common Objectives and Pitfalls

There are bound to be objections to quality circles in any organization. Initially, the concept can seem too time-consuming, too costly, or too idealistic. The following are some common objections and suggested responses regarding quality circles:

Objection: Circle meetings during work hours will decrease productivity.

Response: This may be true at first, but, in a short time, solutions generated by circle meetings and increased motivation by members will enhance productivity.

Objection: We don't have time for quality circles. We're already too busy to get our normal work done.

Response: Quality circles meet only one hour per week. In the long run, quality circles save time, energy, and money by solving work-related problems.

Objection: Supervisors and management will lose authority and power.

Response: Employee input does not replace management decisions. It allows management to make better-quality decisions.

Objection: Quality-circle meetings will just turn into useless social sessions.

Response: Training of leaders and members will ensure that circles make productive use of discussion time.

Objection: It is not my job to solve problems. Supervisors, managers, or quality-control experts get paid to do that.

Response: Employees often are most aware of the problems that need solving. Why not offer your knowledge on paid time to make your company a better one?

There are also pitfalls to avoid in implementing quality circles in an organization. As previously discussed, the conditions must be right for quality circles. Companies should avoid starting a program that will be doomed to failure because the appropriate organizational atmosphere does not exist. The quality-circle program should begin on a small scale and expand gradually. Being too impatient or too aggressive with the program will lead to difficulty. It is crucial that an organization do more than pay lip service to a quality-circle program. Employees can feel set up if their input is solicited but not actually used. Circles should not be instituted without adequate training for all involved. Discussions will be a waste of time if members do not have an agenda and problem-solving scheme to follow and if leaders cannot solicit meaningful and well-balanced interaction in the group.

Benefits of Quality Circles

There are many advantages to both individuals and organizations involved with quality circles. By discussing issues of quality and productivity, circle members develop a heightened sense of excellence that carries over to their on-the-job behavior. They experience increased pride and loyalty in their work and feel a greater sense of belonging to an organization. The training that participants receive makes them more skilled employees. Quality circles produce improved communication and more realistic attitudes among workers. They develop a better understanding of the difficulties faced by supervisors. And supervisors often increase their respect for their subordinates. Overall, a more collaborative spirit develops in the workplace. The organization moves toward improved participation, thereby benefiting from the knowledge and insights of a larger pool of people, its most valuable resource.

Suggestions for Making Quality Circles Work

Based on the insights of individuals experienced in implementing quality circles, some final tips for promoting success follow:

- Acknowledge that quality circles may require changes in management styles.
- Keep the program voluntary.
- Make sure circles work on problems in their areas of expertise.
- Make sure circles solve problems, not merely identify them.
- Keep circle projects small and uncomplicated.
- Realize that training is crucial.
- Provide frequent open and positive information about circles.

[See also Meetings; Quality; Team Building]

For Additional Information

Dewar, Donald L. The Quality Circle Guide to Participation Management. Englewood Cliffs, N.J.: Prentice-Hall, 1982. An overview of all the steps of implementing quality circles, including a sample leader manual, member manual, and forms for administering a program. Unique information includes actual results documented by organizations with quality circles, sample job descriptions for facilitators, and implementation timetables.

Fitzgerald, Laurie, and Joseph Murphy. Installing Quality Circles: A Strategic Approach. San Diego, Calif.: University Associates, Inc., 1982. A 134-page guide that gives a theoretical framework, history, and implementation plan of quality circles. There are chapters on selling the concept to senior management, middle and line management, and unions. The book includes information on preparing a budget, common objections, and a sample charter for a quality-circle program.

Hutchins, David. Quality Circles Handbook. New York: Nichols Publishing Company, 1985. General information to help the reader implement quality circles, a thorough history of quality circles, highlights of the quality-circle movement, answers to 152 questions most asked about quality circles, case studies, and a thorough bibliography.

Ingle, Sud. Quality Circles Master Guide. Englewood Cliffs, N.J.: Prentice-Hall, Inc., 1982. A workbook-style volume covering the history, objectives, and implementation procedures for quality circles. There is a thorough section on data collection and analysis techniques to be used by circles. Additional chapters cover group dynamics, communication skills, case studies, quality circles for service industries and management, and the future of quality circles. A bibliography of books, articles, and periodicals is included.

Portis, Bernard, David Fullerton, and Paul Ingram. "Effective Use of Quality Circles." *The Business Quarterly*, Vol. 50 (1985), No. 3, pp. 44–47. Reports on a systematic study of how quality circles relate to strategic concerns of companies, why companies undertake these programs, union and management support for these programs, and how companies evaluate their programs.

Recruiting and Selecting New Employees

RECRUITING AND SELECTING NEW EMPLOYEES are very important functions in organizations. Increasingly, organizations are coming to regard people as their most important asset. By developing appropriate hiring practices, you can avoid the costly error of hiring the wrong person for a particular job. Poor hiring decisions can cost thousands of dollars in advertising, interviewing, travel, training, and administrative expenses. Then there is the lost time devoted to the selection process, the disruption to the work unit because of a position needing to be filled, and the negative effects on productivity and morale when a new hire performs a job unsuccessfully. Obviously, it is advantageous to make careful and correct recruiting and selection decisions initially in order to avoid costly and demoralizing errors.

Many managers believe that recruiting and selection are functions of the personnel specialists in their organizations and that operating managers need not be involved in the process. Nothing could be farther from the truth. There are many reasons why all managers should be skilled in recruiting and selection procedures. First, in many small companies, sophisticated personnel departments do not exist. Managers are expected to do their own hiring. Even in large organizations where personnel departments have selection specialists, managers should also be involved in the process. Personnel departments can never know as much as departmental managers do about the requirements of the position, the nature of the department with the opening, or the type of individual who could best perform the job. At the very least, managers must educate the personnel department about their hiring needs. Only in very low-level, routinely filled positions should managers consider leaving the whole process to the personnel department. You should work with personnel departments to conduct recruiting efforts, screen applications, interview candidates, and make hiring decisions. In short, recruiting is an essential skill for all managers.

Elements of the Recruiting and Selection Process

The key steps in recruiting and selecting new employees are discussed in the following sections.

Preparing a Job Description

You must be thoroughly familiar with the duties and requirements of a job before you can select the best person to perform it. In order to acquire familiarity, you must conduct a job analysis, which entails learning about the daily tasks and special assignments required of the employee. Observe the incumbent employee at work, interview the employee, administer a questionnaire about job requirements, and use previous written job descriptions. All of these methods will provide you with an accurate and comprehensive picture of the job.

In addition to outlining job duties, the analysis should determine other job specifications such as education level, prior work experience, specialized abilities, and necessary personality characteristics. It is essential that these determinations not be arbitrary. For example, if the job could be done by someone without a college degree or without five years of experience, then to demand such specifications would be discriminatory. All requirements must be directly linked to job performance.

After analyzing what the job entails, prepare a realistic and specific job description. This should include all the duties and responsibilities performed in the job, arranged in order from most often to least often performed. Some job descriptions include the percentage of daily time devoted to each specific responsibility. Other items to include on a job description are job title, reporting relationship, salary grade and range, and work schedule. These elements are especially important for job descriptions you provide to candidates.

Delineating job specifications is an essential step in the planning process that precedes the actual recruiting. By identifying job duties, necessary skills, and important personality characteristics ahead of time, you can make more efficient use of your interviewing time and enhance your hiring decisions. This step also can reduce the number of unqualified applicants, since some people will not apply if they lack certain skills or do not want to perform certain job duties.

Selecting Recruiting Sources

There are many sources you can use to find job applicants. Some sources lend themselves to certain types or levels of jobs; others produce large numbers of applicants who may or may not be qualified. Common sources for recruiting job applicants include:

- *Newspaper advertising.*   This method is inexpensive and produces large numbers of applicants in a very short time. But it is time-consuming, because help-wanted ads can attract many unqualified applicants. Someone must then take the time to screen a potentially large number of applications.

- *Job posting.*   This entails advertising a job opening within your own organization. In many companies, jobs must be made available to insiders before jobs can be advertised externally. The advantage is that you are able to hire someone who is already familiar with the company and whose performance record is known. Disadvantages include the fact that the company still has another opening to fill and that employee applicants not hired may become disgruntled.

- *Internal referrals.*   Current employees recommend candidates for a job. Some organizations provide bonuses for employees whose referrals are hired. Because employees know the realities of a company, they can provide an accurate description of a job to potential applicants. On the other hand, the method can create "inbreeding," with close friends and relatives working together. Organizations using this method should combine it with other recruiting sources. Word-of-mouth alone is an insufficient recruiting practice, according to equal employment opportunity (EEO) requirements.

- *Campus recruiting.*   Many organizations turn to college campuses for a large pool of talented applicants for entry-level professional positions. Likewise, high school and vocational schools can provide a pool of qualified applicants for secretarial or technical jobs. These sources provide, for the most part, applicants who lack work experience, however.

- *Employment agencies or executive search firms.*   While these two methods differ in the level of employee they recommend, they both locate qualified applicants for job openings. Using these outside sources can save a manager or a personnel specialist a great deal of time but can be very costly to the hiring organization. In each case, the outside agency should take the time to learn of your staffing specifications, scout the market for qualified talent, and carefully screen applicants so that they refer only the most qualified candidates. Executive search firms have the advantage of locating talented employees who are already employed and may be difficult to recruit through any other means. Because these recruiting sources vary in quality, you should screen them as carefully as you would any other employee or resource.

- *Government agencies.*   State or federal employment agencies can provide, at no cost to organizations, a pool of applicants for entry-level positions. Since these applicants are unemployed, they can usually start work immediately. Government agencies can only provide qualified applicants for limited types of jobs, however.

- *Professional societies and trade or business associations.* People in professional careers or skilled trades usually belong to associations affiliated with their speciality. Such associations may offer job-placement services, hold conventions where you can scout for qualified candidates, or publish job advertisements in their newsletters, magazines, or journals. This method is useful for recruiting for highly specialized positions such as engineering, law, architecture, medicine, and so on. Also, highly motivated individuals in a particular field are most likely to be members of professional associations. The method is limited, obviously, by the type of job you need to fill.

- *Walk-in applicants.* Frequently, people will apply for jobs in a particular organization even if no openings exist. These applications can be kept on file and examined when a job opening occurs. While this recruiting method does not cost an organization, accepting large numbers of unsolicited applications can be time-consuming, especially if they are acknowledged and taken seriously.

- *Other sources used less frequently, which can nevertheless prove effective for certain jobs or organizations.* Career days, job fairs, open houses, networking, or help-wanted signs can all recruit new employees. Career days are events sponsored by educational or community organizations to highlight certain types of careers. Employers in a particular field can meet individuals employed in or interested in the field. When an organization holds open house, it invites the public to its facility, provides information about the company and about available jobs, conducts tours of its facility, and accepts applications for employment. Some managers are so well immersed in their fields or so well-known in their communities that they can find qualified job candidates by calling acquaintances in their professional network for referrals. Keep in mind that personal referrals alone tend to exclude minority candidates. Finally, in service organizations subject to substantial public traffic, help-wanted signs can provide a large pool of applicants from which to select new hires.

Screening Application Materials

After the application deadline for an open position has passed, you begin to examine the pool of application materials. In most cases, each applicant will provide a completed application form and a résumé. Depending on the position and the organization, a large number of application materials may have to be reviewed. You can solicit assistance from the personnel department or other qualified individuals to screen out the obviously unqualified applicants. In some cases, this will reduce the applicant pool substantially.

It is important that the hiring manager take the time to review the materials of all qualified candidates. While this may be time-consuming, time spent in the careful evaluation of written materials prevents unnecessary interviews and reduces the possibility of an inappropriate selection decision. You can review application materials in an unstructured fashion to determine the most preferred and least preferred candidates or develop systems for awarding points to applicants according to important job criteria, thereby rank-ordering the applicants. Whatever the method, you must screen application materials so that a limited number of top candidates emerge to be interviewed.

Naturally, the requirements of the particular job and culture of the hiring organization will dictate the criteria you use in screening applications. However, there are some standard considerations to use as you review a pool of application materials:

1. *What is the appearance of application materials?*   The application form should be complete, legible, and neat. The résumé should look professional, should be easy to scan, and should be free from grammatical or spelling errors. An applicant who is careless about the appearance of application materials is likely to be sloppy in work habits.

2. *Are there inconsistencies in information presented?*   For example, are the dates of previously held jobs sequential and without interruption? If there is a gap in the work or educational history of an otherwise qualified candidate, ask the candidate for an explanation. Does it appear that the candidate was involved in activities in two widely different geographic locations during the same time period? Has the candidate been obviously overqualified or underqualified for previous positions? You need not disqualify an applicant because of perceived inconsistencies in written information; however, inconsistencies should alert you to seek clarification. If candidates cannot provide satisfactory explanations for unusual information on an application or résumé, they may be attempting to hide a problem.

3. *Is there evidence of an irregular employment history?*   An excessive number of job changes in a short time period may indicate a problem employee. This may be confirmed if the applicant is ambiguous about the reasons for such job changes. Keep in mind, however, that some applicants have justifiable reasons for making frequent job changes. An erratic career pattern can result from company mergers

or relocations, the job transfers of a spouse, changing employment trends in society, or ambitious career goals.

4. *Are there indications that the applicant is particularly well-suited to your job or organization?* Perhaps the person has performed very similar duties in a previous job or has worked for an organization in a related field. Volunteer or civic activities may have helped the applicant develop relevant job skills.

The role of the manager in screening applications is to objectively review materials to determine possible strengths and weaknesses of each applicant and to decide if that applicant should be interviewed.

Interviewing Candidates

Interviewing candidates is a key step in the selection process. This is when the majority of information about a candidate is obtained, when the candidate develops impressions about the organization, and when decisions about the match between applicant and position occur. It is important to allocate enough time to prepare for, conduct, and summarize each interview.

1. *Prepare.* You should prepare for selection interviews by reviewing job descriptions and job requirements, by familiarizing yourself with the applicant's written materials, and by preparing some standard and specific questions. Managers who are unprepared for interviews make inefficient use of interview time, present a poor image of the company, and fail to obtain pertinent information.

2. *Establish rapport.* The first step in the actual interview is to establish rapport with the candidate. This is an important ingredient in calming the applicant and in showing a positive work atmosphere. You should realize that job interviews are transactions in which each party gathers information to make a decision about the other. Both sides give and seek information to influence each other. You can establish rapport by greeting the candidate in a warm and friendly manner, by using a comfortable and private place to conduct the interview, and by beginning with some small talk. The more that you can reduce intimidating aspects of the situation and show genuine interest in the candidate, the more likely it is that you will get honest and thorough information.

3. *Ask questions.* After a few minutes of small talk to put the candidate at ease and to establish a relationship, move into the actual interview. It is wise to begin with broad, open-ended questions to get the applicant talking. For example, you can ask about daily duties at the last job. Then you can get more specific information by

probing specific statements that the applicant makes. In this way, the interview resembles a conversation rather than an interrogation. Essentially, you want to converse with the interviewee in a relaxed style while obtaining specific information about work experience, educational background, and relevant skills and personality characteristics. You can achieve a conversational tone by occasionally commenting on, but not evaluating, the person's remarks. Of course, you will have a strategy and ask very direct questions without making the strategy apparent.

Open-ended questions are always preferable to questions that can be answered with yes/no responses. The key is to get the candidate talking, at length, in areas of interest to you. Focus the interview with prepared questions and keep it moving smoothly with well-placed follow-up questions to obtain elaboration or clarification in certain areas. Beware of leading questions that cue the applicant to provide the answers you want to hear. Such questions provide little information about the candidate's actual abilities, motivations, or characteristics. The applicant and not the interviewer should do the majority of the talking. You must be a careful observer and listener. Interviewing is a complex process. The ability to obtain all pertinent information in a comfortable, conversational style during a limited time period develops with experience.

4. *Give information.* In addition to obtaining information, you must be skilled in providing thorough and accurate information to the job applicant. Here, the more candid you can be, the better. It is counterproductive to paint an unrealistic picture of the job or the organization to job candidates. Both the positive and negative features of the job should be explained. Do not minimize, for example, the demanding deadlines, the extent of travel, or the amount of overtime associated with the job. Qualified candidates need to know the realities of a job so they can determine if the position fits their goals, life-style, or temperament. Some organizations arrange for potential new hires to talk with employees in similar positions or to observe part of a workday in the company. Providing an accurate rather than an attractive picture of the company will improve both the effective selection and the eventual retention of new employees.

Besides providing information about job expectations, this phase of the interview process also involves answering the interviewees' questions. Encourage the applicant to ask questions by providing enough time for dialogue, by making the interviewee feel comfortable throughout the interview, and by soliciting questions in an unintimidating manner. Consider, for example, two ways of soliciting questions from a job applicant: "Any questions?" versus

"I'd be happy to answer the questions you must have about the job." The first approach can cause a person with questions to feel inadequate or foolish, while the latter style encourages questions as a natural part of the interview process. Candidates may have questions about salary, benefits, work schedules, training, or growth opportunities. You can gain additional insights into candidates by the number and types of questions they ask about a job.

5. *State the next steps.* The final part of the face-to-face interview is to indicate what the next step will be. Will there be call-back interviews, reference checks, or physical exams? Should the applicant provide more information or submit a portfolio of work samples? To conclude an interview, thank the applicant. Escort the applicant out of the room and indicate how soon the decision will be made.

6. *Summarize information.* It is common for interviewers to take a few notes while the candidate talks. But note taking should be limited and inobtrusive during the interview. Then, immediately after the interview, take some time to elaborate on your notes. Your purpose is to summarize the person's answers, to record factual information, and to describe the candidate's appearance and mannerisms.

Avoid subjective evaluations. Both to make an unbiased decision and to comply with legal aspects of the selection process, you should refrain from recording opinions and unsubstantiated judgments about applicants. Personal interpretation by the interviewer can never be totally eliminated from hiring decisions, but subjective bias must be minimized as much as possible.

The post-interview summary is used as a memory aid after you have obtained information from many candidates. The manager who conducts more than a few interviews for a vacant position will find it difficult to associate information with particular candidates without the aid of detailed, objective notes on each person.

Administering Standardized Tests

Some organizations use standardized testing as part of the selection process. These may include tests of intelligence, aptitudes, skills, job information, or personality. But testing should never be the sole means of making hiring decisions; it can be a valuable tool to provide precise, objective information you cannot obtain through other means. For example, judgments about a person's intelligence from an interview would be highly suspect, but administering a standardized intelligence test would give more objective information. Likewise, if you want to know how skilled a person is as a typist, you could obtain a quantifiable score from a standardized typing test. Tests for job information are frequently used to award certification or a license in a particular field.

If you use selection tests, they must be relevant to the job qualifications, they must be valid in measuring what they claim to measure, they must be administered and scored consistently for all applicants, and they must be administered by a qualified person. You can use selection tests initially to screen qualified applicants prior to scheduling interviews or test preferred candidates emerging from interviews to help distinguish among them. Whatever the method, if selection tests conform to professional and legal standards, they can provide a valuable source of additional information to employers.

Follow-Up and Evaluation

Even after scrutinizing written materials, conducting and summarizing the interview, and obtaining test scores where applicable, the manager involved in selection has other tasks to perform. You should check references, verify degrees, and confirm previous employment. It is wise to check with at least three references to see if consistent evaluations of the candidates emerge. In many cases, you must be perceptive in noticing what the reference does not say about the candidate, as well as noting what comments are made. Degree verification is becoming increasingly common in the selection process and companies now exist to provide this service. The candidate's previous employers should be contacted to verify the dates of employment. In many cases, personnel departments will provide little additional information. Because of the fear of litigation, they are less willing to disclose evaluations of previous employees.

In some jobs or organizations, security clearances, physical examinations, or drug testing is performed. Certain categories of jobs require these additional screening measures and candidates may be rejected for failing them.

Once all the information from these various sources is available for candidates, it is time for you to evaluate qualifications, compare candidates, and make hiring decisions. This step should not be taken lightly. Avoid the tendency to make snap judgments, rely on personal biases, or make premature decisions. The evaluation of applicants should be systematic and as objective as possible. Some managers develop elaborate point systems for evaluating candidates. In each case, the applicant's job qualifications should be compared against job factors. You can develop lists of strengths and weaknesses for each candidate, based on factual information. The goal is not to hire the most stellar candidate, but to make the best match between a job and a candidate. The brightest and most motivated applicant, for example, may quickly become bored with your position and resign.

By carefully comparing the qualifications of the various candidates and matching them to job requirements, you can rank-order the candidates. It is important to consider several top candidates, should the most preferred candidate reject the job offer. Once your decision is made, you can make the job offer and notify applicants once the preferred candidate gives written acceptance of the offer.

Legal Considerations

Anyone involved in the selection process should be familiar with equal employment opportunity (EEO) laws and practices. This is a complex and constantly changing area, so you should stay abreast of EEO regulations by subscribing to personnel publications, consulting EEO specialists, or seeking legal counsel in this area. Some general guidelines for EEO compliance include the following:

- *Job qualifications must be realistic.* Requiring a college degree or five years of experience is legal only if the employer can show that someone without the specified degree or experience cannot perform the job satisfactorily.
- *Only job-related questions should be asked.* These questions may be about experience, skills, job or educational history, motivation, or personal characteristics. But every question must be directly related to the performance of the specific job. Asking if the applicant has a car, for example, is appropriate only if a car is necessary to the performance of the duties of the job.
- *Interview questions must be consistent across applicants.* You cannot ask certain questions of female applicants that you would not ask of male applicants, for example. Specific questions cannot be targeted to applicants of certain age-groups, races, or ethnic backgrounds.
- *Certain interview questions are illegal.* Interviewers cannot ask questions about marital or family status, religion, physical health, financial status, national origin, age, or native language. The wording of questions in the areas of citizenship, criminal record, disabilities, and military experience often determines the legality of the question.

[*See also* Assessment Centers; Interviewing]

For Additional Information

Arthur, Diane. *Recruiting, Interviewing, Selecting, and Orienting New Employees.* New York: AMACOM, 1986. Aimed at managers who find themselves involved in the personnel-selection process as well as practicing human-resources development professionals. Chapters cover the areas of job analysis, recruiting, interviewing, selecting, and orienting employees. Arthur also provides a thorough examination of EEO guidelines. Sample job-description forms, job advertisements, application forms, evaluation forms, and reference forms are included.

Dobrish, Cecelia, Rick Wolff, and Brian Zevnik. *Hiring the Right Person for the Right Job.* New York: Franklin Watts, 1984. Information on such topics as creating job descriptions, advertising and recruiting, employee testing, and interviewing. The authors review over 100 standardized tests in various categories and provide the addresses of test publishers. Additional checklists for employment interviewers are included.

Hendrickson, John. "Hiring the Right Stuff." *The Personnel Administrator,* Vol. 32 (1987), No. 11, pp. 70–74. Proposes collaboration, with line management and human resources sharing perspectives by assessing job candidates.

Phillips, Jack J. *Recruiting, Training, and Retaining New Employees.* San Francisco: Jossey-Bass Publishers, 1987. Focuses primarily on the selection of and transition process for new college graduates. Phillips discusses transition problems of the new college graduate, delineates the turnover costs for organizations failing to retain college graduates as new hires, and provides guidelines for employers doing campus recruiting.

Wanous, John P. *Organizational Entry.* Reading, Mass.: Addison-Wesley Publishing Company, 1980. Uses case studies and organizational examples to examine the stages in organizational entry, from recruitment to entry to socialization of new hires. The author contrasts the practices of traditional and realistic recruitment, analyzes the interview process from an individual and an organizational perspective, and examines the concept and practice of assessment centers.

Sexual Harassment

MANAGERS must be aware of the issue of sexual harassment in the workplace. Equal Employment Opportunity Commission (EEOC) guidelines mandate that companies must be responsible for creating a working environment free from harassment and must have mechanisms for dealing with reported incidents of sexual harassment. Clearly, sexual harassment is not just an issue between two people, but an organizational issue. Because you can be held responsible when your subordinates are sexually harassed, you must know what constitutes harassment and be able to take steps to eliminate it from your organization.

What Is Sexual Harassment?

The November 1980 EEO guidelines clarify sexual harassment as an unlawful employment practice under Section 703 of Title VII of the Civil Rights Act of 1964. The legal definition of sexual harassment is as follows:

> It is illegal for a supervisor or co-worker to engage in unwelcome sexual advances, requests for sexual favors, or verbal or physical conduct of a sexual nature. Such behavior constitutes sexual harassment whether submission is made an implicit or explicit condition of employment; whether employment decisions are based on submission to or rejection of such behavior; or whether such behavior substantially interferes with work performance or creates an intimidating, hostile, or offensive work environment.

Additionally, an employer is responsible for the behaviors of all its employees regardless of whether those behaviors were forbidden and regardless of whether the employer knew or should have known of the occurrence of those behaviors. The employer is also responsible for the behaviors of nonemployees if the employer knew or should have known of the harassing behavior. The employer has the defense of having taken immediate and corrective action in the cases of harassment by co-workers and nonemployees.

You should examine certain aspects of the legal definition to fully understand its ramifications.

1. Sexual harassment is *unwelcome* behavior. Sexually harassing behavior differs from behavior that expresses sexual interest. Welcomed expressions of sexual interest or mutually entered sexual relationships do not constitute sexual harassment.

2. Sexual harassment may be *verbal, nonverbal, or physical.* Nonverbal harassment includes such forms of behavior as leering, offensive gestures, or whistling. Verbal harassment includes such forms of behavior as sexual innuendos, sexual jokes, and suggestive comments. Physical harassment includes such forms of behavior as touching, pinching, and assault.

3. *Employment decisions need not be tied to the harassment.* The harasser does not need to threaten some work-related consequence in order for the behavior to be considered harassment. Obviously, making employment, promotion, or compensation decisions contingent on sexual behavior is harassment. But so are unwanted sexual behaviors with no job-related contingencies. Any unwanted sexual behavior that creates an intimidating, hostile, or offensive work environment can be considered harassment.

4. The employer *cannot claim ignorance.* The legal definition indicates that employers should know about the existence of sexual harassment in their work environments. This means that you must make sure that such behavior does not take place—you are responsible for providing a harassment-free work environment. You must be able to recognize and detect harassing behavior.

5. You can be held accountable for the behavior of *nonemployees as well as employees.* You must make sure that vendors, clients, customers, and delivery or repair personnel do not create an offensive work environment through their behavior toward organizational employees.

Why You Should Be Concerned

Evidence reveals that sexual harassment affects not only the parties involved but the entire organization. A harassed worker is likely to take more sick leave, become accident-prone, and resort to abuses in alcohol and drug consumption. An organization with sexual harassment problems faces worker stress, lower employee morale, higher rates of absenteeism and turnover, and productivity problems. In short, sexual harassment is extremely disruptive and costly.

Another vulnerability for you and your company is the possibility of a lawsuit related to instances of sexual harassment. Obviously, the harasser will be named and will be held liable for damages in successful sexual harassment litigation. But even managers who are not themselves harassers, and the company as a whole, can be liable in cases where blatant harassment was tolerated or where reported cases were handled inappropriately. As a representative of your organization, you can be implicated along with the actual persons engaging in harassing behavior.

The Nature of Sexual Harassment

Sexual harassment is a complicated issue and does not always have clear-cut boundaries. Unwanted behavior is not always distinguishable from reciprocal behavior. The same behavior may be defined as friendly by one person and as offensive by another. Experts disagree about whether the accusor should confront the accused to communicate that certain behaviors are offensive. Despite the ambiguities surrounding the issue of sexual harassment, some patterns emerge to create a typical sexual harassment scenario.

An examination of reported cases of harassment reveals that the typical complaint is filed by a female employee against a male employee. While there have been reported instances of females harassing males, females harassing females, or males harassing males, the majority of cases involve a female accusor and a male accused.

There is no clear-cut demographic profile of sexual harassment victims, but some factors seem more prevalent than others. Besides being female, targets of sexual harassment tend to be young and unmarried. Education, income, and occupation do not predict incidents of sexual harassment. Highly educated women in high-status jobs are just as likely to be harassed as are less educated holders of lower-status jobs.

Another trend, discerned from confidential surveys of employees, is the tendency for victims not to report harassment. Whether or not companies have policies and procedures for dealing with sexual harassment, nonreporting is common. Employees who have perceived themselves to be victims of sexual harassment offer several reasons for not reporting the incidents. They often feel that they will be blamed for the incident, believe that nothing will be done to stop the harassment, feel too embarrassed to report the incident, fear they will suffer personal repercussions or job reprisals from complaining, or feel guilty if the accused is hurt by the complaint.

The most common response to harassment is to leave the organization. Many victims quit their jobs without complaint once sexually harassing behavior has created a stressful work environment. In such cases, you have no way of knowing the extent of turnover due to harassment in your organization. Even in instances of formal complaint or litigation, many victims opt to leave the organization. Women may quit if, after lodging a formal complaint, insufficient action is taken to stop the harassing behavior. Litigation may take so long and result in such a deteriorated employer-employee relationship that the victim feels there is no recourse except to leave the organization. In some cases, women are fired after reporting sexual harassment.

Outdated Managerial Attitude

One outdated approach to sexual harassment is that harassment does not occur in "our" company and that women who accuse men of sexual harassment are overreacting to or misinterpreting certain types of behavior. That view trivializes the subject, maintaining that allegations of sexual harassment stem from romances that have gone sour, from women taking offense at well-intentioned compliments, or from overly sensitive woman employees who are not tough enough to handle a normal work environment. Managers who hold this view will dismiss reports of sexual harassment by indicating that boys will be boys, that the accuser must have behaved provocatively, that women have no sense of humor, or that no harm was intended. In short, sexual harassment is regarded as nonexistent, as an overreaction, or as a misunderstanding between two people. By perceiving harassment as an interpersonal rather than an organizational matter, managers who adhere to this school of thought either refrain from getting involved or try to protect the accused party.

Although some organizations seem to operate smoothly with this perspective, there is no way to determine the costs of absenteeism, medical benefits claims, turnover, or decreased morale or productivity resulting from unresolved incidents of sexual harassment. Such organizations and their managers clearly expose themselves to financially disastrous lawsuits, in light of contemporary EEO guidelines.

Recommended Managerial Responses

Enlightened organizations take the view that sexually offensive behavior of any type is unprofessional and cannot be tolerated in the workplace. Such a position is a good business practice because it reduces disruption in the workplace and eliminates legal liability. By establishing the following practices for preventing sexual harassment, you can create a safe, comfortable, and productive work environment for all employees.

1. *Establish and publicize a policy statement about sexual harassment.* Sexual harassment policy statements should communicate the EEO definition of harassment, provide examples of behavior constituting harassment, and explain the organizational procedure for reporting and dealing with sexual harassment complaints.

   Have employees report their complaints to the immediate supervisor, to the personnel or human resources manager, to a company EEO officer, to the chief executive officer (CEO), or, where appropriate, to a union representative. Complainants must be assured confidentiality and the freedom from reprisal. Policy statements may be communicated through personnel policy manuals, employee handbooks, company newsletters, bulletin boards, or memos.

2. *Establish investigative procedures.* Typically, the person responsible for EEO in an organization will follow these steps in investigating a sexual harassment complaint:

   a. *Interview, in separate sessions, the complainant and the accused.* Try to ascertain, from each person's perspective, what happened, when it happened, who else might be aware of the events, the background of the incident, and each person's prior and current attitudes toward the other.

   b. *Interview witnesses.* To gather documentation, you may have to talk with others who were aware of the alleged harassment. Realize that third parties will tend to take sides. Try to get the facts rather than opinions.

   c. *Act as a mediator in a meeting of the accusor and the accused.* Some organizations do not take this step either because they investigate anonymous complaints or they feel that forcing the victim to confront the accused is too traumatic or sensitive. In some cases, however, such a meeting can clarify perceptions, can show the seriousness of management's concern about harassment, and can resolve the incident.

   d. *Make an objective decision.* The person investigating a sexual harassment complaint often must decide the merits of the case or must head a decision-making body. Objectivity is imperative. The decision must be based on the facts, not on personal attitudes or relationships with the people involved.

3. *Take disciplinary action.* Once a sexual harassment complaint has been judged to be accurate, some disciplinary action should be taken. Depending on the nature and the extent of the harassment, disciplinary actions can include warnings, reprimands, suspensions, or terminations. Where the harasser is a nonemployee, verbal warnings, notification of supervisors, or discontinuation of the relationship may be warranted. Some organizations take disciplinary action against employees who knowingly file false allegations of sexual harassment or against managers who do not follow established procedures for handling reports of harassment.

4. *Educate employees about sexual harassment.* Because sexual harassment is a complicated and sensitive issue, preparing a policy statement and reporting procedures may not be sufficient. Organizations can provide training to clarify the definition of sexual harassment, to show top management support in preventing sexual harassment, to encourage employees to discuss their feelings on this issue, and to teach employees how to deal with sexually offensive behavior in the workplace. In addition, managers should be taught how to detect early signs of sexual harassment, how to intervene to prevent harassment, how to monitor their own behavior, and how to process any sexual harassment complaint that they receive from a subordinate.

[*See also* Women and Minorities in the Workplace]

For Additional Information

Cohen, Cynthia Fryer, and Joyce P. Vincelette. "What To Do About Sexual Harassment Complaints." *Supervisory Management*, Vol. 30 (1985), No. 2, pp. 25–29. The form that harassment takes, employee concerns affecting the investigation of harassment, remedial action, and effective responses.

Deane, Richard H. "Sexual Harassment—Is Your Company Protected?" *Business—The Magazine of Managerial Thought and Action*, Vol. 36 (1986), No. 2, pp. 42–45. The significance of the problem, a preventive program for employers, and important ethical and managerial questions arising from sexual harassment issues.

Gutek, Barbara. *Sex and the Workplace.* San Francisco: Jossey-Bass Publishers, 1985. The results of a survey of 800 working women and 400 working men concerning issues of sexual activity at work. The book examines reciprocal sexual relationships as well as sexual harassment on the job. It presents data on the nature and frequency of harassment, characteristics of harassers and reactions of victims, employees' attitudes about sexuality in the workplace, working environments that affect sexuality, and recommendations to management for dealing with sex-related workplace issues.

Meyer, Mary Coeli, Inge M. Berchtold, Jeannene L. Oestreich, and Frederick J. Collins. *Sexual Harassment.* New York: Petrocelli Books, 1981. Defines sexual harassment, presents statistics on its prevalence, discusses its impact on individuals and organizations, examines theories of behavior that explain the origins of harassment, and presents a variety of individual and organizational responses. The authors use case studies to illustrate points and they provide an appendix of sample policies and procedures, court cases, a list of special-interest groups, a self-help bibliography, and a sexual harassment survey.

Neugarten, Dail Ann, and Jay M. Shafritz, eds. *Sexuality in Organizations.* Oak Park, Ill.: Moore Publishing Company, 1980. A collection of contributed articles that explore issues of romantic relationships at work as well as sexual harassment. Section III, "Organizational Responses to Sexual Harassment," covers responses of fair employment practice agencies to complaints, company policy statements, and action plans for management and unions. The final section of the book examines the legal status of sexual harassment under Title VII. Information covers the public as well as the private sector.

"Sexual Harassment: Employer Policies and Problems." Washington, D.C.: The Bureau of National Affairs, 1987. A fifty-five-page booklet that presents the results of a survey of 156 organizations regarding their sexual harassment policies, complaint and investigation procedures, education programs to prevent harassment, and actual harassment cases. The survey data, combined with sample policy statements, training materials, and investigation forms, provide a comprehensive resource for organizations to model in establishing a program to prevent sexual harassment.

Stress

STRESS is a state of physical or mental tension resulting from factors that alter the body's equilibrium, or, in other words, the body's reaction to either pleasant or unpleasant stimulation. We think of stress as a negative reaction, but pleasant experiences or positive changes can also cause stress. Likewise, both overstimulation and understimulation can produce stress—for example, too much or too little to do on a job, or any sort of deviation from a normal routine occasioned by factors related to both the job and the person.

Effects of Stress

Both individuals and organizations are becoming aware of the serious consequences of stress. At the human level, it can have a variety of effects ranging from mild irritability to total disability or death. At an organizational level, stress can limit productivity and therefore be costly. Such effects reveal the need for stress-management intervention at both levels.

Much research recently has documented the relationship of stress to certain diseases. The medical community largely agrees that cardiovascular disease, hypertension, ulcers, headaches, backaches, depression, gastrointestinal problems, allergies, sexual dysfunctions, alcohol and drug dependency, and certain forms of cancer are stress-related illnesses. Chronic stress is obviously taking its toll on people and has become a major health problem costing millions of dollars and countless lives annually.

Stress can also impair people's relationships and life-styles. Stressed workers are more likely to be irritable, to withdraw from social situations, to engage in conflicts with others, to have emotional outbursts, and to have problems with families and friends. Not only do stressed individuals suffer; so do the people around them. It is difficult to estimate the extent to which work stress contributes to turbulent family relationships and divorce, but an association seems likely.

The effects of stress on the organization are numerous. Studies have documented that it leads to more workplace accidents; higher workers' compensation, disability, and medical insurance costs; higher rates of absenteeism and turnover; lower group morale; more labor unrest including grievances, strikes, and sabotage; and losses in productivity. The costs of such outcomes are staggering.

Extensive studies on the relationship of stress to productivity reveal that too little stress as well as too much stress impairs performance. Moderate amounts of stress seem to result in optimum performance. People in boring or repetitive jobs with little challenge report feeling just as much stress as do workers in demanding, pressure-filled jobs.

Because stress has serious consequences for both the individual and the organization, both groups must understand the issues in stress management. Individual employees must take action to alleviate their own stress, and organizations should implement stress-management programs for their work force. It is in the best interest of both groups to work cooperatively in managing workplace stress. Such efforts can save relationships, money, and lives. Effectively managing stress means understanding the sources of stress, recognizing the symptoms of stress, and utilizing strategies to reduce stress.

Sources of Stress

Various factors create stressed employees. Stressors can be personal (intrinsic to the individual's personality and private life), organizational (intrinsic to the job and the organization), or environmental (intrinsic to the physical surroundings and working conditions). Studies have shown that stress factors may be different for white collar and blue collar employees.

Personal Sources of Stress

Personality and perception play important roles in the level of stress. Some types of people are more prone to stress than others. Two people with similar jobs, family, and working conditions can vary in the extent to which they feel stress. Individual variations in stress tolerance and anxiety level clearly affect perceptions of stress.

Highly emotional people and those characterized as Type A

personalities report high levels of stress. Type A persons exhibit extreme competitiveness, sense of urgency, aggressiveness, constant striving for achievement, impatience, perfectionism, inability to relax, desire to control, the performance of multiple activities simultaneously, irritability, and restlessness. While many Type A individuals enjoy a great deal of job satisfaction and success, their behavior does correlate with high stress, increased incidence of coronary ailments, and workaholism.

Personal problems can contribute to stress. Psychological, financial, marital, sexual, or child-rearing problems are common types of personal stressors that can adversely affect work performance. Employees have responded to this problem by creating employee-assistance programs.

While family and friends often help alleviate stress caused by work, they can also cause stress. Troublesome relationships, communication difficulties, or illnesses of loved ones all produce stress, as do joyous life events such as a marriage, the birth of a child, the purchase of a home, or holiday celebrations. A myriad of personal factors can therefore produce stressed employees.

Organizational Sources of Stress

The stress level of certain occupations has been found to be particularly high, such as police officer, fire fighter, physician, dentist, farmer, miner, secretary, nurse, teacher, social worker, air traffic controller, machinist, and customer service representative. Nor is this list exhaustive. Many other occupations are stressful.

Work relationships are a potential source of stress. The quality of our relationships with bosses, co-workers, and subordinates clearly affects our perception of a job as stressful or not. Stress is likely to result if we feel distrust, threat, hostility, or a lack of support in these relationships. Communication difficulties and personality clashes are a major source of workplace stress. Sometimes we like our jobs but don't like the people with whom we work.

Unclear or conflicting job responsibilities present another source of organizational stress. Stressed employees often report uncertainty about what is expected of them. Many people work without job descriptions and with little awareness of the criteria by which their performance will be evaluated. Managers, for example, may be unsure of the extent of their responsibilities and the scope of their authority. Secretaries may work for many managers who simultaneously put conflicting demands on them.

Stress may also stem from the structure and philosophy of an organization. Organizations with strict chains of command and cumbersome rules, policies, and procedures can be very stressful places, as can those with authoritative and impersonal styles of management where there is little chance for employees to have input into decisions that affect them. In other organizations, politics, game playing, and the lack of straight answers cause frustration. Some organizational cultures make it difficult for newcomers, women, minorities, or older workers to succeed. This category of stressors is broad and pervasive. A wide variety of issues related to organizational structure, management style, and workplace climate have been found to cause stress.

We have already stated that both overly demanding positions and unchallenging positions can be stressful. We are all familiar with the harried manager who must work excessive hours, face constant deadlines, juggle multiple projects, make important decisions, and travel frequently. Such jobs make extraordinary demands in terms of work overload and allow little time for personal relationships, exercise, hobbies, and rest. It is no wonder that burnout or physical or mental collapse occurs. High levels of stress also occur in jobs with little fulfillment or challenge. Boredom can produce as much stress as a taxing job can. Highly specialized, repetitive, low-skilled jobs often are stressful because they lack challenge.

Certain issues related to career development can be sources of stress. Someone who is inadequately trained for a particular job will experience stress trying to perform the job. Being overqualified for a position has its own frustrations. Many managers, especially high achievers, feel stressed when their desires for promotion are thwarted or postponed. Both stagnation in a job and urgency in climbing the career ladder are career-development stressors. Rapid career development via training opportunities, frequent promotions, special projects, or transfers can be quite stressful. Questions of job security inevitably produce anxiety.

Environmental Sources of Stress

Certain aspects of the physical surroundings in a workplace can create stress. For example, noise, crowded conditions, uncomfortable temperatures, inappropriate lighting, uncomfortable furniture, awkward working positions, air pollution, or safety hazards contribute to worker stress. While federal regulations limit excessive noise or toxic chemicals in the workplace, many other environmental stressors go unnoticed. Working all day under fluorescent lights or sitting for long periods of time at a computer terminal can produce tension, headaches, dizziness, and fatigue. Environmental features of the workplace not only create stress but also cause accidents, disability, and death. In recent years, more companies have been paying attention to environmental stressors. Indeed, a speciality area called ergonomics has emerged to examine ways to adapt the work environment to human requirements, capabilities, and needs.

Some studies have delineated different stress factors for management and nonmanagement positions. Managers are more likely to be stressed by deadlines, take-home work, responsibility for other people, competition, job instability, and the need for achievement. People in nonmanagement positions are more likely to be stressed by shift work, job monotony, insufficient responsibility, social isolation, little recognition for achievement, fear of unemployment, and environmental conditions. These categories of stressors are not necessarily mutually exclusive; that is, an individual may be affected simultaneously by personal, organizational, and environmental stressors. Obviously, coping will be more difficult for a person with Type A behavior who has family problems and is in a highly demanding job. In fact, there seems to be a contagious effect: family problems can lead to job stress or vice versa.

Symptoms of Stress

In order to detect stress early enough to prevent serious consequences to the individual or to the organization, we must be able to recognize stress symptoms. Stress manifests itself through certain feelings, behaviors, and illnesses. Chronic anger, despair, anxiety, and depression can all indicate stress. While it is inevitable that we feel some of these emotions occasionally, their persistence may be warning signals of stress.

Defensive or aggressive behavior can be a sign of stress. Stressed individuals have trouble dealing with life's little irritations and tend to have frequent emotional outbursts. Other behaviors potentially indicative of stress include difficulty concentrating; increased use of alcohol, caffeine, nicotine, or drugs; frequent nightmares; insomnia; loss of appetite or compulsive eating; or nervous tics. Work-related behaviors also change due to stress. For example, a decline in job performance, sudden increases in absenteeism, preoccupation with busywork, or an obsessive concern for work can all signal stress, as can the onset of typical stress-related illnesses.

Stress-Management Strategies

To be effective, a stress-management program must take a two-faceted approach. First, individuals must learn how to identify, monitor, and reduce stress in their lives. Second, the organization must revise its personnel procedures, managerial styles, and physical environment to be less stressful to employees.

Individual Practices

An ongoing, dualistic approach to reducing stress will reap benefits for individuals and organizations alike. The following are some specific stress-management strategies for individuals and organizations to consider:

1. *Recognize your stress.* The first step in managing stress is to realize its attitudinal, behavioral, and physical signs. Many highly stressed people are immune to the messages their bodies are giving them. Be aware of individual stressors and unique symptoms of stress. On a regular basis, ask yourself what aspects of your personality, job, or private life cause you to feel stressed. Make note of how you show the early warning signs of stress.

2. *Monitor your pace.* Periodically, you need to examine the pace of your life. Are you trying to do too much? Does your life offer too little stimulation? Remember that Type A personalities take on too many tasks and even rigidly schedule their leisure time. Setting realistic limits on work and social responsibilities is essential to stress management.

3. *Practice relaxation techniques.* Relaxation provides a temporary but important break in a period of stress. Medical approaches to stress management typically recommend relaxation techniques such as meditation, yoga, self-hypnosis, progressive muscle relaxation, or biofeedback. Most of these techniques take just a few minutes and can be done in any quiet place at work. Each offers physiological and emotional therapy. In fact, some companies now provide relaxation or exercise breaks in lieu of coffee breaks during the workday.

4. *Develop an exercise program.* Exercise is one of the best stress-reduction strategies available. It provides cardiovascular benefits, helps control weight, can boost energy levels, and induces relaxation. The type of exercise need not be strenuous or time-consuming. The choices range from energetic options such as running or racquet sports to milder forms such as walking or gardening.

5. *Practice good nutrition.* Sound eating habits help you resist certain diseases and survive stress. A simple plan would be to moderate intake of fat, sugar, salt, calories, and caffeine and to consume recommended portions from the four basic food groups.

6. *Socialize with people other than co-workers.* For some people, work is the exclusive source of socializing. While friendships with co-workers can be enjoyable and relaxing, associating only with work colleagues can be detrimental because of the tendency to exclusively talk shop with co-workers and therefore never escape the workplace even away from it.

7. *Develop a network of social support.* We all need people whom we can approach, trust, and depend on. While family typically fulfills this role, it does not always provide the social support necessary for coping with stress. In some cases, family may be the very source of stress. Confiding in various people, such as family, friends, work associates, or professional counselors, can provide a buffer to stress.

8. *Moderate life changes.* Too much change, unexpected change, and uncontrolled change produce stress. Where possible, anticipate and pace your major life changes. Combining a promotion, the purchase of a home, and the birth of a child probably will be too much to cope with at once, no matter how positive each single event is. While we cannot control all life's changes, we can pace certain decisions with stress-management goals in mind.

9. *Practice time management.* Stress management and time management go hand in hand. We feel stressed when we lose control of our time. Setting reasonable goals, planning ahead, establishing priorities, scheduling tasks, resisting interruptions, delegating work, and avoiding perfectionism are all effective time-management techniques.

10. *Protect idle leisure time.* Sometimes we structure our free time as much as our workday. Hobbies and social life should not be as taxing as a job. Unstructured leisure time is more relaxing than a tightly scheduled itinerary. A little idleness each day and some larger blocks of unplanned time for spontaneous activity on the weekends is essential for relieving tension.

Organizational Practices

Because many stressors are intrinsic to the job itself or to climates in organizations, individual strategies are not sufficient for managing stress. Organizations can adopt several practices to reduce employee stress. Obviously, the best stress-management program combines both individual and organizational interventions. Some suggestions for organizations include the following:

1. *Provide stress-management training.* Organizations can teach supervisors and managers to identify signs of stress in themselves and in their subordinates. Equipping employees with stress-management skills can reduce the company's medical benefits costs and help to maintain productivity.

2. *Improve internal communication.* The more that information flows smoothly in an organization, the less anxiety and uncertainty there will be. Employees should be encouraged to communicate upward with managers, who should provide information to employees. Employees should know what is expected of them, should receive regular performance feedback, and should feel free to bring problems and recommendations to the attention of supervisors. Open communication can produce better decision making as well as help to reduce stress.

3. *Clarify role expectations.* Because employees need to know their job duties, responsibilities, and authority, they should receive detailed job descriptions with explicitly stated reporting relationships. This is especially important for employees who receive assignments from several different people or groups. When an employee has more than one supervisor, strategies for resolving conflicting demands must be developed.

4. *Implement an employee-assistance program.* For troubled employees, professional counseling is necessary. Some sources estimate that as much as 20 percent of a work force will have personal problems that significantly affect productivity. Providing counseling to troubled employees can be cost-effective, reducing turnover and maintaining productivity.

5. *Develop people-oriented management styles.* Rigid, authoritarian management styles ought to give way to more flexible, democratic approaches. Employees should be treated fairly and humanely rather than like machines. Not only will people-oriented management styles reduce organizational stress, but evidence suggests that companies with democratic cultures attain higher levels of productivity. To change their management philosophy, some companies may need to begin a program of organizational development.

6. *Redesign jobs, where necessary.* You can enlarge or enrich unstimulating jobs. In cases of work overload, reduce responsibilities or delegate them to others. Periodically solicit employees' perceptions about the amount of challenge, stimulation, and fulfillment in their jobs.

7. *Provide a safe and comfortable physical environment.* The Occupational Safety and Health Act mandates that working environments be free from extreme noise, toxic substances, and safety hazards. Employers can go further, however, in developing a comprehensive awareness of ergonomics. Employers should consider the relationship of spatial arrangements in the workplace to stress and productivity factors.

[*See also* Employee Assistance Programs; Time Management]

For Additional Information

Brief, Arthur P., Randall S. Schuler, and Mary Van Sell. *Managing Job Stress.* Boston: Little, Brown and Company, 1981. Research findings of physicians, psychologists, sociologists, and other professionals concerned with human stress. Topics include the antecedents and consequences of job stress, self-help techniques for coping with work strains, organizational conditions contributing to stress, and managerial strategies for reducing stress. One chapter examines the unique stress on women in the workplace.

Dubinsky, Alan J. "Managing Work Stress." *Business—The Magazine of Managerial Thought and Action,* Vol. 35 (1985), No. 3, pp. 30–35. Approaches employers can take to help employees reduce stress as well as approaches employees can implement on their own.

Gmelch, Walter H. *Beyond Stress to Effective Management.* New York: John Wiley & Sons, 1982. Written to help managers and their employees deal with organizational and personal stress. Through numerous exercises and self-tests, you can recognize stressors and symptoms of stress and then can develop a comprehensive stress-management plan.

Ivancevich, John M., Michael T. Matteson, and Edward P. Richards. "Who's Liable for Stress on the Job?" *Harvard Business Review,* Vol. 64 (1985), No. 2, pp. 60ff.

Levi, Lennart. *Preventing Work Stress.* Reading, Mass.: Addison-Wesley Publishing Company, 1981. Examines the worker's interaction with the work environment and the relationship to emotional and physical health. The author suggests a restructuring of the social systems of the workplace and offers policy recommendations for local, national, and international levels.

Pelletier, Kenneth R. *Healthy People in Unhealthy Places.* New York: Delacorte Press, 1984. Organizational responsibilities and benefits of a healthy workplace. Chapters cover work and stress, toxic hazards in the workplace, and model health-promotion programs.

Yates, Jere E. *Managing Stress.* New York: AMACOM, 1979. Sources of stress, symptoms of stress, the consequences of stress, and actions for alleviating stress.

Team Building

BECAUSE OF ADVANCES IN TECHNOLOGY IN AN IN-
CREASINGLY COMPLEX SOCIETY, MANY JOBS require the
collaboration of people across departments or specialities. Team building is the process of unifying a group to work effectively toward a
common goal. It involves motivating the members to take pride in the
accomplishments of the group. By cooperating to share knowledge and
skills, a team can often complete work more effectively than an individual can. Teams are often intact, relatively permanent work groups; they
can also be temporary groups designed to complete a particular project.
To help both permanent and temporary groups develop motivation,
cohesiveness, and productivity, many organizations are turning to team
building as an aspect of organizational development.

Objectives of Team Building

Team building helps a group function more as a unit. Because of
the sense of individualism and competitiveness fostered in many
organizations, a work group is not automatically a team. Just because
five or six people are working on the same project does not ensure that
they can work cooperatively toward a common goal. Specifically, team
building enhances the morale, trust, cohesiveness, communication,
and productivity of a work group.

- *Morale.* Morale is the degree of confidence a group has about its
  ability to get a job done. The higher the group's morale, the
  more motivated it is to perform well.
- *Trust.* Trust is a willingness to take risks based on a belief in
  others' abilities or integrity. Team members must have faith in
  each other if they are to function effectively as a team.

- *Cohesiveness.* Cohesiveness is the feeling of unity that holds a group together voluntarily. A cohesive group is one in which members want to belong. They feel much loyalty to the group. Cohesive groups are more productive.
- *Communication.* In order for a team to function well, members must be able to develop good interpersonal relationships, to speak openly with each other, to solve conflicts, and to confront issues.
- *Productivity.* Teams can accomplish goals that cannot be met as well by individuals. Through sharing resources, skills, knowledge, and leadership, the team is greater than the talents of its separate members.

The Team-Building Process

There is not one method of team building. The objectives of morale, trust, cohesiveness, communication, and productivity can be met in a number of ways, and a wide variety of activities can help a group understand and improve its functioning. Whatever the methods, it is important that the team itself develop the ability to identify its operating problems and to solve them. The steps commonly used in team building are discussed in the following sections.

Step 1: Collecting Information

Team building should begin with group self-assessment, which provides the starting point for team development and helps to both determine strengths and weaknesses and set goals for improvement. Consultants are often used to help a group through the team-building process. They can be either organizational employees or independent contractors. Because they are not actual members of the team, consultants can challenge the assumptions and behavior of team members. They can be more objective and take more risks, and may have greater freedom of operation when helping the group.

Information collection is necessary to diagnose problems of group functioning. Team-development needs can be determined through various data-gathering techniques, including attitude surveys, interviews of members, standardized questionnaires, role-play analysis, or the observation of group discussions. These techniques are useful in assessing a number of content areas, such as communication climate, motivation, leadership ability, group consensus, group values, knowledge of team goals, and role conflicts. Needs-assessment areas and methods should be tailored to fit the team's purpose, composition, and workplace culture. Any information that sheds light on how to improve team functioning is valid. Be careful to use only objective and valid data-gathering methods in order to pinpoint real and important team problems.

Step 2: Discussing Needs

Information gathered in step 1 should be summarized and fed back to the team. The team should openly discuss and interpret trends that emerged from the needs assessment. According to the data-collection process, what are areas of team strength? In what areas does the team need improvement? It may take several meetings for the team to grasp the results of the data collection and to agree on team-development needs. These feedback sessions are essential in order for the team to establish its own goals rather than have the goals imposed externally. By participating in what can be sensitive discussions of strengths and weaknesses, the team is already on its way to self-sufficiency in problem diagnosis and solution.

Step 3: Planning Goals

Once issues are clarified, the team should define its goals and establish some general priorities. It is essential that the team work on issues that are most important to members. By setting its own agenda, the group will be more committed to the process of team development. The group should develop a tentative schedule and action plan for meeting its goals. Consultants can be helpful here by suggesting techniques or activities through which the group can meet its goals. Organizational development or training specialists should know of exercises, films, instructional modules, or case studies to help a group develop skills necessary for effective team functioning.

Step 4: Developing Skills

The bulk of the team-building process will focus on activities to develop skills needed for high-performance teamwork. Just as an athletic team must learn plays, develop moves, and practice skills, so a work team must develop performance skills. The following are some common skills developed through team-building activities:

An Awareness of Group Development It may be fruitful for a team to realize that groups progress through predictable stages. Being able to recognize these stages can help the group deal with problems and prevent frustrations. The organizational-development literature includes activities to help a group cope with the typical developmental phases of orientation, evaluation, and control. The orientation phase is characterized by confusion over what roles members ought to play, the task to be performed, and the emergence of leadership. Members exchange information in order to orient themselves to the team project. During the evaluation phase, members tend to be opinionated and experience much conflict. They disagree about how to approach the task and must frequently take sides in struggles for leadership. The group may be fragmented by coalitions. In the final stage, the group begins to coalesce. Members accept influence from others and from the leader in order to achieve team objectives. The group takes on a personality and an energy of its own. Deliberations are coordinated and directed toward a common goal.

Putting a newly formed group through a case-study discussion can trigger the emergence of these typical phases. Careful processing of the discussion by an experienced group facilitator can help the group understand them. Replaying a videotape of group sessions can provide vivid illustrations of the group's progression through the phases. By developing an awareness of this crucial aspect of group dynamics, teams can function more smoothly and more productively.

Role Clarification In achieving a group task, it helps if everyone knows their individual responsibility and areas of authority. Even if the team has been working together for some time, there may be confusion over who is doing what and who has the right to do what. Formal job descriptions may not correspond to people's expectations of roles and rights. Early on, group members ought to discuss their expectations of the group's role within the organization and of individual members' roles within the group. What is the group's mission? Whom does the group report to? What types of power does it have? Who is the designated leader of the group? Do members agree on the division of responsibility? Do members' roles complement one another or do they conflict?

Just like members of a sports team, work-group members need to know who is playing what positions and how to play together smoothly and effectively. Role-clarification questionnaires or discussions can help members see how their performance depends on the performance of someone else. This understanding creates a strong sense of unity and loyalty within the team.

Consensus Decision Making Most decisions in the workplace are made by deferring to the views of powerful people. At best, democratic decision making means majority rules. When a majority decides, some people find themselves "going along" with, but not agreeing with, the majority. In a true teamwork approach, the group makes decisions by deliberating until everyone agrees. By taking extra time to reach consensus, more options are considered and all members have complete input into the decision. Not only does consensus decision making tend to produce better decisions, but members feel a greater commitment to the decision.

Most groups have to work at developing the skills of consensus decision making. Case-study discussions, followed by analysis of group process, can give groups practice in decision making. Do members listen objectively to each other? Do all members have the chance to contribute? Does domination, ambivalence, or naysaying occur? Does the group mediate its own conflicts? The goal is to systematically and patiently consider information and opinions until the best decision, not the quickest or obvious one, is reached. When a group can reach consensus, the true potential of teamwork is being utilized.

Conflict Resolution It is inevitable that a group of people working closely together will experience conflicts. If the people fail to handle these conflicts properly, the group will fall apart. By developing conflict-management skills, though, the group can realize productive outcomes of conflict. By disagreeing openly without becoming defensive, members can see opposing viewpoints, can develop respect for each other, and can arrive at better decisions.

A team can develop its capacity to handle conflict by openly discussing the values of conflict, by removing negative consequences that typically surround conflict, by playing devil's advocate in discussions, and by encouraging skepticism and debate. Questionnaires, role plays, or exercises can help the team develop the open communication necessary for productive conflicts. A high-performance team is characterized by members who can strongly disagree over ideas and still like and respect each other.

The team should do as many activities to develop as many specific skills as necessary. In the process of team-building activities, members may discover additional problems or needs of the group. Skill-building areas may emerge as the team performs its organizational tasks. Because the team is developing its own capacity to diagnose and solve problems, it can channel new goals into the team-building model.

The consultant may be a valuable resource in helping the group to conduct skill-building activities. The consultant can lead the group through discussions, suggest exercises, and encourage the group to analyze its own process. Also, an expert in team building may be needed to teach concepts such as phase development, role clarification, consensus decision making, and conflict resolution.

Evaluating Results

The team should evaluate whether or not it is functioning effectively. Does it have high morale, trust, cohesiveness, and productivity?

Are there additional areas that need improving? Evaluation should take place at several stages in the team-building effort. Initially, the team undergoes evaluation to determine needs and set goals. Also, periodically throughout the skill-building activities, the team should assess its progress. The ability to systematically assess its progress is a crucial element of team development. This is a major means by which the team becomes self-sufficient in determining its own growth. In the workplace, most people are accustomed to being evaluated by others. But the skill of self-assessment makes people and organizations adept at change and growth.

Evaluation can take many forms. In some cases, the effects of team building can be measured by standard workplace criteria of productivity or output. If the team is producing more units than it did before team building, then it must be performing more effectively as a team. Less error, lower production costs, and less turnover of employees may be signs of effective team functioning. Less tangible measures of team-building effectiveness include surveying members' attitudes and perceptions regarding team morale, trust, and cohesiveness. The team-building cycle continues as the evaluation results feed into needs assessment and the team proceeds again through the team-building model.

Characteristics of a High-Performance Team

A successful team-building effort should create a team that functions effectively based on these characteristics:

1. All members are committed to the team goals that they helped to develop.
2. The team possesses the necessary skills to make goal achievement possible.
3. All team members understand their roles and responsibilities.
4. The team uses consensus decision making.
5. Team members communicate openly and directly and listen to one another objectively and patiently.
6. The team can handle conflict without resentment or hostility.
7. Team members are loyal to the team and proud of its accomplishments.

[See also Conflict Management; Motivation]

For Additional Information

Bennett, Dudley. *Successful Team Building Through TA*. New York: AMACOM, 1980. Management styles conducive to and antagonistic to team building. Bennett offers transactional analysis as an approach to changing behavior and building skills of team members. He gives advice for structuring team-building work groups and using TA in performance appraisals.

George, Paul S. "Team-Building Without Tears." *Personnel Journal*, Vol. 66 (1987), No. 11, pp. 122ff. Team-building strategies that might be pursued by managers interested in developing work relationships.

Patten, Thomas H., Jr. *Organizational Development Through Team-building*. New York: John Wiley & Sons, 1981. Information and exercises from team-building seminars the author has conducted. Topics include setting goals, assessing needs, building group dynamics, managing conflict, managing time, and examining management styles and reward systems of organizations as they affect team-building efforts.

Shonk, James H. *Working in Teams*. New York: AMACOM, 1982. Provides concepts and materials for developing and managing teams. Shonk covers factors that influence team effectiveness, as well as the team-building steps of setting goals, implementing activities, and evaluating results.

Terminating
Employees

MANAGERS FREQUENTLY regard employee terminations as the least desirable aspect of their jobs. Termination is the most traumatic and disruptive event an employee faces in the workplace. In addition, it is costly to an organization and upsetting to colleagues who retain their jobs. For these reasons, you must be aware of the proper methods of terminating employees from a legal, psychological, and communication perspective.

Employment-at-Will Doctrine

The employment-at-will doctrine, in effect for nearly a century in the United States, allows an employer to fire an employee for any reason or for no reason at all. The doctrine is based on the rationale that if an employee can quit at any time, then the employer can discharge at any time. Unionized workers, civil service employees, and executives or professionals with individual employment contracts receive protection from arbitrary dismissals. Also, federal employment statutes as well as some state laws provide exceptions to the employment-at-will doctrine. It is illegal to fire someone based on reasons of sex, race, creed, ethnic origin, age, or handicap. Additionally, within the past few years, court decisions have provided further exceptions to the employment-at-will concept, which fall into two legal categories: public policy exceptions and implied-contract exceptions.

Public policy exceptions protect employees who blow the whistle on company violations of environmental, safety, or health laws; who try to start a union; who file a discrimination charge; who file a workers' compensation claim; who refuse to perform criminal acts on behalf of the company; and who take time off to serve on a jury.

Implied-contract exceptions indicate that company literature such as a policy statement or a new-employee manual that discusses terms and conditions of employment may constitute an implied contract with an employee. To prevent wrongful-discharge litigation, personnel directors should review recruiting and employment literature to eliminate statements that could be interpreted as promising job security. An employer should regard written statements in offer letters, on employment applications and contracts, and in employee handbooks and personnel files as legal commitments to employees. Likewise, oral promises made in selection interviews, performance appraisals, and exit interviews may be binding on the employer.

So while the employment-at-will doctrine still guides employment practices, numerous exceptions have eroded the concept. You must be aware of the doctrine and its exceptions as they relate to employee terminations.

The Psychology of Termination

Because terminating an employee is unpleasant, many managers do not want to examine their own feelings regarding this duty. Being aware of the psychological effects of termination, though, can make the process less stressful for the manager and more humane for the discharged employee. Managers experienced in terminating employees report resentment at having to perform the task, guilt for making the wrong hiring decision or for inadequate training of the employees, compassion for the dismissed employees and their families, anger at supervisors or the organization, blame and anger toward the fired employees, and fear that they themselves may be fired someday.

The psychological effects of being fired seem to follow a predictable pattern not unlike the stages of grief. Awareness of these effects can help discharged employees cope with the situation and can assist managers in dealing with typical employee reactions. Terminated employees initially experience shock, disbelief, and denial. The suddenness of being part of an organization one moment and being ousted the next moment can be overwhelming. They may have difficulty comprehending the reason for termination and feel that their lives have been shattered. They may also be quite dazed, have a confused sense of identity, and feel anger toward the manager and the organization. Terminated employees may feel mistreated and want to retaliate against the company. The third stage is bargaining. Some individuals perceive that a mistake has been made, try to appeal the decision, or cling to a hope of being recalled. When the employee fully realizes the finality of the decision, depression is likely to ensue. Termination can lead to feelings of failure, bruised egos, and anxiety about financial or career consequences. There may be guilt over errors, shame with family and friends, and hopelessness about finding a new job. Finally, the employee accepts the reality of the situation, rebuilds confidence and esteem, and plunges into the task of finding new employment.

One area frequently overlooked concerns the psychological effects of termination on co-workers. Whether dismissal involves one person or a mass cutback of personnel, co-workers who remain will be affected. The manager who realizes this can better deal with morale issues resulting from terminations. Third parties to terminations report immediate shock and increased communication about the dismissal, relief at retaining a job coupled with the fear that "I might be next," empathy for the discharged worker, and an opinion about the fairness or unfairness of the firing based on whether the terminated person was perceived as competent or not.

Conducting a Termination

There is no one way to fire an employee. Many of the decisions and methods of carrying out the task depend on the reason for termination, the status and seniority of the employee, and the individual organization's human resources orientation. While the fine points of conducting a termination will vary case by case, all terminations will include the elements of planning, communicating, and follow-up.

From a legal standpoint, careful planning is crucial and can make the difference between a dignified firing and a brutal one. You must make the decision to fire, determine the reason(s) for dismissal, and gather the evidence to document and explain your decision. If you have followed a system of progressive discipline with the subordinate, you will find this stage of the process easier and less stressful. A progressive disciplinary system includes a series of rules and regulations regarding work behavior and performance, progressive warnings to employees who violate those rules, counseling to improve work behavior, and criteria for termination. Progressive discipline allows open and objective communication about poor performance so the employee knows that specific actions must be corrected within a certain time frame or termination will result. Under this system, the employee receives advance warning that dismissal is being considered and is less likely to perceive unfair treatment in the event of a termination. You, then, have written records to document the reasons for dismissal. In the event of litigation, these records assist in the defense that the termination was fair and not abusive. Of course, the progressive disciplinary system does not apply if the termination is based on economic reasons beyond the employer's control.

Additional questions involved in planning a termination include:

- Who will communicate the termination?
- When will the employee be terminated (time of year, day of week, hour of day)?
- Will third parties be present at the termination (immediate supervisor, member of personnel)?
- Where will the termination occur?
- How will the message be delivered?
- How will the news be communicated to the rest of the company?
- What credible and agreeable cover story (reason for separation) should be proposed?
- What severance package or outplacement assistance will be provided?
- How might the terminated employee react? How will the terminator handle all possible reactions?

After planning these aspects of the process, someone must communicate the decision to the employee. Careful communication is necessary to help the employee save face and cope with the news. Consideration must be given also to the legal implications of what is said. Face-to-face communication of the dismissal is often called the exit interview. The content of the actual message of termination depends on whether the dismissal is based on economic, organizational, or employee behavior factors.

When the termination is due to reasons beyond the employee's control, you should explain the company's problem (economic, relocation, reorganization), indicate other necessary actions already taken by the company, state the decision to release the employee, express confidence in the employee's abilities, indicate the extent to which the company will provide help with finding new employment, and state the company's financial terms of separation (severance pay, benefits continuation). Then you must listen to the employee and allow feelings to surface. At the conclusion of the exit interview, take the employee to the personnel office to complete the necessary paperwork.

When the termination is based on incompetent performance or unacceptable behavior by the employee, you should inform the employee of the decision to terminate, explain the reasons for dismissal, avoid blame by indicating there was a misfit between the organization's needs and the employee's attributes, show confidence about the employee's ability to find new employment, and explain severance and outplacement options. Again, listen patiently and deal calmly with the employee's reactions.

The exit interview should be direct and concise. It should be absolutely clear that the person has been fired and the decision is irreversible. Dwelling on past mistakes and effusive demonstrations of sympathy should be avoided. It is important that the terminator remain aloof and avoid defensiveness whatever the reaction from the dismissed employee. Reactions can run the gamut from tears, accusations, threats, self-pity, pleading, disorientation, to delight. When the message has been delivered, the reaction shown, the questions about severance answered, and the cover story coordinated, then the exit interview should be brought to a quick close. The final remark should refer to the employee's next step and future success.

The wrap-up part of termination involves the package of assistance given to the dismissed employee, a mutually agreeable cover story for prospective employers, and the dissemination of information about the termination to the rest of the company.

Some companies have specific policies regarding severance benefits. Others design severance packages to suit individual employees. Whatever the method, a severance settlement is important for helping the employee during a transition to a new job. The attention given to this aspect of termination can significantly affect the morale of retained workers and the overall image of the company. Most severance packages include a continuation of salary for a certain time period depending on the employee's position, length of service, and age. Typically, higher-level, older individuals with longer tenure in the organization receive larger settlement amounts. Other areas for discussion include the eligibility period for unemployment benefits and health and insurance coverage.

There are other types of separation assistance in addition to severance pay and benefits. Middle- and upper-level employees may be offered special termination perks such as office space, secretarial help, and outplacement counseling for finding a new job. Outplacement counseling provides professional assistance to help dismissed employees cope with termination, assess career strengths, set goals for future employment, and conduct the job search.

The manager and dismissed employee should agree on a reasonable story to tell others both inside and outside of the organization regarding the termination. The story should put both the individual and the organization in a good light, thereby protecting co-workers' morale and the employee's chances of obtaining a good position elsewhere. Prepare a draft of this story to offer the employee for approval.

The termination process is not complete until you write a summary of the exit interview and communicate information about the termination to co-workers. While all the details of the exit interview are still vivid, make a record of all that transpired. Include all remarks exchanged, the emotional climate that prevailed, and decisions regarding severance benefits. Your accurate summary could prove invaluable should the employee decide to challenge the termination decision. Finally, provide a written announcement of the termination to co-workers, stating merely that the individual is no longer an employee of the company. Provide the effective date and indicate the process for determining a replacement. Do not discuss reasons for the termination.

Advice for Handling Terminations

Here are some additional suggestions to consider regarding the termination of employees:

1. Make sure the termination takes place in a private setting. Never conduct a dismissal over the phone, by a memo, or by a pink slip in the pay envelope.
2. If there is a possibility that the employee could make a case for wrongful discharge, seek advice of counsel before terminating the employee.
3. Consider whether the employee may try to retaliate against an individual or against the company. Make sure the employee cannot endanger other people, important documents, or equipment. Request the help of security if necessary.
4. Give the termination process the attention it deserves so that effective communication, dignity, and respect can prevail.

[See also Disciplining Employees; Interviewing]

For Additional Information

Coulson, Robert. *The Termination Handbook.* New York: The Free Press, 1981. Information for employees being fired, for supervisors who have to fire, and for managers making termination decisions. The book includes examples of numerous actual terminations, court cases, employment practices abroad, a survey of corporate termination practices, and employee arbitration rules of the American Arbitration Association.

Employee Termination Handbook. New York: Executive Enterprises Publications, 1981. Legal and psychological guidelines for employers regarding termination. The contributors include lawyers, human resources specialists, and psychologists. Chapters cover the employment-at-will doctrine, protective labor legislation, federal antidiscrimination acts, the uniform guidelines on employee selection, record-keeping requirements, progressive discipline, and the psychology of termination and outplacement.

Fulmer, William E. "How Do You Say You're Fired?" *Business Horizons,* Vol. 29 (1986), No. 1, pp. 31–38. Reviews the issues of how frequently executives fire managers, how they do it, and what legal liabilities they incur. The author also makes recommendations for firing effectively.

Kingsley, Daniel T. *How to Fire an Employee.* New York: Facts on File Publications, 1984. The psychology and communication of termination. Kingsley examines the process of termination from the views of the manager, the terminated employee, and co-workers. He discusses legal factors of performance appraisal as they relate to firing, alternatives to dismissal, appealing terminations, outplacement, as well as protective legislation and court cases.

Michal-Johnson, Paula. *Saying Good-Bye: A Manager's Guide to Employee Dismissal.* Glenview, Ill.: Scott, Foresman and Company, 1985. Focuses on communicating a dismissal, including practical advice, case studies, role plays, and checklists for constructing the termination message, handling employee reactions, assisting the dismissed employee, and detecting troubled employment relationships.

Time Management

THE SKILL OF EFFICIENTLY USING TIME is essential to your success. Unlike other resources, time cannot be saved or accumulated. A manager who wastes this elusive resource cannot regain it. Your role typically places numerous and diverse demands on you. In order to achieve goals, meet deadlines, and deal with unexpected problems, you must make effective use of limited time. To be skilled in time management, you must recognize your time robbers and develop habits that protect and maximize the time you do have.

Common Time Robbers

Managers who work excessively but merely spin their wheels with little tangible accomplishment may be victims of three types of pitfalls: poor planning and organizational skills, external time robbers, and negative personal traits. Let us examine each category to see the specific unproductive habits that waste time.

Poor Planning and Organizational Skills

Harried managers often feel a loss of control in their workday and in their lives. They complain that they cannot get organized, they cannot get a handle on things, they cannot complete any one task, and they cannot prevent interruptions. Poor time managers act as if someone else controls their time and they are puppets whose strings are being pulled by others. Clearly, others do have legitimate claims on our time. Bosses and customers, for example, have the right to expect us to work for them, but we ultimately control whether we will respond to their requests, how we will respond, when we will respond, and how much time we will devote to their requests. Then there are all the times

314

when we allow, if not invite, others who do not have legitimate claims on our time to take a piece of our valuable time. The first step in understanding our time-management pitfalls is to realize all the ways that we give up responsibility for and control of our work time.

Another sign of poor planning and organizational skills is the lack of clear priorities. Poor managers of time hop from one project to the other without successfully completing any. This is classic wheel-spinning. Managers who feel that all tasks are equally important are not efficient masters of time. They spend as much time on routine, trivial, or low-payoff tasks as they do on significant tasks with important consequences. Poor time managers have difficulty distinguishing between work they should do immediately and work they can delay or eliminate altogether. A key ingredient in becoming organized is establishing and adhering to priorities.

Some managers are disorganized because they do not have a system for keeping track of duties and deadlines. Work piles up on their desks, important requests become buried, they cannot find things, and they perform tasks haphazardly and inconsistently. Usually, these people waste hours searching through incomprehensible filing systems or through towering piles of paperwork to find an elusive document. Such disorganized managers feel overwhelmed and anxious, and their credibility plummets in the eyes of others. Systematic methods of cataloging and retrieving information are essential to the wise use of time.

Another sign of poor planning is to let work expand to fill the available time. Ineffective time managers begin a project and work on it until the project is complete. If you have all day to do a report, the report will take all day to do. If you have a week to do the report, the report will consume your entire week. Ironically, if you allot two hours to do the report and then protect those two hours from interruption or distraction, you are likely to complete a quality report close to that two-hour deadline. By devoting unlimited time to tasks, you let the task control your time. Planning projects and schedules realistically is an important tactic for becoming a good time manager.

Managers who lack planning and organization skills usually jump into projects with little purpose or preparation. They begin work without adequate thought, outlines, or strategies to guide their work. Without clear direction, it takes longer to complete the work and the quality will suffer. Then they lose even more time because the poor-quality work will have to be redone. Planning means giving advance thought and direction to a project. Taking a little time to conceptualize a project and to arrange a sequence of steps for its accomplishment will save much time overall.

The several pitfalls related to lack of planning and organization include relinquishing control of your time, failing to establish priorities and record-keeping systems, letting tasks consume too much time, and insufficiently preparing and strategizing work. If you want to better utilize your time, analyze whether you fall victim to these types of pitfalls.

External Time Robbers

A typical workday for most managers involves responding to mail, originating correspondence, preparing reports, attending meetings, making and receiving phone calls, and interacting with others who drop by the office. Less routine duties include putting out fires and business travel. The majority of a manager's day is spent responding to external stimuli. Large portions of time are encumbered by mail, calls, visits, and meetings that other people impose on you. You originate very little of this type of work. Many managers have trouble protecting their time from these external interruptions. Keep in mind, however, the notion that you control your own time and that you often allow the interruptions that frustrate you. These external demands are considered pitfalls of time management when managers fall prey to interruptions and do nothing to control them.

Out of habit, you may respond to mail that is unimportant and undeserving of reply. Or you may interrupt a significant project to deal with a request that could be handled at a more appropriate time. It is amazing how frequently managers will allow phone calls to take precedence over more important matters. By not limiting when you will take phone calls, you invite constant interruptions. The same principle applies to people who drop by the office without an appointment. A manager who promotes a total open-door policy probably has to take important work home to get it done. Obviously, you need to be accessible to subordinates and colleagues. But this does not necessitate giving everyone immediate access to you all day long! Having specified periods of the day when people are free to drop by as well as other periods of private time can combine approachability with effective time utilization.

You can also control, to some extent, the amount of your time consumed by meetings. Even when you are not leading the meeting, you can steer a meeting toward more productivity. By asking for an agenda, by being prepared and asking others to be prepared, and by helping the group stay on target during discussions, you can contribute to meeting effectiveness. You can also skip unnecessary meetings or ask subordinates to attend certain meetings in your place. It is a myth that we must attend all meetings to which we are invited or that we must sit through an entire unproductive session.

Finally, in terms of external time robbers, is the pitfall of taking on subordinates' problems or work. Frequently, subordinates bring problems to your attention and expect you to solve them. By taking on the problem or agreeing to do some part of the subordinate's work, you have reversed the supervisor-subordinate role. In effect, the subordinate has delegated work and you have willingly accepted the delegated assignment. In most instances when subordinates dump problems on you, you should guide or assist them in solving the problems themselves. This strategy not only protects your time but helps develop subordinates as well.

External time robbers include doing unnecessary paperwork, allowing a steady stream of phone calls and drop-ins as interruptions, tolerating meetings that waste time, and taking on subordinates' problems or work. You should examine the ways in which you allow others to encumber your time.

Negative Personal Traits

Some time-management pitfalls relate to your personality or attitudes. For example, anxiety, indecisiveness, procrastination, perfectionism, lack of concentration, and feelings of indispensability contribute to poor time-management practices. We will examine how each of these traits or attitudes undermines the effective use of time.

Some people spend more time worrying about certain tasks than actually doing them. Anxiety about your ability to handle a project can sap energy and time that could be better spent on the project. We all have unpleasant tasks. Fretting about them or imagining dire consequences makes them doubly unpleasant. Being an effective time manager requires a certain amount of confidence and risk-taking ability. Effectively using time means plunging in and completing even those dreaded assignments.

Another personal pitfall is indecisiveness. The indecisive manager shuffles paper all day while trying to decide what task should be tackled first. Or indecisiveness may manifest itself in chronic uncertainty about how to proceed on a project. By delaying getting started on anything, this person appears busy but is just wasting time. Indecisiveness about work may be related to anxiety or may be a result of a lack of priorities. By being confident and having well-established priorities, you know what needs doing and can embrace the task without delay.

We are all familiar with the classic enemy of time management: procrastination. Some managers will claim that their procrastination habits are effective because they work best under pressure. What do such people do with their time until deadlines approach? Do they think about the task and engage in several false starts? If so, they have wasted time already. Also, procrastinators can rarely be counted on to meet deadlines. Sure, they will meet some deadlines. But the rush to do a project at the last minute inevitably means that some deadlines will be missed and some quality will be sacrificed.

Perhaps one of the biggest impediments to effective use of time is perfectionism. Perfectionists will claim that to do a project right, you must give it 100 percent. Their personal ethic will not allow them to submit work that is less than perfect. Indeed, they claim to devote 100 percent effort to everything they do. The irony is that despite such ideals, no piece of work can reach perfection. The time spent striving for the elusive ideal of perfection usually does not result in a noticeable quality difference. There comes a point of diminishing returns regarding time spent on a task and the quality of the task's outcome. Achieving excellence in your work takes a considerable amount of concentrated, well-directed time. But beyond that amount of time, only miniscule and unrecognizable improvements in quality result from additional inputs of time. Besides being an ineffective use of time, perfectionism can be an excuse for accomplishing less than adequate amounts of work. The perfectionist who delays completing tasks until all details are flawless rarely finishes anything at all.

Another culprit of time is the inability to concentrate. Some people can have large blocks of uninterrupted time and still not achieve results. Daydreaming and self-imposed distractions plague these individuals. They find it difficult to focus on one task at a time. They are unable to work on a project for more than just a few minutes without losing interest or feeling the urge to take a break. Ironically, they may be able to give concentrated attention to hobbies or leisure activities. The lack of concentration, therefore, may be linked to the lack of will power to stick to a task, no matter how unpleasant or boring the job.

Ineffective time managers believe that they are indispensable. They have the attitude that they must be directly involved in all work if that work is to be done correctly. These individuals cannot get caught up because they essentially are doing the jobs of several people. Managers who fall into the trap of doing it all are not effective managers. Management means getting others to do the work while you coach, support, oversee, and evaluate. Managers who think they are indispensable not only make poor use of their time but impede their subordinates' growth and hinder their own credibility as well.

Clearly, there are numerous traps managers can fall into when trying to make effective use of their time. The lack of attention to planning and organization, the allowance of external intrusions, and negative personal traits can undermine your use of time significantly. A thorough self-analysis of current habits regarding time can help you avoid these pitfalls. After realizing poor time-management practices, you should adopt some of the following strategies to become a master of your own time.

Time Management Strategies

Eliminating Unnecessary Tasks

Some of the tasks we do each day are essential and some are unnecessary. We may not realize the unnecessary ones because we feel compelled to do them or because we have been doing them for years. It takes an objective look at a work routine to distinguish indispensable duties from unimportant ones. Begin by listing all work-related tasks for one day on a piece of paper. Then cross off at least two listed tasks. Do not rationalize that they all are essential. No matter how imperative it seems to be to do all the listed tasks, select the two least important ones to eliminate. Note that these should be eliminated altogether, not merely postponed for another day's "To Do" list. You may need to enlist the help of a colleague to provide objectivity in streamlining your daily routine. One way to select items for elimination is to assess the costs versus the payoffs in doing the task. Tasks that take a great deal of time but provide little reward should be dropped. In the majority of cases, no negative consequences result from eliminating them. It is unlikely that anyone will even notice that they were not accomplished.

When you practice this technique, try to avoid anxiety and guilt that may accompany your initial attempts at breaking old work habits. Likewise, it is important to use this strategy repeatedly with the goal of increasing the number of discarded items each day. Eventually, you will learn to streamline your perceived obligations and to avoid including unnecessary tasks on "To Do" lists in the first place.

Setting Priorities

Priority setting is essential to effective time management. Most managers, however, do not make conscious decisions about the order in which tasks are tackled. You may let daily demands determine priorities. As questions, calls, memos, or visitors grasp your attention, you respond to whatever task someone else hands you. Then you feel frustrated because you didn't have time to get to the really important demands.

Some managers let past habits dictate current priorities. They may handle correspondence first every morning because they have always begun their day in that manner, not because correspondence is the top priority. Another illogical way of establishing priorities is to do favorite tasks first and to put off unpleasant ones. The dilemma is that preferred tasks may not be important ones and vice versa.

Rather than letting others, past habits, or personal preferences determine priorities, effective time managers make conscious decisions to establish and to adhere to priorities. To begin establishing priorities, make a list of what you want to accomplish for one day. Eliminate some according to the previously discussed strategy. Then decide which ones you can delegate. For each remaining entry, label top-priority tasks as "A," items medium in importance as "B," and low-priority items as "C." Use the costs-versus-payoff formula for deciding A's, B's, and C's. Obviously, tasks with approaching deadlines that were delegated to you by a boss should be top priorities. Tasks that seriously affect others, impinge on your credibility, or would result in dire consequences if ignored are likely to be high priorities. These are the things you must get done that day. "B" items have moderate payoff or importance. "C" items have little value or importance associated with them. They are important enough to do, but not immediately.

Once you have labeled each task on a priority basis, begin with the top-priority ones. Give them ample time and attention and as much uninterrupted time as possible. Some people intersperse an occasional "B" or "C" item as a mental break from the top-priority projects. After concentrating for an hour on a financial report, for example, making a less important but enjoyable business phone call will provide a rest. An alternate approach to doing top-priority jobs first is to schedule these during your peak-efficiency time. Some people are mentally sluggish early in the morning and would not have the capacity to work on "A" items then. So they do a few "C's" and switch to the top-priority tasks when they feel fully alert.

You must work out your own systems for deciding priorities and for determining a schedule for accomplishing your priorities. Some errors in judgment may occur at first. With practice, however, assessments about what can be reasonably accomplished in a given day will become accurate. Then fewer items will be carried over from one day to the next as you learn to master your own time.

Improving Concentration

Being able to concentrate is a key to the effective use of time. Strive to eliminate both external and internal distractions. To create an undistracting environment, close the door, hold phone calls, and have all necessary materials and information at hand. To free yourself of internal distractions, clear your mind of all thoughts except the particular project. Immerse yourself in the task at hand. If you feel frequent urges to turn your attention to something else or to take a break, force your attention back to the task. Set minimum times to concentrate on the task and then reward yourself for reaching that designated goal. Over time, strive to increase the minimum periods of concentration. What may start out as 15-minute periods may evolve into hours of concentrated work. But there are no foolproof techniques for improving concentration. It takes motivation, will power, inner drive, and a great deal of practice.

Finding Extra Time

Managers who are very busy find that they must utilize all their available time. With some analysis, you can find pieces of time throughout the day that could be put to better use. Time spent commuting to and from work could be used for planning or for mental problem solving. Some people listen to tapes or dictate while driving. With the increased popularity of car telephones, commuting time provides an opportunity for conducting business calls. For those who use public transportation, commuting time can be spent reading, writing letters, or handling paperwork.

In addition to commuting time, there is waiting time. This is the time spent waiting for appointments, waiting in line to do business, or waiting for service somewhere. Wise time managers carry newspapers, paperback books, or notebooks with them to occupy such delays.

There may be other wasted time during the day. Could some long lunches be shortened to make the workday more productive? Could you reduce some social chitchat at work? The time spent getting ready in the morning could be used for planning or for mentally preparing a talk, a letter, or a report. The point is that there is extra time during the day if you search for it and use it productively.

Changing Your Attitudes

For those who believe that they are indispensable or are perfectionists, some change in thinking will have to precede the attempt to be better time managers. People who can't say no in order to protect their time may have to look inward to understand their lack of assertiveness. Likewise, workaholics should examine their beliefs about self-worth, work, and leisure. Some people may have to overcome anxiety, indecisiveness, or procrastination. The chronic need to be overworked, compulsive guilt associated with relaxation, or unrealistic views regarding work quality and career advancement frequently interfere with effective time management. Self-defeating attitudes may have to be dealt with before other time-management strategies can be successfully employed.

Distributing Time Effectively

It may be wise to block out certain times for particular types of tasks. This can provide a comfortable routine and maximize concentration. For example, you could set aside the same hour each day to handle correspondence or to make phone calls. Perhaps Friday afternoons could be devoted to reading professional journals. Maybe certain periods could be publicized as open-door time in which drop-in visits are encouraged. By establishing and communicating a schedule whenever possible, you protect your time and create predictability for work associates.

Scheduling Relaxation Time

When trying to become a better time manager, you can fall into the trap of becoming compulsive about every moment of the day. When this happens, you feel even more frustrated and harried. Sometimes the best use of time is to do nothing—to daydream, to look at the clouds, to meditate, to take a walk. By seizing time to relax through both planned and unplanned activity, you revitalize your mind and body. Treating yourself to a favorite relaxation technique, even under time pressures, can improve motivation, concentration, and endurance to get the work done.

[*See also* Delegation; Meetings]

For Additional Information

Cummings, Paul W. *Open Management.* New York: AMACOM, 1980, chapter 12, "Time Management," pp. 199–215. Pitfalls of time management, techniques to overcome the pitfalls, and a checklist for measuring the value of time.

Douglass, Merrill E., and Donna N. Douglass. *Manage Your Time, Manage Your Work, Manage Yourself.* New York: AMACOM, 1980. The essentials of time management, including preventing others from abusing your time, clarifying objectives, planning, eliminating busywork, and conquering indecision.

Oncken, William, Jr. *Managing Management Time.* Englewood Cliffs, N.J.: Prentice-Hall, 1984. How to use organizational leverage to concentrate efforts on doing the right things; how to resolve conflicts between planned priorities and urgent, last-minute tasks; and how to avoid frequent intrusions on your time.

Rutherford, Robert D. *Just In Time: Immediate Help for the Time-Pressured.* New York: John Wiley and Sons, 1981. Time-management questions and answers on such topics as identifying common time wasters, improving concentration, setting priorities, getting started in the morning, avoiding procrastination, delegating, and getting others to respect your time.

Training

To EFFECTIVELY DEVELOP YOUR EMPLOYEES, YOU must understand the training function. You must know when, how, and where to find training for yourself and your subordinates. From time to time, you must train your staff by yourself. Managers in organizations with training departments must know how to work effectively with the in-house training staff. By understanding the functions and methods of training as well as its benefits and drawbacks, you can make enlightened decisions about this employee-development tool.

Making Training Decisions

There is a logical decision-making process that you should use to make training decisions, which involves five questions.

Is There a Need for Training?

Usually some type of actual or anticipated problem or deficiency in the work unit leads you to consider training as a solution. For example, if a work team is not functioning effectively, you may consider training in team building as a possible solution. A supervisor who has stormy relationships with subordinates may be recommended for supervision training. An organization with sexual harassment problems may use training as an intervention. Because managers rarely select training unless there is a perceived need for it, training can be selected as a reaction to a problem or as a proactive measure to prevent a problem. The more specifically you anticipate or pinpoint the need or problem, the more sound the decision-making process about training.

Is Training the Best Solution?

After determining the specific problem, examine all possible solutions to decide if training is the best option. Some problems are best solved by training; others are not. For example, a manager who is effective in all areas except delegation will profit from a training session to develop delegation skills. But a supervisor who is prone to emotional outbursts may need an employee-assistance program as opposed to a communication-training program. In some cases, training is selected to solve a problem when a better solution would involve job enrichment, individual coaching or mentoring, discipline, or termination.

What Type of Training Is Needed?

If you determine that training is the best solution to a problem, then your next step is to identify the type of training needed. Training can be used to change attitudes, affect behavior, develop skills or technical competence, or provide information.

What Is the Most Effective Means of Delivering the Training?

Training options are enormous. The categories typically include self-instruction methods, an in-house training department, public seminars, or outside providers who train employees inside your organization. Often, the range of choices within each category is broad. A brief overview of each type will help you make appropriate training decisions:

Self-Instruction Self-paced manuals such as user manuals for computers or equipment, individual-instruction workbooks, audiocassettes, videotapes, or computer-assisted instruction are fast and inexpensive. They need not interrupt an employee's daily work routine but can be used during free time. For certain purposes with certain people, self-instruction can be effective. There are limitations to self-instruction training methods, however. The element of human interaction, often crucial to learning, is missing. The user may feel isolated and demotivated. There is no one to check and correct mistakes. Self-instruction is therefore not always appropriate.

In-House Training Staff Internal training departments provide a valuable service to managers and employees. They provide or assist in finding the training that managers need for their subordinates. In deciding whether internal trainers are the best option, assess the competence of the training staff. Even large training departments do not always have expertise in all training topics. Are there employees inside the company who can provide the type of training you need? Does their schedule permit them to provide the training when you need it? Is the problem a politically sensitive one that would be handled best by an outsider? Can the internal trainer be objective regarding the problem that training should solve? Can you work with the training staff? This is not an option for all managers, because small organizations do not always have training departments.

Public Seminars   Public seminars include speakers doing programs at local hotels or motels; courses sponsored by colleges, universities, and vocational schools; vendor-supplied education in conjunction with the purchase of equipment; and public programs provided by independent consultants, trade or employers associations, professional companies, or management-information companies. Public training offers much diversity in topics, facilitators, and cost. It allows your employees to meet people from other companies. Much can be learned from hearing about the experiences of other organizations. On the other hand, sensitive company information may be disclosed. Also, because public seminars must meet the needs of participants from various levels, functions, and types of organizations, the content must be general. Training from public seminars may not be applicable to the specific situation of a particular company.

Outside Providers Who Train Inside Your Organization   Many of the facilitators of public programs will also provide training to specific organizations. They may offer the same seminar as the public version brought to your location for a number of employees, or they may create a training program unique to your needs. In the latter case, the outside provider can create the training program for someone in your company to deliver, deliver the training for you, or train someone on your staff to deliver the training in subsequent sessions after presenting the initial training session. Outside providers who train inside your organization offer many advantages. They can tailor the training to meet your specific needs and provide objectivity and credibility. On the negative side, this type of training can be very expensive and is time-consuming for you to coordinate. Also, the trainer is still an outsider who will never know all the nuances of your organization.

How Much Can You Spend for the Training?

You must analyze the cost of training against the probable returns. The cost includes the actual training fees, the time that trainees spend away from the job, and possible travel expenses. It is difficult to put a dollar figure on the benefits that training provides. Try to assess the tangible returns after employees participate in training. Perhaps there are fewer customer complaints, less signs of stress and absenteeism, fewer disputes or grievances, higher morale, better-quality products, or higher rates of productivity.

How to Select a Public Training Program

To carefully select a public training program for themselves or their subordinates, managers can use a number of criteria, including the following:

- *The program content.* Before selecting a public training program, you should receive a course outline that specifies objectives, content, and training formats to be used. The outline should be detailed enough so that you can identify the exact topics to be covered and the amount of attention devoted to each. Likewise, the outline should indicate how each topic will be covered, for example, through lecture, discussion, case study, audiovisual, role play, or simulation activities. To what extent will participants work with the information or practice the skills? This may depend on how many participants are included in a session. Feel free to ask questions about the program content. In some cases, the person or organization sponsoring the program will provide sample written materials for your perusal in making a training decision.

- *The trainer's ability.* A training program, despite excellent content, is only as good as the person delivering it. Before selecting a public training program, you should feel confident about the trainer's expertise, prior organizational experience, familiarity with the topic, and platform style. Some trainers will provide sample videotapes or audiotapes of their work.

- *Evaluation system.* Evaluation may involve both the trainer's evaluation of participants and the participants' evaluation of the trainer and the program. It is helpful if participants receive from training some assessment of their own abilities or knowledge on the training topic. Some sessions will provide pretest and posttest evaluations, rating forms, or self-tests for participants. Such evaluation of participants is not possible in short programs with large numbers of participants, which are more akin to a speech than an actual training seminar.

All training programs should include a means for participants to evaluate the program. This can include a few questions on which trainees rate certain features of the program after completing the session, open-ended written or oral feedback to the trainer about program strengths and weaknesses, or follow-up evaluations after the participants are back on the job to determine how much they are applying program content. Whatever evaluation tools are used, you should solicit informal reactions or written reports from subordinates about the perceived value of the training. Additionally, you can observe, through relevant on-the-job measures, whether the training had an impact.

• *Participants' recommendations.*   Before selecting a public training program, you should obtain a list of previous participants in similar programs. Contact these previous participants to obtain their perceptions of the program. Ask them specific questions about it. This is the best way to get an accurate picture of the program. Be suspicious of public program facilitators who will not disclose the names of people and organizations that have previously used their training services.

• *Price and location.*   The price of public sessions can range from under $100 for a full day to several thousand dollars for a week-long program or for a nationally renowned trainer. Public training programs are held at local motels, hospitals, community centers, or educational institutions. Or they may be in posh resorts or training facilities anywhere in the world. Naturally, you will want to consider price and location in selecting a public training program.

Selecting an Outside Provider to Train Inside Your Organization

Many of the same issues of content, trainer ability, evaluation system, references from previous clients, and price apply when you choose an external provider. However, there are some criteria unique to choosing outside trainers to work within your company, such as:

• *Needs assessment.*   With this type of training, you should expect the training organization to conduct a needs assessment or training audit. The trainer should distribute surveys, conduct interviews, lead focus-group discussions, or observe the dynamics of the organization. The more familiar the trainer becomes with the structure, the mission, the people, and the problems in your organization, the more effective the training will be. This pretraining phase may or may not include a fee and ranges from a few hours of work to several months of research and analysis. The nature of the needs assessment depends on the organization, the scope of the training program, and the organization's training budget.

- *The training program itself.* Do you want a standard program brought to your location so that your employees do not have to travel to a public place? Or do you want program objectives, content, and delivery formats designed to your specifications? Do you want a program delivered once to a group of employees or do you want a program that your organization can use repeatedly in the future?

- *Follow-up consultation.* You should expect more ongoing assistance from an outside provider who trains inside organizations than from public training seminars. The trainer should not disappear once the training program has been delivered. Instead, this type of training should include periodic visits from the trainer to assess the impact of the training, to monitor the progress of participants, and to offer additional coaching or training to increase effectiveness. The follow-up phase may or may not include a fee.

Working With an In-House Training Department

Managers with a trainer or a full-fledged training department in their organizations are fortunate. Nevertheless, they sometimes do not realize or take full advantage of this employee-development tool. It is important to realize that internal trainers are an asset to your work unit. Managers who do not understand their role as human resources developers or who do not appreciate the benefits of training will see training as a waste of time. Some managers see training as an added luxury or as an unnecessary interruption to the work routine. In this age of business competition, information explosion, technological advancements, and rapid career change, training is an essential ingredient of organizations.

You can also use internal trainers to create or to locate the training you need. By working closely with your training department to pinpoint training needs, to structure materials and content, and to evaluate the impact of training, you can be assured of quality training for your staff. If in-house trainers cannot provide the service needed, then you can work with them to find and evaluate quality, cost-effective programs elsewhere. In either case, good managers take advantage of the training resources within their organizations.

Advantages and Disadvantages of Training

An analysis of some of the advantages and limitations of training will present a balanced perspective for managers making training decisions. Training offers many advantages to individuals and organizations alike. It is an excellent avenue for employee development because it can improve attitudes, develop skills, and impart information. Providing employees the opportunity for training can serve as a reward and improve their morale. Those who have participated in training usually return to work with heightened enthusiasm, as well as ideas and suggestions for improving the work situation. Organizations with excellent reputations for providing employee training are likely to have better public relations images and recruiting opportunities. All of this translates into organizational development. The organization with an enlightened view of training usually enjoys better employee relations and higher productivity.

This is not to say that training is a panacea. One limitation is its expense. Some companies can afford no more than the most minimal of training efforts. And because the return on the investment in training is difficult to calculate, other companies cannot justify large expenditures for training. Still other departments or organizations simply cannot afford to take someone off of a job to send to a training program. Training can also result in employee misuse of information gained. Employees may even take jobs with other organizations once you have paid to upgrade their knowledge or skills.

The Manager as Trainer

All managers face the task of training their employees, in the broadest sense of the term. In addition to knowing how to select training for subordinates, you must know how to perform the role of trainer. Managers are called on to help new hires, for example. Even if the personnel department provides general orientation training, it is the duty of the unit manager to see that the new employee learns to perform the new job correctly.

Too many managers take this task too lightly. Ineffective managers typically hand new employees a manual and tell them to read it. This hardly suffices as on-the-job training. Another on-the-job training error is to tell the new hire to watch a seasoned employee to learn how the job is done. There is no guarantee that the experienced employee is doing the job correctly or can teach someone else how to do the job. In the meantime, the new hire feels like a pest and is reluctant to ask too many questions. Some managers, like drill sergeants, dictate job procedures and command new hires to perform these correctly without asking too many questions. Rather than adopting these procedures, you must work closely with new employees to see that they develop the right work skills and attitudes.

You should also train in the event of employee-performance problems, when an employee's job is expanded or changed, or when you want to develop a subordinate for a new project or promotion. In essence, whenever you provide feedback, coach, or serve as a mentor, you are training.

In addition to directly training employees, you must provide support to subordinates who return to the job after attending a training seminar. It is your job to help them transfer what they have learned from the training program to the work situation. This may mean letting them try a new approach or test a new idea. It may mean removing attitudinal or structural barriers so that employees can incorporate training concepts into the daily work routine.

[*See also* Consultants; Orienting New Employees]

For Additional Information

Cothran, Tom. "Build or Buy." *Training*, Vol. 24 (1987), No. 5, pp. 83–85. Addresses the question of whether you should design a training course in-house or shop for a packaged program. The author offers some answers for novice managers and trainers.

Gee, John N. "Training Program Haute Couture." *The Personnel Administrator*, Vol. 32 (1987), No. 5, pp. 69ff. Information on choosing the most effective and appropriate training tools and courses from the myriad selection on the market. The author suggests that selection decisions carefully consider four basic training issues: people, content, budget, and timeliness.

Wehrenberg, Stephen B. "Supervisors as Trainers: The Long-Term Gains of On-the-Job Training." *Personnel Journal*, Vol. 66 (1987), No. 4, pp. 48ff. An argument that skills learned in the workplace, tied directly to the job to be done, are learned faster, retained longer, and result in greater productivity gains than skills learned in a classroom. The author discusses some benefits of the supervisor as trainer.

Turnover

TURNOVER can be defined as the total number of separations of employees from an organization during a given time period. Separations are both voluntary (resignations or retirements) and involuntary (terminations). Most organizations maintain turnover statistics, if only to recognize the extent to which they lose employees. Such data can also be used to calculate costs of personnel replacement, document reasons for separation, and project future labor demands.

Positive and Negative Consequences of Turnover

Most people think that turnover is bad for a company. Indeed, organizations with high rates of turnover will probably suffer, but there are some advantages to it: When employees leave a company, they are replaced with new hires who bring new knowledge, practice, experience, and skills into the organization. Turnover can also allow for organizational renewal. With little or no change of personnel, there may be stagnation in the workplace.

While too much turnover is costly, a certain amount of it can save an organization money. Employees with large salaries may be replaced with less expensive, but equally qualified newcomers. Some positions may be eliminated, merged, or automated. Through turnover, an organization can rid itself of marginal performers, unmotivated workers, and people who are difficult to get along with. Turnover does sometimes result in the loss of a valuable employee, but often employers are pleased to be rid of the discharged employee. Likewise, many employers breathe a sigh of relief when certain employees quit or retire. So turnover may provide vitality, may have financial advantages, and may serve a housecleaning function for organizations.

The potential negative effects of organizational turnover are many. Clearly, there are tangible and indirect costs associated with turnover. Organizations can calculate original and replacement human resources costs. Recruiting, selecting, and training new employees is costly. Exit interviews, severance benefits, and outplacement services also cost money. Temporary help may have to be hired. Then there are the costs of reduced productivity while positions remain vacant and new hires become oriented to the job and to the company.

Turnover, no matter how necessary to organizational vitality, is also disruptive. Remaining employees may have to take on more work until the separated employee is replaced. Special projects and work teams may be disrupted when turnover affects their membership. If a valuable and well-liked person leaves, group morale, cohesion, and communication can be negatively affected. Separations put companies into a temporary state of imbalance. Remaining employees find themselves preoccupied with the change and spend work time discussing the former employee and the reasons for separation. A period of anxiety and uncertainty ensues. Additional turnover can result when disgruntled employees identify with separated employees and follow their lead in leaving the organization. Turnover is especially disruptive if qualified replacements in certain job categories are difficult to find.

Organizations with high rates of turnover earn reputations as less desirable working environments. Replacing employees becomes an even more difficult and costly task. Because turnover can have a serious impact on organizations, it must be managed or controlled. Managing employee turnover involves not only being aware of the consequences of turnover, but understanding the reasons for turnover and trying to control it.

Reasons for Turnover

A complex array of factors affect an individual's decision to voluntarily leave an organization, including personal circumstances, the job itself, the larger work environment, and the perception of alternatives.

A variety of personal reasons can precipitate the decision to resign or to retire from a job. Marriage, personal illness, childrearing, family problems, the job transfer of a spouse, or the desire to relocate are common reasons for quitting a job. By having fair parental leave policies, child-care benefits, and employee counseling programs, an employer can prevent some turnover. Many personal reasons for turnover are beyond the employer's control, however.

In many cases, dissatisfaction with the job itself propels employees to quit. They may not be challenged by their jobs, they may find the work repetitive or boring, or they may not be using their knowledge or abilities adequately. Dissatisfaction with salary, benefits, work schedule, and job security is also a powerful motive for leaving. Such factors of turnover, in which the employer has more control, relate directly to selection, placement, and personnel-policy decisions made by managers.

Sometimes people like their work but have difficulty with the company itself. The larger work milieu cannot help but affect their perception of a job. Employees who are unhappy with working conditions, with supervisor and co-worker relationships, with organizational policies and procedures, and with career opportunities in the company are likely candidates for separation.

Employees may also leave because they perceive better alternatives elsewhere. They may take a similar job in a different organization as a career-development strategy. They may give few reasons for their departure other than the opinion that it is time to move on. Other reasons for separation are the goal of starting a new business, the desire to return to school, an interest in military or volunteer service, or the option of early retirement.

Strategies for Controlling Turnover

Managing turnover does not mean intervening just before an employee decides to quit. Nor is it simply a matter of helping employees with performance problems so termination becomes unnecessary. While these actions help to prevent separation, they are not sufficient to effectively manage turnover because they are reactive, that is, they involve waiting until a problem surfaces and then responding. In order to manage employee turnover, organizations must realize that almost all managerial decisions can relate to turnover. In order to control turnover, companies must examine their recruitment, selection, and placement decisions; their performance evaluation and reward system; their salary and benefits plans; their promotion and career-development opportunities; their supervisory styles and relationships; their work environments; and how they handle the special needs of certain segments of their work force. The following sections discuss ways in which each of these organizational features affects turnover and presents strategies in each area for retaining employees.

Recruitment, Selection, and Placement

Companies may experience turnover because of hiring mistakes. If you hire the wrong person for a job, the individual will be unable to perform satisfactorily and is likely to quit or be fired. The more that the selection process can match an individual with an organization, the more successful that process will be and the more turnover will be reduced. Many companies fail to be specific when creating job descriptions, if they create them at all. Likewise, it is difficult to hire the most qualified applicant if you have not delineated the behavioral criteria for success. Typically, in selection interviews, candidates try to portray themselves in the best possible light while interviewers focus on style and image rather than on performance-related characteristics. The applicant's desire to get the job and the interviewer's desire to fill the position cloud the real task of making a good match between a person and a job.

To improve the match between applicant and job, both interviewers and applicants must be more realistic and more honest. Job requirements must be clearly specified, valid and reliable selection techniques must be used, job expectations and risks must be disclosed, and significant time and resources must be devoted to the selection process. Money spent at this stage will be money saved later if the amount of turnover is reduced.

Improving the selection process also depends on effective recruiting techniques. The best person cannot be hired if few qualified individuals apply. You may need to upgrade your recruiting procedures. Do ads in newspapers, professional magazines, and journals represent the best investment of recruiting dollars? Could employment agencies, executive search firms, and placement offices associated with educational institutions increase the pool of applicants? Develop creative ways of reaching minority applicants. Encourage current employees to recruit potential applicants.

The placement process is another factor of personnel selection that can ultimately affect turnover. Once an employee is placed in a work assignment, the orientation and training process must be adequate preparation for the job. Employees who start off on the wrong foot with rushed, vague, or stressful orientation periods may remain disenchanted. Some companies assume that new employees can immediately do the job or can learn the job through casual observation. Thus, they provide no systematic orientation for new hires. Orientation training should provide a realistic but supervised portrayal of actual job conditions. The new person should learn correct procedures, ask questions, and rectify mistakes.

Organizations with turnover problems should consider whether their recruitment, selection, and placement procedures are contributing to high rates of turnover. Improving hiring practices may help prevent voluntary and involuntary separations later on.

Performance Evaluation and Reward

Many employees quit because they are unhappy with their performance reviews or because they perceive they have been passed over for a promotion. Likewise, organizations typically fire employees whose performance is below expectation. Thus, the performance evaluation and reward system in an organization directly relates to its rate of turnover. Yet many performance evaluation systems are vague and subjective, leading to arbitrary decisions about workers' performance. Inadequate performance-appraisal methods can contribute to employee turnover if they fail to identify real performance problems early enough for correction or if they frustrate employees to the point of quitting.

To be effective, a performance-review system should have well-defined, measurable criteria of performance for each job in the organization. Reviews should occur frequently and results communicated directly. Most importantly, employees whose performance falls below standard should receive coaching until their performance improves. Identifying problems early and coaching to solve performance problems makes termination unnecessary. Employees know what is expected of them and what they have to do to earn rewards such as merit bonuses or promotions. Employees report feeling treated fairly under this type of system and are less like to file grievances, quit, or complain about the company to others.

Companies can also reduce turnover by encouraging frequent informal discussions about performance. Routine, unthreatening feedback about job-related behavior can prevent performance problems from developing. Supervisors who routinely praise and criticize their subordinates' job performance support the formal performance-review system. Open communication leads to fewer surprises and complaints about formal performance appraisals. When decisions about performance are clear, valid, and fair, there will be fewer disgruntled employees who feel bypassed for a promotion.

Because complaints about performance reviews and promotions cannot be eliminated totally, organizations should have systems for handling grievances. Impartial reviews and reconsiderations of performance-appraisal and promotion decisions can help reduce grievances, legal battle, and separations.

Organizations can therefore manage turnover through their performance review and reward systems by having behaviorally based and explicitly stated job-evaluation criteria; by identifying performance problems early and coaching for improved job performance; by encouraging frequent, open communication about work behavior and promotion possibilities; and by establishing unbiased procedures for handling employee complaints.

Salary and Benefits

Some employees leave jobs because they are dissatisfied with their salaries or benefits. While it is idealistic to think that employers can provide compensation packages that will completely satisfy a work force, it is important to realize the relationship of compensation to turnover.

Organizations that want to retain valuable employees must make sure their salary ranges are competitive with industry and regional standards. Not only do employees compare their salaries and benefits with those of comparable positions in other companies, but they compare across jobs within an organization. Employees will be dissatisfied and will consider leaving if they perceive that their salaries are less than those of colleagues in similar job categories with similar experience or longevity in the company. Perceived salary inequity within companies is a major factor affecting turnover. Organizations can intervene by making sure that salary equity exists both externally and internally.

Organizations also must determine if their benefits are competitive and equitable. Spending more in attractive benefits plans can save turnover costs. In addition, many companies are opting for flexible benefits packages that allow employees to select the benefits they need and to reject unnecessary options. While this does not necessarily increase the costs to employers, it does mean offering a wider range of benefits from which employees can choose. It may represent a simple strategy for retaining certain categories of employees.

Career Development

Some employees leave their present jobs because they do not anticipate satisfying future roles in the company. High achievers especially want clear and attainable paths to career development. Organizations can implement career-development programs as a strategy for retaining valuable employees. Such programs should provide information on realistic career-progression paths within the company; opportunities for self-assessment, education, and training for individual development; career counseling; and posting of available positions within the organization. Opportunities for personal growth and promotion within an organization can be a powerful motive for remaining with a firm for a large portion of an employee's career history.

Supervisory Relationships

Another factor affecting whether an employee remains on a job or not is the relationship with the supervisor. Many reasons cited for voluntary separation involve supervisory problems. Conversely, an attachment with a supervisor can retain an employee even if other dissatisfactions occur. Employees report that they are less likely to quit a job if they have a positive personal relationship with their supervisor and if the supervisor shows them consideration and creates a supportive working environment.

It is easy to see why the relationship between supervisors and workers has such a direct relationship to turnover. Supervisors play a major role in orienting employees to their jobs; supervisors typically conduct performance reviews and recommend or withhold performance rewards; supervisors shape salary decisions; and supervisors are the ones to offer praise, coaching, and career-development opportunities. They also affect most of the other factors related to employee retention or turnover.

This means that organizations should encourage effective and satisfying supervisory relationships. Resources should be provided for supervisory-skills training. Supervisors must be encouraged to set good examples, to communicate openly and regularly, and to treat their subordinates fairly. Making first-line supervisors a high human-resources priority can significantly impact employee turnover.

Work Environment

Certain types of work environments or climates drive people away. The work environment encompasses many of the elements already discussed and entails a wide variety of aspects that shape employees' perceptions of their jobs. People who quit their jobs because of dissatisfaction with the work environment cite these factors: mutual distrust between managers and employees, lack of communication, inconsistent policies and procedures, stress, competitiveness, unreasonable deadlines, job responsibilities interfering with personal life, and uncertainty about job security. Employers should examine whether aspects of their work environments contribute to turnover in their organizations.

Special Needs

Certain segments of a work force may have special needs that affect their abilities to remain in a particular job. Troubled employees may be fired or may quit if counseling or employee-assistance programs are not available. Many organizations have found it more cost-effective to offer employee counseling than to replace employees due to high rates of turnover.

Organizations perceived as inhospitable to minorities may face alarming rates of turnover among minority employees. Such a trend can damage a company's reputation or result in charges of discrimination and costly litigation. Some practices to retain minority employees include recruiting minority applicants, fair employment practices that comply with guidelines put out by the Equal Employment Opportunity Commission, and mentoring or career-development strategies that meet the special needs of minorities in the workplace.

Dual-career couples, which represent an increasing proportion of the work force, may need child-care benefits or flexible work schedules in order to remain employed. Spouse relocation assistance may be needed for a valuable employee to accept a transfer. A company wishing to retain its older employees should implement preretirement counseling or offer alternative working arrangements.

The days of loyal employees who spend their entire career with one employer have passed. Increased mobility, career changes, and emphasis on work gratification make changing jobs a common and sanctioned behavior. Progressive employers realize the need to carefully select, train, evaluate, and reward their employees. By combining such practices with equitable compensation plans, career-development opportunities, good work environments and supervisory relationships, and attention to special needs of employees, organizations can control employee turnover to a manageable and beneficial rate.

Exit Interviews

Organizations should establish the procedure of routinely scheduling exit interivews with employees who have resigned or been dismissed. This allows managers and employees to discuss the reasons for separation and to make separation agreements. Some organizations hold exit interivews in the case of terminations but do not schedule them for voluntary separations. This section will discuss advantages and disadvantages of exit interviews following resignations and will present guidelines for conducting exit interviews after an employee quits.

There are many compelling reasons for holding an exit interview in conjunction with a resignation. By soliciting the employee's reasons for quitting, the organization can compile data on the causes of turnover. Through this information, the organization can monitor and adjust its personnel practices. It is difficult to know what changes should be made to retain people if disenchanted employees do not communicate the source of their frustration.

In some cases, the exit interview can be used as a vehicle to dissuade a valuable employee from leaving. Managers may not know of employees' dissatisfactions until the intention to quit is announced.

Managers may be able to intervene to solve employees' concerns, thereby preventing separation.

The exit interview can reduce the disgruntled employee's hostility and can serve a goodwill purpose. Organizations that provide opportunities for employees to air their feelings prior to leaving and that take some responsibility for a person-job mismatch will have fewer vengeful people complaining about them in the community. The departing person is likely to be hired by a competitor, so it is important that the person leave on good terms. The exit interview can clear the air and can show the organization's concern for people.

In some cases, employees leave an organization with no ill feelings. In that case, the departing employee can be an excellent source of referrals for replacement.

Some turnover analysts are skeptical of exit interviews following voluntary separations because resigning employees are often emotional, lack objectivity, desire revenge, or fear reprisals via recommendations for subsequent positions. It is therefore difficult to know how much validity to attach to the information provided in an exit interview. Departing employees may hide their real reasons for leaving or may inflate their negative perceptions of the organization. Because of the credibility problem surrounding exit interviews, some organizations hold them when the employee leaves and then conduct follow-up interviews to verify information at a later date.

Exit interviews in conjunction with voluntary separations ought to solicit the following information:

- Positive aspects of the job
- Negative aspects of the job
- Reasons for leaving
- Other factors contributing to dissatisfaction
- Perceptions of the relationship with supervisor
- Perceptions of the organization
- Recommendations for improvement
- Factors that could have prolonged the employment

In addition, terms of separation must be discussed. The atmosphere should be professional and the goal should be to exchange information. The interviewer should allow the departing employee to vent emotions and should not become defensive. The interviewer must assure the departing employee that all remarks will be confidential and that the information can serve as a basis for correcting problems in the workplace. No resigning employee can be forced to participate in an exit interview. An employee who is willing to discuss reasons for resigning should be encouraged to speak honestly, objectively, and thoroughly.

The interviewer should express appreciation for the cooperation and should wish the departing employee well in future employment.

[*See also* Career Development; Feedback; Interviewing; Recruiting and Selecting New Employees; Performance Appraisals]

For Additional Information

Mobley, William H. *Employee Turnover: Causes, Consequences, and Control.* Reading, Mass.: Addison-Wesley Publishing Company, 1982. A research-oriented discussion of employee turnover that covers four major components: causes and correlates of employee turnover, conceptual models, consequences of turnover, and analysis and control of turnover.

Roseman, Edward. *Managing Employee Turnover: A Positive Approach.* New York: AMACOM, 1981. Written to help managers understand their responsibility in controlling turnover. The book includes information on how managerial actions affect turnover, early-warning systems regarding turnover, retention strategies, improving interpersonal skills, and societal changes affecting turnover. Each section includes commonsense actions to help managers retain valuable employees.

Wohahn, Ellen. "In Search of the Retentive Incentive." *Inc.*, Vol. 6 (1984), No. 5, pp. 211ff. Procedures and policies to attract and retain a committed and stable work force.

Whistleblowing

WHISTLEBLOWERS are individuals who expose what they consider to be illegal, dangerous, or immoral practices of the organization in which they work or formerly worked. Whistleblowers serve as inside watchdogs to monitor organizational policies and practices.

Whistleblowing situations tend to follow a typical scenario. Managers who are aware of the steps in the whistleblowing process may be able to intervene early enough to prevent public exposure of company practices. A potential whistleblowing event begins when an employee perceives a company policy, practice, or product to be dangerous, unethical, or illegal and expresses concern to a supervisor or manager. If the supervisor or manager does not act on the complaint, the employee will try to bring the charge to the attention of a higher-level executive or administrator. If attempts to contact senior officials fail, or if the organization refuses to consider the complaint, the employee is likely to become a whistleblower. Such employees feel compelled to go public with their allegations when they perceive that the company is not seriously considering their complaints. Employees become whistleblowers by alerting a regulatory body or the media to the perceived questionable practices of the company. Typically, the whistleblower is ostracized within the organization and either resigns or is fired.

Legal Considerations

Whistleblowers are protected by federal statutes, laws enacted by several states, and by some recent court decisions. Occupational health and safety legislation as well as environmental laws enacted by Congress protect whistleblowers. Within the public sector, the Merit Systems Protection Board and the Offices of Inspector General handle complaints and protect whistleblowers who expose practices within the government. Several states prohibit employers from retaliating against whistleblowers. Court decisions have eroded the employment-at-will doctrine by allowing whistleblowing as an exception to the general rule that employers can terminate employees at any time for any reason. In essence, this means that case law prohibits employers from firing employees who blow the whistle on company practices. While individuals discharged for whistleblowing must appeal those actions in court, the courts seem to consider the factors of motive, internal complaint, and discretion when rendering decisions. A whistleblower probably will receive protection if the motive for blowing the whistle was not personal vengeance, if the person used internal mechanisms of complaint first, and if the whistleblower did not recklessly harm the organization.

Organizational Mechanisms to Prevent Whistleblowing

Whistleblowers are not merely disgruntled troublemakers in organizations. An examination of whistleblowing incidents shows whistleblowers to have high ideals and to be quite committed to their organizations. They are often dedicated, competent individuals who are strategically placed in the company. Their knowledge and position is what allows them to discover potential wrongdoing in the first place. The evidence also reveals that they become disillusioned when their companies are unresponsive to their well-intentioned dissent. We can add to this portrait the fact that whistleblowing is more common in large organizations with centralized power. The more bureaucratic the organization, the harder it is for complaints to be heard and corrected.

Granted, some whistleblowers are not well-intentioned, highly principled people. Likewise, whistleblowing can occur in small or decentralized organizations. Because whistleblowing incidents typically follow consistent descriptions, however, organizations can extract preventive guidelines from past whistleblowing situations.

Organizations wishing to establish mechanisms for reducing the chances of whistleblowing incidents should follow these guidelines:

1. *Realize the value of dissent within an organization.* Harmful or unethical practices are more likely to occur when employees do not feel free to routinely voice concern or disagreement on the job. Better decisions can result when differences of opinion and rational debate are encouraged. When professionals can serve as critics of each other's work, a system of checks and balances then reduces the chance of questionable practices developing at all.

2. *Establish strategies for internal dissent.*   Ongoing disagreement can be worked into the channels of communication and chain of command. Informal conversations or formal meetings can be avenues for exchanging diverse views regarding workplace practices. Work at creating an open environment where employees can express controversial opinions.

3. *Establish grievance procedures.*   Organizations should have formal mechanisms by which complaints can be heard. All employees must be aware of the grievance process and feel comfortable making complaints without fear of reprisal. Impartial review boards comprised of a cross-section of employees, ombudsmen, consultants, or appeal boards within professional societies provide a variety of ways of evaluating formal allegations in companies. Fair and effective internal means of considering complaints can be the major deterrent to public whistleblowing.

4. *Realize the dangers of organizational reprisals against whistleblowers.*   The tendency of company officials to react defensively to employee allegations of wrongdoing is a dangerous stance. In most instances, the whistleblower has legal protection. To retaliate in any way will just complicate the situation. Companies should seek legal advice in the initial stages of employee complaints capable of escalating into whistleblowing incidents.

5. *Conduct periodic social audits.*   Progressive companies take a proactive stance in reviewing how conscientiously they manage health, safety, employment, and environmental concerns. They are aware of and comply with regulations in these areas. By periodically reviewing and revising policies and practices, organizations can ensure that no questionable activities occur. Organizations that operate safely, legally, ethically, and fairly will not have to deal with whistleblowers. There will be no reason to blow the whistle.

Advice to Whistleblowers

Individuals who consider going public with allegations of company wrongdoing should be aware of the personal and professional implications of their actions. Realize that blowing the whistle on your company is stressful. Colleagues may resent and reject you. You may not get much public support even from fellow employees who agreed with you or encouraged you. You may be fired from your job and have to appeal to the courts for reinstatement. The professional network within your occupation or industry may brand you as a troublemaker, thereby hindering your chances for future employment.

This is not to completely discourage whistleblowers. In many cases, whistleblowers are vindicated and have the satisfaction of knowing they served a crucial role of watchdog in an organization. Their actions may save tax dollars, preserve the environment, or save lives. They can be regarded as heroes in a company or in the community.

Individuals who consider the consequences and choose to blow the whistle on perceived questionable practices should follow these guidelines:

1. *Get your facts straight.* When making a formal charge internally or publicly, you must have evidence. Keep records and obtain documentation to verify your concern before approaching anyone with it.

2. *Use internal channels.* Try all means of rectifying the concern within the organization. Be persistent in getting supervisors, managers, executives, and administrators to listen to you. Carefully follow established complaint procedures where they exist. Make whistleblowing a last resort after all internal attempts have failed.

3. *Seek support.* It is tremendously difficult to be the lone fighter. Try to get other highly principled, concerned colleagues to join you. Check to see what laws, court decisions, regulations, or codes of ethics support your position. Having an established group take up your cause will alleviate some of the personal stress and will strengthen your case.

[*See also* Terminating Employees]

For Additional Information

Elliston, Frederick, John Keenan, Paula Lockhart, and Jane Van Schaick. *Whistleblowing: Managing Dissent in the Workplace.* New York: Praeger Publishers, 1985. The strategies used inside and outside organizations to express professional dissent. Sections cover the historical backdrop, actual whistleblowing cases, and recommendations for individuals and organizations.

Westin, Alan F., and Stephen Salisbury, eds. *Individual Rights in the Corporation.* New York: Pantheon Books, 1980. Articles written by individuals from business, law, government, public-interest groups, labor unions, and the social sciences examining employee rights within corporations. Section IV covers free expression on the job and includes eleven articles related to whistleblowing.

Westin, Alan F., Henry I. Kurtz, and Albert Robbins, eds. *Whistle Blowing: Loyalty and Dissent in the Corporation*. New York: Mc-Graw-Hill Book Company, 1981. A series of articles presenting a representative group of whistleblowing incidents in corporate employment and discussing organizational and social policies to deal with whistleblowing.

Women and Minorities in the Workplace

WITH INCREASING NUMBERS OF MINORITIES AND WOMEN IN THE WORK FORCE, MANAGERS must develop the awareness and skills to deal appropriately and effectively with a diverse organizational population. This means not only possessing knowledge about antidiscrimination laws and current equal employment opportunity (EEO) requirements, but also helping to create an environment of positive attitudes, flexibility, and opportunity for all members of the organization. Likewise, women or minorities who are managers or who aspire to the ranks of management must be aware of the unique challenges they face or the different roles they must fulfill. By understanding individual strategies for success that women and minorities can adopt as well as organizational strategies that can be implemented in terms of company policies and procedures, you and your organization will be able to capitalize on the potential of all employees.

Individual Challenges for Women in Organizations

The experiences of women employees, managers, and executives reveal some common dilemmas of being "different" in a traditionally male environment. The notion of a workplace dominated by men is disappearing in many industries, so that the extent to which women can identify with these problems will vary. Nevertheless, when women in the workplace report the challenges they face, the following issues repeatedly emerge. This list is not exhaustive or universal, but merely representative of the experiences of women in organizations.

Token Dynamics

Token dynamics occur when someone is a member of a social category (sex, race, age, religion) that is scarce in the workplace

347

environment. Being the only woman or one of a few women in a department or organization will create token status which carries with it many unique circumstances. For example, token employees face increased visibility, greater performance pressure, polarization, stereotyping, and loyalty tests.

Look at the effects of each one of these token dynamics. Organizations frequently place their women (or minorities) in highly visible positions as a way to publicly demonstrate their commitment to affirmative action. Each task force, board, committee, or project must have a woman (or minority token) on it to show diversity. Even if organizations do not consciously showcase their tokens, women and minorities are visible because they are different. Their presence is noticed automatically. The advantage of visibility in organizations is that your competence is recognized and you are singled out for opportunities. People who have experienced this token visibility, however, report feeling pressure to represent their entire social category. Thus, the one woman on the board is expected to present the women's perspective. The lone woman department head cannot fail without feeling that she has ruined the opportunity for all other women. At the very least, the token employee feels greater pressure to perform in order to dispel the assumption that she was hired not for her competence but because of her gender. The effect of increased visibility is therefore greater performance pressure for token employees, whether their token status results from sex, race, or other reasons.

The existence of token employees inevitably creates two polarized groups, no matter how sharp or negligible the division: the women and the men, the blacks and the whites, the majority and the minority. Each group overemphasizes its similarities and exaggerates its differences from the other group. Even if the two groups have similar expectations, perceptions, or goals, the polarization phenomenon provides the illusion of wide differences. Misunderstandings occur where they should not. Tensions exist for no real reasons.

With polarization comes the tendency to stereotype. If one group feels alienated from another, each group will categorize the other. Instead of dealing with the uniqueness of people, there is the tendency to lump people into groups and to make assumptions about the entire group. Often, those assumptions are offensive and wrong.

Another effect of tokenism is loyalty tests. With stereotyping comes defamatory remarks or offensive jokes. The token faces a dilemma when subjected to a put-down remark or joke. To object is to further alienate herself from the majority group. If each member of the majority group appreciates the joke and the token is the only one offended, then the token further distinguishes herself from the "in group." The woman who laughs at a sexist joke or remark, on the other hand, is allowing herself to be put down. The effect of this behavior on a woman's self-esteem can be devastating. A token is in the bind of showing loyalty to her social or cultural identity or to the majority work group, but not both. Token dynamics are not unique to women in organizations, but can be experienced by anybody who is demographically different in an organization.

Sexual Harassment

Surveys have shown that large numbers of working women have experienced some form of sexual harassment on the job, ranging from offensive verbal comments to physical overtures or propositions that jeopardize job security. Despite the illegality of sexual harassment, women often face dilemmas when dealing with it in the workplace. Their complaints are not taken seriously, they are told they are too sensitive, or they are dismissed from the organization, albeit for fabricated reasons, if the complaint is against a valuable member of the organization. In any case, they are likely to experience stress, health problems, and diminished performance while coping with sexually harassing behavior. Despite organizational attempts as well as legal recourse for dealing with this problem, sexual harassment is still a workplace fact of life for many women.

Balancing Work and Family

Working women with husbands and families face the extraordinary challenge of performing well in the two arenas of work and home. While men, as well, face a conflict of roles between workplace and family demands, women still bear most of the responsibility for family duties. Women who want to excel in their careers inevitably face the pull of family concerns. There is great stress on working women who wrestle with issues of childbearing, child care, career competition with spouses, guilt, social stigma, and exhaustion.

Femininity

Because most organizations embody masculine norms and behavior, many women are confused about the appropriate behavior for them in the workplace. This translates into questions about how to dress, what types of behavior to allow or to suppress, or how to avoid alienating male colleagues. Men can "be themselves" in organizations, since workplace structures and norms have derived from the masculine culture, but for some women in organizations, being themselves may mean violating workplace norms and expectations. The question of femininity is particularly relevant for women managers, and the question of appropriate management style for women has received much discussion. Should women managers emulate traditional male management styles or develop their own management styles that incorporate traditional notions of feminine behavior? While there is no definitive answer to this question, it represents a host of dilemmas facing women in the workplace.

Confidence

Many competent women in organizations find their confidence challenged by societal expectations, organizational constraints, or co-workers' attitudes. Women who penetrate traditionally male occupations may find the obstacles overwhelming. They may experience self-doubts about their capacity to handle career and family demands. Those who encounter token dynamics or sexual harassment in their organizations may be worn down by the stress. Sexist attitudes or treatment from others in the workplace erodes confidence. It is not uncommon for women in organizations to feel doubts about "doing it all."

Power and Authority

Women supervisors, managers, and executives must frequently deal with issues of power and authority. Some women managers, by virtue of traditional sex-role socialization, lack the skills of assertiveness, power, delegation, or competitiveness necessary to perform well in the managerial role. Others who display appropriate power and authority are perceived negatively by employees who have difficulty dealing with women managers. If the woman manager herself does not have problems with power and authority, her colleagues or subordinates may.

Individual Strategies for Women in the Workplace

While there are not specific remedies for each of these dilemmas common to women in the workplace, there are some mechanisms by which working women can cope with the unique demands they face. Each of these strategies requires action on the part of individual women rather than organizational changes. Each should be a positive step in improving both career success and emotional well-being.

1. *Gain access to informal networks.* Because most working women are so busy managing careers and households, they may not take the time to cultivate informal alliances in the workplace. Yet networking

is a valuable investment of your time. The time spent having lunch with colleagues or attending a professional meeting will pay off later in terms of well-placed contacts, professional favors, or valuable information. At the very least, networking with other women is likely to provide a sounding board and empathic understanding for your stresses and role conflicts.

2. *Acquire role models and mentors.* It is helpful if women in organizations have other women to serve as role models. Learning how other women have coped with career and family demands can be a valuable lesson. While any ambitious member of an organization can learn from observing the behavior of others, women especially need to observe other women functioning effectively in the workplace. Effective mentoring relationships can be a career boost to any organizational newcomers. There is some sentiment that women, being organizational newcomers in general, can especially benefit from having mentors.

3. *Learn stress- and time-management skills.* Because women in organizations seem to face unique challenges, stress- and time-management techniques can be useful. Programs in both of these areas can help women determine whether they are taking on too much or practicing perfectionism. Saying no to certain requests, depending on others for help and support, and maintaining some amount of leisure time can go a long way in promoting emotional well-being and, consequently, workplace productivity.

4. *Develop androgynous management styles.* Women managers can cope with the dilemma of adopting masculine versus feminine styles of behavior by developing an androgynous management style. Androgynous management is a flexible style that combines typically feminine and masculine styles. Androgynous managers are assertive yet supportive, confrontative yet collaborative, competitive yet cooperative, and authoritative yet participative. This style is often comfortable for both men and women managers because it is moderate and suitable to the variances in personalities. It allows a manager to have flexibility in behaving appropriately according to the demands of the situation rather than artificial role prescriptions. Androgynous management is synonymous with good management, regardless of the manager's gender.

Individual Challenges for Minorities in Organizations

It is difficult to generalize about minority experiences in organizations because there are vast cultural differences between such groups as blacks, Asian Americans, Native Americans, and Hispanic Americans. However, being a member of a racially or ethnically distinct group in the workplace does present some common challenges.

1. *Token dynamics.* Token dynamics are probably more pronounced for racial minorities than they are for women in organizations. For example, the only black manager in a company has tremendous visibility. While all the men in an organization have had lifelong interaction with women, few may have had any experience interacting with minorities. Thus, polarization, stereotyping, and loyalty testing become more pronounced. Being the lone woman minority member in the workplace can further accentuate token dynamics.

2. *Resentment from members of the majority group.* Many fear that affirmative action plans will displace white men from jobs and favor minorities. Periods of large-scale immigration create panic about minorities taking jobs away from nonminorities. Stereotypes about racial inferiority or intellectual superiority fuel this resentment. Minorities who enter organizations characterized by blatant or covert hostility face tremendous obstacles to their career success.

3. *Cultural pull.* In some cases, achieving occupational and financial success alienates minority employees from their cultural community. They may be seen as selling out or abandoning their cultural heritage. Minority managers or executives whose roots are in lower-income, blue collar, working-class environments may feel guilt and stress as a result of their professional success. This notion of cultural pull manifests itself in such questions as "In what neighborhood should I live?" "Should I abandon unique accents and grammatical structures in favor of standard speaking styles?" "What cultural traditions should I maintain?"

4. *Reality testing.* It is not uncommon for minorities to experience prejudice in the workplace, to confront it, and to be told that it does not exist. When your perceptions are different from almost everyone else's in the workplace, it is easy to begin questioning your own sense of reality. There is the inevitable problem of distinguishing between personal and racial problems with others. It is not easy for minorities to determine whether they are being treated as individuals or as members of a demographic category.

5. *Self-doubt.* Just as women in organizations question their ability to handle it all, minority members of organizations also frequently experience self-doubt. It is a rare minority employee who does not ask, "Can I make it in the white corporate United States?" You may wonder whether you were hired because of your minority status.

You may doubt that you are tough enough to handle the obstacles you will face as a minority member of an organization.

6. *Racial loyalties.* Minorities in organizations may be unsure about whether they should confront instances of racism or discrimination. How much should you concern yourself with internal issues of equity? Is it appropriate to network with other minorities in the company, or would that be seen as antithetical to organizational loyalty? Some black managers, for example, adopt conservative behavior at work but practice social activism on their own time. There is no way to know to what extent being true to yourself and your personal ideals will help or hinder the career progress of minorities in the workplace.

7. *Opportunities for social contact.* At certain organizational levels, opportunities for social contact outside of work are imperative for career success. Many minority employees feel a sense of isolation from informal social get-togethers, which may impede their job mobility.

8. *Feelings of rage.* Some individuals with minority status report feelings of powerlessness, exasperation, and rage as a result of their participation in predominantly white organizations. While members of the majority group may feel uncomfortable with such statements, it is virtually impossible for whites to know what it is like to be a minority in an organization. Obviously, minorities must cope with their powerful emotional reactions if they are to remain where they are currently working and function successfully.

Individual Strategies for Minorities in Organizations

As a minority, you may want to adopt these strategies for dealing with minority status and achieving organizational success:

1. *Look at your situation accurately.* This involves both realistic self-appraisal and accurate perceptions of others in the workplace. Some minorities tend to underestimate their potential because of limitations placed on them in the past. As a minority member of an organization, you must be realistic about how much you can do to enlighten others or affect the organizational culture. Disappointment will stem from an expectation that you can eradicate prejudice in your company. It is important to enter an organization with an open mind and to avoid making assumptions about colleagues. Avoid the tendency to selectively perceive obstacles where they do not exist, but be prepared to deal with them if they do exist.

2. *Recognize and deal with racism.* For your own well-being as a member of a minority in an organization, it is important to recognize racism and to develop some personal strategies for coping with it. Observe how majority group members interact with you as opposed to how they interact with each other. This does not mean that you should look for racism in every remark. Just be cognizant of the realities of your organization. Denying prejudice if it exists in order to avoid problems is unrealistic and stressful. Minorities who accurately assess organizational behavior and discover incidents of racism must develop their own coping mechanisms. For some, this means confronting stereotyping attitudes and discriminatory behavior. Others cope by avoiding confrontation but disclosing feelings to family or minority colleagues. Still others leave the organization to find a more enlightened environment in which to work. Coping strategies will vary according to individuals, the extent of the racist behavior, the degree to which one feels able to affect the organization, perceived opportunities within the organization, and career alternatives.

3. *Cultivate mentors and a support structure.* Because minorities may experience more isolation and obstacles than women do in organizations, it is crucial that they have a support system. Find powerful, competent members of the organization whom you can trust. Having a mentor who is also a minority group member is ideal, although that is not always possible in organizations. Surely there are some individuals in the organization with whom you can develop mutually beneficial relationships. There may be professional organizations in the community that offer access to successful individuals who can provide career assistance and a professional friendship. Assuming leadership roles in the minority community helps develop valuable job skills and cultivate a support network.

4. *Understand cultural differences.* The more you know about the variances in human behavior, the more you will be able to deal appropriately with different people and situations. Just as whites may respond inappropriately because of their ignorance of minority cultures, members of minority groups may misunderstand the majority culture. Try to understand why people behave the way they do. Learn the best ways of dealing with particular people.

5. *Be flexible in your behavior.* Each situation calls for a different response. Just as women managers can use androgynous behavior as a middle ground between feminine and masculine sex-role behavior, minorities can draw on both their cultural learnings and observations of the majority culture. At times it is appropriate to rely on

your instinctive behavior and to act in ways consistent with your cultural background. At other times, the preferable approach is to discard traditional patterns in favor of new behaviors learned from observing majority group members.

6. *Be persistent in obtaining resources.* Minorities in organizations have to work harder to obtain the resources necessary for career success, including access to information, social contacts, power, credibility, respect, and promotion opportunities. Minorities often report a feeling of success once they obtain a good position in an organization. The reaction is fleeting, however, once the organizational obstacles present themselves. Then there is the tendency to feel defeated and to resign yourself to career constraints. Successful members of organizations, be they minorities, women, or majority group members, do not give up. They continue to display competence, to fight for what they want, and to be persistent in achieving goals. Employees with minority status especially need persistence and stamina.

Organizational Strategies for Women and Minorities

While there are many ways women and minorities can improve their situations in organizations, the complete burden of removing obstacles should not have to rest with women and minorities themselves. Organizations have legal, ethical, and social obligations to create the best environment possible for their women and minority members. By necessity, most companies realize the need to behave equitably toward women and minorities in hiring, promotion, salary, and termination practices. Being aware of and trying to comply with EEO requirements is not sufficient, however, for organizations to create hospitable working environments for all their members. There must be fairness and equal treatment in all day-to-day aspects of organizational decisions. There must be nonprejudicial attitudes among all members of the organization.

The following are some strategies organizations can implement to deal with a diverse work force. Such interventions will pay off in terms of organizational morale and productivity.

1. *Create and enforce company policy statements regarding workplace diversity.* These set the tone for appropriate behavior in the workplace. While company policy statements are typically vague and do not provide remedies to specific problems, they do help structure expectations in an organization. Progressive organizations make statements, in employee handbooks, about equal employment op-

portunity. Further, statements outlining company policy on discrimination, harassment, sexism, and racism are useful. An open
attitude about such issues lets women and minorities know that the
organization supports them. It also helps shape a workplace culture
of equity and opportunity for all.

2. *Try to meet the unique needs of women and minorities.*
Organizations that want to recruit and retain women and minorities
implement policies and benefits to meet the needs of such employees. Such companies are aware of possible cultural biases in selection or assessment-testing procedures; are willing to accommodate
nontraditional religious observances; and offer options of flextime,
child-rearing leaves, or child-care benefits. Progressive companies
establish special mentoring or career-development programs geared
to women and minorities. Such companies have mechanisms, such
as training programs, roundtable discussions, minority-affairs specialists, or dispute-resolution boards to resolve problems of discrimination before they escalate.

3. *Create numerical balance between women and men and whites and
minorities in an organization.* The best way for companies to
eliminate all the problems of token dynamics is to avoid having
tokens in organizations. Being proud of having a few women in the
company or a few Hispanic managers is foolhardy. Once organizations make a real commitment to workplace diversity, then problems of discrimination disappear. Issues of sexism and racism
diminish as the division between a visible, powerful majority and
an equally visible, powerless minority disappears.

4. *Practice multicultural management.* This means helping all managers to deal effectively with diverse subordinates. It means equipping them with the tools of open-mindedness, sensitivity, cultural
awareness, and behavioral flexibility. Organizations cannot expect
this to happen without intervention. Because employee demograph-
ics are changing rapidly and societal as well as workplace norms
are in flux, there is confusion about standards of behavior. Managers
may not know how to adapt to such change. To understand the
needs of women and minorities and management's responsibilities
in these areas, organizations must educate themselves. Using EEO
consultants, developing training programs, and locating appropriate
personnel, psychology, or women's studies and minority studies
courses in the community are a few ways of educating managers in
multicultural management. By practicing multicultural management, organizations reap the benefits of the unique talents, different

perspectives, fresh insights, and creative approaches of a diverse work force.

[See also Mentoring; Networking; Sexual Harassment; Stress; Time Management]

For Additional Information

America, Richard F., and Bernard E. Anderson. *Moving Ahead: Black Managers in American Business.* New York: McGraw-Hill Book Company, 1978. Despite the publication date, offers practical advice for helping black managers succeed in contemporary corporations. Data are drawn from 100 interviews with black managers in a variety of workplace settings. Suggestions cover such areas as conducting self-appraisals; acquiring sponsorship; developing relationships with supervisors, subordinates, and peers; understanding corporate loyalty and diplomacy; being a skilled politician; and managing personal emotions.

Dickens, Floyd, Jr., and Jacqueline B. Dickens. *The Black Manager: Making It in the Corporate World.* New York: AMACOM, 1982. A four-phase structured model of development for black managers in white corporations. The model, developed from interviews with black managers, identifies and organizes the experiences of black managers and provides a means of understanding the personal dynamics that occur on the job.

Jones, Edward, Jr. "Black Managers: The Dream Deferred." *Harvard Business Review,* Vol. 65 (1986), No. 3, pp. 84–93. An assessment of the progress of black managers in United States corporations. Jones provides data and anecdotes to illustrate the problems encountered by many black managers in the workplace.

Kanter, Rosabeth Moss. *Men and Women of the Corporation.* New York: Basic Books, 1977. A classic that was the first to raise many questions about the status and nature of interaction between men and women in the corporate United States. Its discussion of token dynamics is just as relevant for contemporary companies as when the book was written.

Lee, Chris. "Training for Women: Where Do We Go From Here?" *Training,* Vol. 23 (1986), No. 12, pp. 26ff. A discussion of some of the subtle and pervasive barriers faced by today's businesswomen. Lee describes some company programs that confront these issues.

Marshall, Judi. *Women Managers: Travellers in a Male World.* New York: John Wiley & Sons, 1984. Based on interviews with women managers, a discussion of the common experiences of women in management. This is not a "how to" book, but a source for helping women (and organizations and society) understand the context and issues surrounding women in management. Covers such issues as stereotypes, social values and power, women managers' employment histories and futures, personal identity and lifestyles, and future reform and alternatives.

Sargent, Alice G. *The Androgynous Manager.* New York: AMACOM, 1981. Explains the concept of androgyny, characterizes the androgynous manager, discusses reasons why androgynous management is the most effective style for men and women in contemporary organizations, and provides strategies for developing androgynous management in organizations.

Index